D1180115

GROUND PLAN OF THE BIBLE

BOOKS BY OTTO WEBER

Published by The Westminster Press

GROUND PLAN OF THE BIBLE

KARL BARTH'S CHURCH DOGMATICS:
AN INTRODUCTORY REPORT

GROUND PLAN OF THE BIBLE

By
OTTO WEBER

Translated by
HAROLD KNIGHT

THE WESTMINSTER PRESS
Philadelphia

Translation of *Grundriss der Bibelkunde,* the fourth German edition, 1956, published by Vandenhoeck & Ruprecht, Göttingen, Germany.

Library of Congress Catalog Card No. 59-9195

TYPESET IN GREAT BRITAIN
PRINTED IN THE UNITED STATES OF AMERICA

SUMMARY OF CONTENTS

Part I

THE OLD TESTAMENT

PART II

THE NEW TESTAMENT

(N.B. Chapters 15, 18, 19 and 20 are intended for more advanced readers)

Chapter 1

WHAT IS THE BIBLE?

1. *A Book*

(*a*) It is obvious that the Bible looks like a book. But what must be stressed is the fact that in reality it is a unity and requires to be *read as a book*. Of course there is something singular about the Bible—we call it "Holy Scripture". But this does not mean that it repels us in lofty aloofness. Only when we read it as a serious book should be read do we experience something of its holiness. Even those who feel they can make nothing of it, ought to read it; such reading demands no special insight but only the attention which a book of such high significance certainly merits.

(*b*) The Bible is not a book which has fallen from the skies; *its authors are men*, and it has acquired its present form through an earthly history. Hence it is a monument of a process of literary growth, and literary criticism must apply to it its usual methods. To some extent the authors of our Biblical books are mentioned in the books themselves (consistently so in the case of the Old Testament prophets or the letters of the apostle Paul) or in titles which have been added later (e.g. the four gospels). Sometimes there exists an old tradition which declares some person to be the author of a book (thus in late Judaism Moses is declared to be the author of the first five books of the Bible). Often we have to rely wholly on surmise. In many cases modern criticism has established the fact that the traditional ascription of authorship is questionable; as with numerous literary documents in the ancient world so also in the Bible there are books which are not authentic, i.e. they are not the work of the author to whom they are imputed by tradition. But this has nothing to do with the intrinsic truth of such books. Thus the great section, chs. 40–66, of the Book of Isaiah is not the work of Isaiah himself; it consists of two later collections which originally circulated independently. But these non-authentic—from a literary point of view, spurious—books are intrinsically among the most important of the whole Bible and no one would think of branding them as false from the point of view of content. Faith does not live by the conclusions of literary-historical criticism.

(*c*) The authors of our Biblical books were like other men *exposed to the changes brought about by time*. More than a millennium was required for the gradual genesis of the two great collections of books which we see before us in the Old and New Testaments. The Biblical authors speak the language of their time, they think as children of their time and share the world-view of their contemporaries. They are neither omniscient nor infallible: their environment has powerfully influenced them. Our two accounts of the creation take into account Babylonian traditions. In the New Testament we can observe the effect of contemporary Jewish and Greek ideas. If we picture the Bible as a building, we must say that various hands have taken part in its construction, and the stones themselves derive from the most diverse quarries. But the most important feature of this edifice is not the quarry from which its parts are hewn. And the more plainly the source—often a very strange one—of the stones has revealed itself to the eye of the critic, the more clearly has the peculiar character of the Bible stood out.

2. *The Book of the Nations*

(*a*) The Bible is distinguished from the multifarious literary monuments of the past and present by its enormous *distribution* and influence. In this respect no other book is at all comparable with it. There is no language, hardly any dialect of importance, into which the Bible has not been translated. The figures of this distribution amount year after year to many millions, and are still constantly on the increase. In this connexion it is significant that the spread and influence of the Bible have grown ever greater in proportion as the State authority has diminished, by which for a long time in Western Europe a dubious support was given to the Church. There must be a strong momentum of inner inspiration indwelling a book which is freely desired by so many millions of men.

(*b*) In its *influence* too the Bible is unquestionably superior to any book of secular literature. This applies in particular to the Western sphere of culture but it is to a large extent true also of Slavonic culture. What we call the West is something which has grown up under the predominating influence of the Bible. There is no important poet or thinker of the West who can be properly understood apart from the Bible. This is true even of those who were reserved in their acceptance of the Christian faith (as, for example, Kant or Goethe) or rejected it completely (e.g. Nietzsche). European culture without knowledge of the Bible is an impossibility.

(*c*) The Bible owes its incalculable influence on culture, on the poetry, the ideas and the music and song of the peoples of the West not however to its literary qualities, but unquestionably to the fact that for centuries it was recognized as "*Holy Scripture*". It moulded the life and thought of Christianity, and even in former ages when its contents were less well known it was the dominant factor in Church worship, in preaching, in Church instruction, and thus it shaped culture which in its origins and depths was sustained by the Church. But the Church recognized the Bible as "Holy Scripture" because it heard in its words the Word of God; not because it was overwhelmingly impressed by its literary or general intellectual character. Hence we must conclude: it was not on account of its great cultural significance that the Bible was recognized as Holy Scripture, but on the contrary it acquired this great cultural significance because it was recognized as Holy Scripture.

(*d*) But Western culture is to-day in the grip of a severe crisis. Its world influence is called in question. We may well wonder whether this is not connected with the fact that the influence of the Bible in the West itself has weakened: Western culture has to a large extent freed itself from the Bible and in consequence has split up into opposing tendencies. This development has no bearing on the certitude with which Christians hear in the Bible the Word of God. On the contrary it is now quite clear that the Christian cleaves to the Bible exclusively from the point of view of faith. But for the West and the wider world the question of what importance is to be attached to the Bible will be a matter of vital moment. Furthermore, the significance of the Bible for those areas which are now more and more closed to Western influence has increased independently of Western culture; the Bible has in fact become the book of the millions of Christians and the ever growing churches of Asia and Africa. As a result, whoever is concerned with the Bible now enters decisively the forum of the world as a whole.

3. "*Holy Scripture*"

(*a*) It is a proved fact that the influence of the Bible on culture depends on its recognition as "Holy Scripture". But that the Bible is in truth Holy Scripture, that we hear in it not the words of men but the Word of God, is something which *cannot be proved*; it is a certitude of a unique kind. This certitude arises not through proof but through the "demonstration of the Spirit and of power", through inner conviction of the truth of that to which the Bible bears witness.

(*b*) What is the meaning of Holy Scripture? In the language of the Bible the word "holy" means "that which belongs to God", "that which is separated unto God", "that which has been sequestrated by God". "Holy Scripture" then means a writing or a collection of writings on which God has laid His hand. Hence it is not that God is the theme of this book, but rather that God is the Lord of this book, and the men who here speak to us from thousands of years ago stand in the service of God. The meaning of this can be most clearly shown by reference to the prophet Jeremiah. He knows that he has not himself conceived the word which it is his mission to speak; he has received it, it became his food as he received it (Jer. 15:16) and God became too strong for him; he cannot shake the Word from himself, although it has brought him nothing but scorn and mockery (Jer. 20:7–9). The situation is the same with regard to the apostle Paul: he cannot fail to preach the gospel—"Woe to me if I do not preach the gospel" (1 Cor. 9:16). What is here said about the message of the prophet or the apostle is similarly true of the Bible as a whole. The authors are not as it were the owners of what they write, but they are the witnesses of that which God has said and done. Thus fundamentally we are faced not by the authors but by God Himself. The authors are not reckoned to be perfect or omniscient or superior to time-conditioning; their world-view, their picture of history, their personal opinions—all that recedes behind the importance of the witness which they have to bear, and we the readers are called on to listen to this witness.

(*c*) *God's Word.* It is this therefore which we hear in Scripture and which alone constitutes its holiness. But what do we mean when we speak of God's Word? and to what extent does the Bible mediate this Word to us?

By God's Word we do not mean a word about God, but a word which God Himself speaks, or better, a word in which He speaks *to man.* The decisive point is that in His Word God does not simply impart truth about Himself, but rather opens His heart for mankind. Hence we can say: the Word of God is the *self-disclosure of God.* God breaks silence! The content of what He reveals to man in His word is secondary; the primary thing is that He opens His mind to man. Accordingly, it is not the thoughts which man must conceive about God which stand in the foreground, but the obedience which man renders to the call of God.

In the Old Testament the Word of God is delivered to particular men, especially the prophets, and it is declared by them; always at the heart of some specific situation. In the New Testament, on the other hand, we are faced by One who *is* the Word of God: "The Word became flesh" (Jn. 1:14). Thus, when we say that the Bible declares to us the Word of God, this really means that it attests to us Jesus Christ who is the Word of God. He is the heart of the book and also the criterion by which all must be measured. What the Word of God is in the many words, sentences, sayings, chapters and books, is recognizable solely in the light of Jesus Christ. The witness of the Old Testament points forward to Him and the men of the New Testament declare their witness to Him. We can only come to understand the Bible in proportion as we come to understand Him.

Chapter 2

THE ORIGIN AND FORM OF THE BIBLE

1. *The Old Testament*

(*a*) *The oldest parts.* Research, especially in the last two centuries, has penetrated more and more deeply into the roots of Biblical literature. Of course its conclusions can never be regarded as final; nevertheless much can be affirmed with considerable certainty. Yet it is not clear when the first essays lying behind extant Old Testament literature were made. Among the present *books* of the Old Testament, regarded as a whole, none goes further than the time of the Babylonian exile (sixth century), or, at most, shortly before that time. What in particular dates from the very earliest times is a number of songs, sayings and laws.

Some law words, such as the Ten Commandments (Exod. 20: the decalogue) and perhaps also the Book of the Covenant (Exod. 20:22—23:33) certainly have the ring of the Mosaic period. Israel in its earliest stages, finding its unity in the service of Yahweh under the leadership of Moses, entered a world marked by a high degree of culture in which it very soon took part; we must not suppose that the Israel of the very earliest period was without culture, and there may well have been at that time a far more extended literature than is suggested by the fragments which remain to us. The so-called song of Miriam comes from the time of Israel's wanderings no doubt (Exod. 15:21), while the song of Lamech (Gen. 4:23,24) with its grim insistence on the most relentless blood vengeance echoes a pre-Biblical age. The song of Deborah (Jdg. 5), one of the finest songs of the world, is inspired by the stern wars of conquest which the Israelite tribes had to wage in order to gain possession of their land. Moreover the so-called blessing of Jacob (Gen. 49) belongs to the oldest parts of the Bible. As we should expect, what we find surviving from these early periods is not ordinary prose but poetry or the lore of proverbs or the codification of law: as in the case of other peoples, artistically moulded literature is found at the origin of Israel's history.

(*b*) *The Period of the Monarchy.* With the monarchy, the origin of which can be placed shortly before the turn of the last pre-Christian millennium (*circa* 1030), literary activity received a powerful impulse. The ancient tradition which affirms that David was himself a poet deserves every confidence, and the songs of lament (especially that on Saul and his sons, 2 Sam. 1:17ff.) traditionally ascribed to him are of compelling power. Likewise it may be regarded as established that David's son and successor Solomon was noted as a poet and speaker of proverbs. Probably at the same period those old collections of songs took shape which are alluded to here and there in the Old Testament: the "Book of the wars of Yahweh" (cf. Num. 21:14) and the "Book of the Upright" (cf. 2 Sam. 1:18). We may observe that now materials which formerly had circulated as fragments were no doubt collected. The same process took place as regards law traditions, except that in this case tentative collections must have been much older.

But above all it is in the early period of the monarchy that the writing of *history* begins. One of the most impressive documents of this early period of historical writing portrays the conflict between David and his son Absalom (2 Sam. 11–20); it is probably the work of a contemporary and shows in what an unvarnished form the figure even of the old king could be presented. Without a doubt it was at that time also that the first collections were made of the reminiscences of Israel's past; traditions about the forefathers, Abraham, Isaac and Jacob, about Moses and the wanderings, about the events of Sinai and the struggles which led to the gradual conquest of the land of Canaan.

In the middle of this monarchic period (i.e. ninth or eighth century) there came into existence the oldest document whose outlines can still be detected within the Pentateuch: the so-called *Yahwistic source*. It owes its name to the fact that from the very first it uses Yahweh as the name of God, and thus sees at work from the most primitive times the God who revealed His name to Israel and granted them His covenant. This Yahwistic source meets us on the very first pages of the Bible; thus we owe to it the second account of the creation (Gen. 2:4ff.), the story of the fall (Gen. 3) and parts of the stories of Abraham and Moses. Not much later arose another similar document, the *Elohistic source*: so called because for the earliest period it gives as the description of God the name Elohim, thus referring to Him as the Lord of the whole world. This source begins with the stories of Abraham; then along with the Yahwistic it is found in the whole traditional text.

Similarly old are some parts of the books of Joshua and Judges and Samuel, linked up with the above-mentioned sources of the Pentateuch. Even the stories which we find in our books of the Kings are to some extent very old. And in the later period of the monarchy the first writing prophets appear (by contrast with their forerunners): Amos, Hosea, Isaiah, Micah belong to the eighth century and are followed in the seventh century by Jeremiah,

Nahum, Zephaniah, all three appearing in the last third of the century. Moreover a considerable part of the Psalms goes back to the time of the monarchy. Hence this epoch, which embraces barely 500 years, is the richest in the literary history of Israel. Judah (the southern part of the kingdom) contributed most to this result.

(*c*) *The Exile.* After the subjugation of the northern kingdom of Israel by the Assyrians in the eighth century, the neo-Babylonians finally crushed the southern kingdom in the year 586. We hear nothing further of the annihilated Israel. But Judah powerfully renewed its life and even its literature from this very experience of exile which overtook tens of thousands of its inhabitants. Among the exiles there were circles which in serious contemplation fathomed the causes of the collapse and learnt to envisage their previous history from a new point of view. There emanated from these circles, in which the thoughts of the older prophets were at work, a third basic source of the Pentateuch, which may have its roots in the decades immediately before the end of the kingdom; it is called the Deuteronomic source because it is found predominantly in the fifth book of Moses, Deuteronomy. Previous extant traditions up to and including the time of the monarchy were remoulded to express the idea of the Deuteronomists.

Prophecy too, whose exponents had long been predicting the coming catastrophe, manifested new power and inspiration in the days of exile. First is the prophet Ezekiel, whose call dates from shortly before the final break-up and who went on prophesying right into the time of tribulation in Babylonia. Later, towards the end of this time, there appears an unnamed prophet whose words have come down to us in a section of the Book of Isaiah (chs. 40–55) and who is accordingly described in a general way as Second (Deutero-) Isaiah. Further, during the exile the oracles of the older prophets were collected and edited. Poetry too, which once in happier days flowed from joyful hearts, now comforted the exiles in their misery; a (small) portion of our Psalms springs from the exilic period. Thus the time of sorrow became productive.

(*d*) *Late Judaism.* The conquest of the Babylonians by the Persian ruler Cyrus (539) removed the yoke from the shoulders of the exiled Jews. Many returned to the land of their fathers. These were especially the men who felt homesick about their destroyed temple, and in whose hearts burned a fervent love for the God of their fathers.

The new Judah arose from religious yearning and was no longer a state but a religious community. At its heart however stood not merely the temple, the sacrificial cultus, the rites, but equally — and in fact governing all—the written, codified *law*. Well before this the men of Israel had not produced their literature merely as a decorative art on the fringes of life, but sternly and seriously in the service of their God. In the time of exile they had learned to treasure the full value of written traditions; their literature had held the exiles together as a community when they were far from their ancestral home and their ruined temple. It had given them the certainty that they were not completely abandoned by Yahweh. The motives which had stirred many thoughtful Jews during the exile remained alive in them in post-exilic times: learned men undertook with new zeal the collecting and editing of old traditions, and a fourth basic source of the Pentateuch was the result: the so-called *priestly source* from the fifth century, described thus because its attention is focused on the priesthood and the cult. It comprises the whole circle of past history and tradition and begins with the creation of the world (first account of the creation: Gen. 1).

Soon afterwards all the writings which had been the fruit of this age's long work at past history and the law were woven together in final shape and there arose, in the fourth century, the Pentateuch as we now have it. About the same time the other historical books, including those which were not written until after the exile (Ezra, Nehemiah and Chronicles) received the form in which we know them.

But the gaze of men was by no means directed backwards merely. Right at the beginning of the post-exilic period of Judaism new prophets arise: Haggai, Zechariah, and no doubt later Habakkuk and Joel. Further, many oracles of other prophetic books were at this time completed by editors. And, above all, this community was in a quite special degree a singing community. It collected the many old songs which had long been in circulation and from the remotest times had been used in divine worship, added new ones and thus composed the Psalter. Also the sententious wisdom of past generations was systematized and gave birth to several books (our Proverbs, Ecclesiastes, similarly too the Song of Songs).

All in all, this late period is distinguished by its work of collecting and sifting, and yet, also—maturing. The poem of Job, which now reached its final form, takes us into the deepest depths. It was certainly not a time of easy comfortable living which produced such a work as this. More than once the continued existence of the community stood on a razor's edge. The most dangerous crisis of all inspired in this period the latest book of the Old Testament: when in the year 168 the Syrian king Antiochus IV desecrated the temple and forbade the possession of religious books, in the midst of this community menaced with extinction there arose, like a comforting and warning voice, the Book of Daniel.

2. *The New Testament*

(*a*) *Paul.* The Bible of primitive Christianity was the Old Testament; that is what is meant when in the New Testament we read of the "scriptures". How thoroughly the early Christians searched the pages of the Old Testament is suggested by every glance at the many verbal quotations of which the New is full; still more numerous are the echoes and allusions. The thought of "doing away" with the Old Testament would certainly not have occurred to any Christian of that time. But what they found in it was not the piety or wisdom of the past, it was the promise of what was now disclosed: Jesus Christ.

The proclamation of the Christ was combined as a matter of course with the study and reading aloud of the Old Testament. But at a very early stage there arose alongside the abundant oral traditions of the words and deeds of Jesus, especially of His death and resurrection, written expressions also and indeed of a quasi-official kind: the letters of the apostle Paul to his congregations. These are historically the earliest components of the New Testament, and they allow us to gain a deep insight into the message of earliest Christianity.

The first epistle to the Thessalonians was written at the beginning of the fifth decade of the first century; it is the oldest New Testament document. In the course of the following ten or at most twenty years there followed Paul's other epistles. Hence we owe our earliest information about Jesus to Paul! But Paul himself invokes an already extant tradition on which he was able to draw, and it is this tradition which is articulated in our gospels.

(*b*) *The Gospels.* There is only one gospel; for gospel means good news and of course refers to the message of Jesus of Nazareth. But this good news was preached in many varied ways, and four quite different compositions have come down to us: our four gospels. The oldest of them is that of Mark (*circa* A.D. 70), then follow Matthew and Luke (both after A.D. 80), and finally that of John (*circa* A.D. 100).

But older collections of words of Jesus and reports about Him lie behind the gospels. If we read attentively the first three gospels (which on account of the extensive similarity of their reporting are called synoptic) we find that many words and deeds of Jesus are described in almost the same terms, though at the same time considerable differences are disclosed. Research has to a certain extent been able to shed light on the affinity and the divergences between the synoptics. It suggests that at an early date there were two main streams of tradition, both of which assumed written form (source-material). One of these streams contained mostly accounts of the deeds of Jesus; it can be recognized especially clearly in the gospel of Mark and is therefore called the Marcan source. Not only Mark but the two other synoptics have utilized this source. The other stream of tradition contained mainly words of Jesus and is accordingly called "sayings-source" (Logia-source, Q), and both Matthew and Luke have derived much of their matter from it. Furthermore, each of the synoptics has material from other sources peculiar to himself, so-called special matter; this special matter is most extensive in the case of Luke, who is in general the most independent of the evangelists.

Such is the general outline of the genesis of the synoptics usually accepted to-day; however, many particular questions are still unanswered. The two sources "Mark" and Q are essentially hardly later than the letters of Paul, and contain the precipitate of the oldest oral tradition that we can detect.

The gospel of John has a quite special character. It presupposes the older gospels, but uses also its own special sources and offers us an outline of the activity of Jesus which diverges essentially from that of the synoptics. It is as it were a vision of the innermost mind of Jesus, and in formal structure resembles a sermon.

(*c*) *The other writings.* The letters of Paul and the gospels can be regarded as the scaffolding of the New Testament. But alongside them there are quite a number of other documents. Closely bound up with the gospel of Luke is the "Acts of the Apostles", which in part reproduces in the first person the personal reminiscences of the author; like the gospel it appeared after the year 80. Further, we have the so-called catholic epistles ("catholic" means in this connexion the totality of Christianity, for in the opinion of the later Church they were addressed to the Church as a whole; unlike the letters of Paul they do not specify the congregations which were intended as their recipients). Among them the epistle to the Hebrews, dating from about the end of the first century, claims quite special significance; then there are the epistles of Peter and John and that of James.

All these writings are post-Pauline; the second epistle of Peter was probably not written until the first half of the second century and must be the latest portion of the New Testament. Most probably also some of the letters circulating under the name of Paul are post-Pauline: the so-called pastoral epistles (the name arises from the fact that they are to some extent concerned with the administration of the communities) appear to have been composed wholly or in part by pupils of Paul, and the same is perhaps true of the epistle to the Ephesians.

The New Testament ends with the mysterious book, the "apocalypse" or Revelation of John, whose tremendous message has only been realized apparently in recent times; the book was probably written shortly before the end of the first century during the reign of the Emperor Domitian.

3. *The Canon*

By the Canon (standard of measurement) we understand the extent of the recognized Holy Scripture as established by the Church. There are in fact other writings too which stood (and still stand) in high esteem but which nevertheless in the judgment of the Church are not to be regarded as of equal value with the books of the Bible. From ancient times such writings have been called "the Apocrypha", and the Apocrypha is included in many editions of the Bible.

Other such writings which are of less value than the usual apocrypha are to be found only in scholarly books; such are the pseudepigraphical writings (i.e. writings which were attributed to great men of early Israel such as Enoch or Baruch but were not written by the latter; they arose in fact in latest post-exilic, and partly in post-Christian, times). Apocrypha are also to be found alongside the New Testament writings: fragments of gospels, letters from the end of the first century and still more from the second century, etc., hence in general early Christian literature which is in part of high historical value.

In face of the existence of such apocryphal literature the limits of our Bible had to be fixed. Furthermore, there were disputes about the recognition of certain books. Thus for instance the admission of the Book of Esther and the Song of Songs was questioned among the Jews, and in the Christian Church there was contention about the full recognition of the epistle to the Hebrews and the Revelation of John. The Canon of the Old Testament was finally established only about A.D. 100. That of the New Testament was not formally fixed until the end of the fourth century: the two disputed writings were then generally admitted. Moreover the Roman Catholic Church has always recognized the Old Testament Apocrypha and does so to-day; the exclusion of such books in Christendom took place only as a result of the Reformation.

4. *The Text of the Bible*

(*a*) *The Language*. The Old Testament, with the exception of only a few chapters (which are in Aramaic), is written in Hebrew.

Hebrew is a Semitic language very closely related to the language of the ancient Phoenicians and Punic (Carthaginian) peoples, but also with affinities to Arabic and the languages of ancient Assyria and Babylonia. The characters of Hebrew are originally connected with those of Phoenicia—it is in that circle of culture that writing with letters in general has been discovered. On the other hand the characters used in the Bible are properly Aramaic (the

Aramaeans are in particular the inhabitants of ancient Syria). The oldest Hebrew writing shows a manifest similarity with that of ancient Greece, and beyond that with our own characters, for the West derived the idea of writing in characters from the Semites. Moreover the Hebrew language was only for a relatively short time the popular language of Israel. As far back as the time of the monarchy a recent form of Aramaic became more and more prevalent, and gradually it replaced the Hebrew with which it was akin. Hebrew, as was the case later with Latin, became the language of the learned and of the synagogue.

The New Testament is written in Greek, not of course in classical Greek but in the current language of the dying ancient world (*Koiné*, i.e. Greek popular speech). It is clear from a study of some of the New Testament writings that their authors were originally Jews. Further, behind our Gospel of St. Matthew there lies an Aramaic draft of which naturally we have no detailed information. The speech of Jesus was Aramaic. Only a few of the words of Jesus have come down to us in the original (e.g. "*Abba*", father, Rom. 8:15, or "*talitha kumi*", maiden, arise, Mk. 5:41). On the other hand Jesus on the cross prays in the words of a Hebrew psalm (at least according to the more convincing rendering of Matt. 27:46: "*Eli, eli, lama asabthani*"). The best Greek of the New Testament is to be found in the Acts of the Apostles and still more in the epistle to the Hebrews.

(*b*) *Translations.* The most important translation of the Old Testament is the Septuagint (LXX), a translation into Greek; its name arises from the fact that allegedly 70 scholars took part in its composition. In fact it came into existence as the result of a long process of development, from about the third century B.C. In its Greek dress the Old Testament conquered the world of late antiquity, and we find it consistently in this form in New Testament quotations. What is more, as we shall see, the text of the LXX has reached us in more ancient manuscripts than those of the original Hebrew text. For this reason the LXX has acquired great importance for scholarly study.

Later the Old as well as the New Testament was translated into Latin; this translation, which after certain improvements is accounted valid today, is known as the Vulgate (the people's Bible). It arose about A.D. 400 and is fundamentally the work of the Church Father St. Jerome. Other ancient translations of the Bible must be passed over here; moreover they have little importance for scholarship.

(*c*) *Manuscripts.* By what process has the Bible come down to us? Printing of course is a modern invention. Before its discovery the Bible, like all other books, could be distributed only by means of manuscripts. In this respect there is a big difference between the Hebrew manuscripts of the Old Testament and all other Biblical manuscripts. The former were considered from a very early date to be "holy"; hence, when they could no longer be used in the synagogue, they were carefully hidden away or even buried, and under no circumstances allowed to circulate freely. For this reason we possess complete Hebrew manuscripts of the Bible dating only from later times;[1] the oldest belong to the early Middle Ages.

It has been established of course that the Hebrew Biblical text just because of its preservation as something sacred has been handed down to us with special care; hence we are compensated for the late origin of the manuscripts. On the other hand manuscripts of both the Old and the New Testaments have reached us in abundance. Since the possession of these manuscripts was greatly desired and since the monasteries in particular expended infinite pains and art on producing them, thousands of them have come down to us. The most costly to produce were those on parchment; in early times they were written throughout in capital letters (Uncial manuscripts).

There are more than 2,500 manuscripts of the Greek New Testament. The oldest parchment manuscripts go back to the fourth century. Foremost stands the almost complete Codex B which is housed in the Vatican Library (hence called "Vaticanus"); scarcely more recent is the so-called Codex Sinaiticus, formerly discovered under adventurous circumstances by a Leipzig professor, Constantine Tischendorf, in a monastery at Sinai. It was once in Leningrad, and is now in London. But the New Testament was also transcribed on cheaper writing material, papyrus, and in our times papyrus manuscripts have been discovered which are far more ancient in provenance than the parchment codices. The oldest of these recently discovered papyrus manuscripts aroused great excitement since it was written as far back as the second century: it contains a chapter of St. John's gospel and is stored at Manchester. On the whole, from the point of view of manuscripts, the Bible has come down to us in far better condition than any other literary monument of antiquity.

[1] However, in 1947 a fairly considerable fragment of a Hebrew manuscript was found, dating from late pre-Christian or very early Christian times.

THE OLD TESTAMENT

Chapter 3

THE OLD TESTAMENT AS A WHOLE

1. *Name and Structure*

(*a*) *Name.* The word testament signifies the *covenant of God.* But this does not imply an agreement between two equal partners; *God* by His own initiative establishes it and allows man to participate in it. Thus the covenant is essentially determined from one side. God makes the covenant, it is not that God and man together make a covenant. It is then the duty of man to keep this covenant. Thus the covenant acquires a connotation which connects it with the modern word testament: a testament is not a contract, implying two partners, but an arrangement made solely by the one who determines it. Hence the word covenant may simply be equated with the word arrangement or disposition or, better, ordering.

The covenant or testament is thus in its essence an act of God. But in that case how comes it that a book bears the title "testament"? Without question the covenant itself is something other than a book. But this book is our primary source of information about the fact that God has made His covenant with man and wills to make a covenant with us. God as it were gives us written testimony that He wills to be our God. He gave such testimony to man in ancient Israel by giving man the law as an authoritative document which could be read and proclaimed. He bears such testimony by giving man the word of the prophets as a warning and a sign that He Himself has spoken. And by these means He gives us written intelligence, offering Himself to us and summoning us to be His partners. Thus the covenant is guaranteed to us by the book, and in this sense it is to be understood that a book can also be a testament.

(*b*) But this book is called *Old* Testament. Hence it guarantees the *old* covenant as opposed to the *new.* How are we to think of this relationship?

In the first place it would be obvious to suppose that the old covenant is now obsolete, that it was the one-time divine covenant which is now superseded. But the Bible does not understand it so. It gives no grounds for the idea that God has suddenly changed His mind. "The gifts and the call of God are irrevocable" says Paul (Rom. 11:29). Even the unfaithfulness of man cannot subvert the covenant of God. "Does their [the Jews'] faithlessness nullify the faithfulness of God?" (Rom. 3:3). Hence we must understand the matter in different terms. The old covenant has been brought to fulfilment in the new and has thus for the first time been fully validated. What was once promise is now, through Jesus Christ, reality. This implies however that all that belonged merely to the sphere of promise, all that was unfulfilled and provisional, is now ended. What is old in this sense is the cultus, the rules about food and cleanliness, the limitation of the divine covenant to a single people. But what was concealed beneath these outward forms is now manifest.

When we see the matter in this light we understand why the New Testament judges the Old in a dual sense. On the one hand we hear a "no"; in the Sermon on the Mount Jesus utters His majestic "But I say unto you" over against Old Testament prescriptions. On the other hand the New Testament is constantly appealing to the Old. For example, Paul finds the true content of the gospel "revealed and attested by the law and the prophets", i.e. by the Old Testament (Rom. 3:21). Whoever wishes to understand the Old Testament must ever bear in mind this dual attitude.

(*c*) *The Structure of the Old Testament.* The Old Testament was customarily divided into the law, the prophets (the history books from Joshua onwards and the prophets in the narrower sense) and the writings. In one respect this division was more accurate, for here the prophets do not appear simply as foretellers of the future but as men with a message for their own time—which in fact is what they were.

The five books of Moses with which the Old Testament begins have for long been described by the Greek term Pentateuch (five books). Most of the individual books of which it is composed are likewise given foreign, i.e. Greek or Latin, titles: Genesis, Exodus, Leviticus, Numbers, Deuteronomy. These titles are better in so far as they give a glimpse of the contents of the books: "the beginning of things", "the departure", "cult-book", "the book of countings" and "the repetition of the law". The traditional description moreover suggests the idea that Moses was the author of these books. Although this is an ancient opinion it is not expressed in the books of the Pentateuch itself. Doubtless many a detail will go back to Moses. But the formation of the Pentateuch was, as we have already said, a lengthy historical process which took many centuries.

2. *The History of Israel*

(*a*) *The origin of the People.* The Old Testament is at the same time an almost complete collection of the literary documents which have come down to us from the old Israelite-Judaic peoples. Not until the last pre-Christian centuries do we find, in growing proportions, literature outside the Old Testament itself. For the better understanding of our book it will be useful to make a survey of the history of the people whose traditions here stand disclosed to us and whose thought, feeling and faith, arising as it were in response to the word of their God, here confront us.

Israel-Judah is a branch of the Semitic family of peoples. From the beginning of the second millennium B.C. "Hebrew" tribes penetrated into the land of Canaan, which at that time was ruled by Egypt. Among them no doubt were to be found ancestors of the Israelites. In the second half of the second millennium a part of the tribes is found however on Egyptian soil, in the border regions of the kingdom of the Pharaohs. The history of Israel begins with the fact that tribes which previously perhaps had not been very closely united encountered, in a way which is not humanly explicable, the God who henceforth became their common covenant God: His name was Yahweh. Among the traditions which part of the tribes cherished were the Sinai traditions and stories (Exod. 19 ff.) with Moses as the focal point. The "covenant" in which the life of Israel as a people was rooted was both "religious" and "political". Israel became a people as a result of the fact that Yahweh became its God. The people of Israel is a sort of confederacy of tribes centring in the rule of Yahweh. The divine covenant is the origin of the people and remains its strength.

This foundation-event from which the history of Israel sprang took place about the fourteenth century B.C. At this time too began also the first attempts of Israel to take possession of its land. There took place the more powerful pressure of the Israelite tribes on the soil of Canaan (i.e. the land promised by Yahweh)—a process which increased the unity of the tribes and led to their gradual consolidation in the land. It was a protracted business marked by the ups and downs of fighting, and is described for us as such in the Book of Joshua and still more plainly in the Book of Judges, though the description is in part highly coloured and distorted. The land was anything but uninhabited. It was indwelt by the Canaanites, a multifarious group of tribes with a fairly high degree of civilization and considerable command of military technique, and for whom the Israelites were in many ways no match. Furthermore, other tribes got busy in trying to displace the over-disciplined and in some ways degenerate Canaanites, and to bring under their control the land between the desert and the coast which for large stretches was very fertile: such were the Moabites, the Ammonites, the Midianites, etc. Soon, coming from the west, the Philistines were to join in the fray; and they proved the most dangerous enemies of Israel. There arose in consequence a turmoil, in which the

Israelites gradually succeeded in wresting into their grasp several strong points, but in no sense did they gain possession of the whole land. The time of the judges is characterized by this confusion and strife, and the rule of Samuel too is still implicated in it.

(*b*) *The first kings.* Saul, the first of Israel's kings, was the first to succeed in organizing its latent powers: he was a military chieftain of a religious stamp. He succeeded in repelling the Ammonites, who were making incursions from the east, and at times also he defeated the more dangerous Philistines. But his rule was really effective only for the times of crisis in war; he was not able to overcome that inner disunity for the emergence of which he was in part responsible. Thus it is in war that he succumbs: he loses the fight and also his life in his struggle with the Philistines.

On the ruins of the reign of Saul, David, shortly before the turn of the millennium, erects his own kingship. He succeeds in uniting the ever centrifugal tribes under his own monarchical power: Judah in the south, and then Israel (which represented a far larger collection of tribes) in the centre, the north and the east. He succeeds in subduing the Philistines and gradually also the other neighbours of Israel. Hence there arises a kingdom whose constant centre and bearer is the king. Very soon he establishes his power independently of the ancient tribal sources of power and secures for himself personal military independence and ascendancy. He conquers Jerusalem which now for the first time—as a royal city!—becomes the capital, and in fact first becomes an Israelite town. He also adopts measures which ensure that the people as a whole finds in Jerusalem a cultic centre: as once the covenant of Yahweh sustained the people, so now the sanctuary in Jerusalem is to be the source of unity. David's son and successor Solomon completes this work. He builds a royal fortress and temple at Jerusalem. This whole process could take place without disturbance because the traditional rulers of the Near East and of Mesopotamia and the Pharaohs of Egypt were weak at this time. In the period after Solomon everything gradually changes both inwardly and outwardly.

(*c*) *The separated states.* Internally there occurs about 932 a rent between the tribal groups which had been held together under David and Solomon. Only the smaller southern state of Judah remains faithful to the dynasty of David. Israel forms an independent political unity with its own Yahweh sanctuaries: Beth-el, Dan and others. The northern state is stronger in external relations. It produces several very powerful rulers: Omri, Ahab, Jehu, Jeroboam II are the best known. But here dynasties change comparatively quickly; about half of the kings of Israel end their reigns through rebellion. Judah is less active externally, and internally is incomparably more stable than the northern kingdom. Of course here too crises are not lacking, but the dynasty remains firm to the end.

In one respect, and that the most important of all, both states go the same way. The heart of the national life was the God of the covenant. But for large sections of this people Yahweh was one God among many. They thought they were not being unfaithful to Him by entering also into cultic relations with local deities, especially the Canaanite "Baalim". Yahweh seemed so inaccessible and they had no image of Him. The native deities were enticing. It had been so ever since Israel took possession of the land. And always religious apostasy, and the breaking of the covenant on Israel's part, was followed by a disruption of internal unity and external power. For Israel-Judah realistic politics meant earnest exclusive loyalty to Yahweh's covenant, apart from which this people ceased to be a people.

Thus these two states, deeply convulsed and decadent, staggered towards a critical situation externally. The great powers were bestirring themselves. In the foreground stood Assyria, whose powerful advances constantly formed a main feature of the history of the ninth century. In the eighth century the menace became an immediate one. The northern kingdom succumbed to it in 722. Judah was hard hit and became liable to pay tribute, yet Jerusalem escaped conquest. Shortly before the danger became pressing—in a period of transition which for a brief spell concealed the critical nature of the times—the first writing prophets appeared: Amos, Hosea, Isaiah: they have been compared to storm birds. The storm battered Israel to the ground and Judah was bereft of all its branches. For the first time Israel-Judah was awakened to the painful realization of the violence with which a great power could strike. But the testimony of the prophets was: your business is not with the great powers but with your God. In the northern kingdom there was hardly an ear to hear the message. In the south King Hezekiah showed himself sensitive to it.

(*d*) *The end of Judah.* In the century which followed Judah remained within the sphere of influence of Assyria. But the pressure was not constant. At this time Assyria itself not only reached the height of its power but also, fifty years later, its downfall. Then the smaller states thought they could breathe again. But other powers took the place of Assyria. First Egypt. In a wave of deep religious inspiration Judah underwent significant religious reforms; King Josiah led his people to concentrate their cultus and all their hopes on the temple at Jerusalem. But the audacious reformer was defeated by the Pharaoh who attacked him from the north (battle of Megiddo, 609). The Egyptian domination however did not last long. The real heirs of Assyrian power were the neo-Babylonians (Chaldeans) who struck all their rivals out of the field. The prophet Jeremiah, emerging in the days of Josiah, declared to his contemporaries: Yahweh Himself, your God, has raised up the Chaldeans: submit yourselves to them! But in an endeavour to be wise, Judah tried to play a game of intrigue: sometimes it yielded, sometimes it laid plots against the world power. The end came when under Nebuchadnezzar the Chaldeans made their final onslaught. In 597 they conquered Jerusalem and sent some of the upper class into exile. When eleven years later the game of intrigue was renewed, the Babylonians made an end: in essentials they destroyed the city and dispatched a great part of the population into exile. The history of Judah as a state finished in the year 586.

(*e*) *The Persian Period.* The exile however lasted only half a century. Once more one world conqueror destroyed another; the Persian Cyrus conquered Babylon. The exiled Jews were allowed to return home. Some of them accepted the invitation, especially no doubt those in whose hearts burned the words of the prophets who were active in this time of exile (Ezekiel, Deutero-Isaiah). The temple at Jerusalem was rebuilt with much trouble and weariness, but it was only a shadow of its former self. Gradually the town rose again from the ruins. Within the framework of the Persian empire the existence of the Jews as a people could be reorganized. But the new Judah never became a state. It was a religious community, although ordered on political lines. In the foreground of events stood the scribe Ezra and the politician Nehemiah, both active in the fifth century. But for a long time numerous members of the old people of Israel had been living scattered over a wide area of the world: Babylonia and Egypt were the points of gravitation for the Jewish diaspora (scattering). Broadly speaking, Jerusalem became for the diaspora also the centre of its hopes and was to become so still more later on. The gaze of the Jewish community not only turned inwards with increased seriousness; it also turned outwards to the wide world and came to cherish a sense of mission and to nurse the hope of an imminent saving action by Yahweh. The tiny community did not give up the idea of the kingdom which had been promised and entrusted to its keeping.

(*f*) *The latest time.* The Persian empire, too, like the empires before it, came to an end. The conquests of Alexander the Great led to Judah becoming part of a political system whose centre lay on Greek soil, in Macedonia. After Alexander's death the land lying between the desert and the sea, the bridge between the Nile and Mesopotamia which from time immemorial had been fought for, became once again the cockpit of the great powers. Finally it fell under the control of the Seleucids who reigned in Syria. Under one of these rulers the monstrous event occurred by which the temple, the nucleus of all Jewish religious hopes, was violently desecrated and the sacred scriptures torn from the grasp of this subject people. For in 168 the temple was turned into a sanctuary of the Greek god Zeus. These events occasioned a fierce rebellion: by a terrible insurrection the tiny people compelled the restoration of the temple and in fact won a certain freedom. Once again a new Biblical teacher and prophet powerfully raised his voice: the Book of Daniel kept alive in this fierce struggle the burning conviction that Yahweh would not allow Himself to be overcome but would destroy the most powerful adversary.

Thus late Judaism which emerged from the exile should not, by an over-simplification, be described as paralysed. It could give vivid tokens of its continuing life. But of course the impulses which stirred up zeal for the law and expectation of the coming saving work of God, and which thus worked inwardly, were dissociated from those impulses which were effective outwardly and which still in case of necessity could seize the sword; seldom were they harmonized and in fact were as a rule in conflict. When this happened the former set of impulses did tend towards petrifaction (later Pharisaism), and the latter towards adaptation to the forms of life and thought in the surrounding world (as we find in the case of the Sadducees of New Testament times). The Old Testament lived on more strongly and purely in the former tendencies, among those whose piety was centred in the law, and still more among the silent insignificant poor of the country. Not from among those who wielded power and enjoyed the prestige of great names, but from the circle of the lowly, the "silent in the land", did the figure of Jesus emerge, the Old Testament's fulfiller. The story of power and dominion finally ended with the shriek of the Jewish revolt against Rome and the conquest of Jerusalem by the Emperor Titus in A.D. 70.

3. *The God of Israel*

The history of Israel-Judah, such as we have surveyed it in broad outline, was the history of a tiny people living on highly contested territory within the framework of surrounding world powers. It appears like an appendix, or an insignificant interlude. What in reality Israel-Judah was it certainly does not owe to its power. The fact that it grew from a group of tribes into a people is only understandable in the light of what constituted the centre of its story: the covenant with Yahweh. "Yahweh, the people and the world"—that is the theme of the history of this nation. In this connexion religion is not an adjunct, or a marginal phenomenon, but the origin and the kernel. The whole life of Israel is bound up with its God. It rests not upon its own intrinsic power, nor upon its share in the power of other peoples and states, but upon the covenant of its God. And the fundamental question which is at stake in the history of Israel-Judah is this: does this people, like other peoples, live by the power which it is able to exert politically or economically or by dependence on the divine covenant? But if the covenant is really believed in, then it gives birth to the growing conviction: it is our God Himself who secretly controls world politics and the peoples' struggle for power. It is not the world empires that rule the destinies of the world, but—Yahweh, the God of Israel! This is the fundamental conviction to which the prophets give expression.

Who is Yahweh? The name, which formerly was mistakenly read as Jehovah, cannot be satisfactorily explained linguistically. The Old Testament itself explains it (Exod. 3:14) with reference to its meaning and theological implications: "I am that I am." Yahweh is a name (whereas "Elohim", i.e. God, is a description) and as such it serves the purposes of invocation and distinction: only this God is to be invoked, not the gods of the peoples. God has a name because He discloses Himself on the plane of earth and wills to be called upon by men. The God of the Bible is no idea, far removed from earthly concerns, but a living "Person" who speaks and is addressed. In other religions it is just the concrete, the living, the earthly, which is the ever-changing. But the Old Testament is borne along by the conviction that God, Yahweh, is living, concerned with the world, and yet at the same time utterly unchanging ("I am that I am"). Later these two aspects, concern with the world and superiority over the world, were expressed by the avoidance of the name Yahweh (which the Jews feared to utter) and the substitution for it of "the Lord". This again is how the Septuagint proceeds, as also the Vulgate. The frequent addition "of hosts" (Sabaoth, e.g. Isa. 6:3) suggests that Yahweh is not only the God of Israel but also the ruler of invisible powers, of the angels. He is not God because His people have chosen Him, no: He who did not need man, has concerned Himself with the human race.

Chapter 4

CREATION AND SIN

1. *The Creation* (Genesis 1 and 2)

(*a*) *The general character of the creation stories.* The very fact that we have been familiar with the creation stories since our childhood days can be a positive hindrance to our understanding of them: we are too easily inclined to relegate them to the sphere of the remote and legendary. On the other hand it is not the purpose of these accounts to be historical and in fact they are not historical. They express the Biblical judgment about the world and man in narrative form. Through this medium they point out that our relation to the Creator does not rest on our own thoughts but upon His deed. Whoever wishes to understand these accounts must be willing to consider what they desire to say. He will not then stumble over the fact that these testimonies have their own characteristic outmoded picture of the world, which they have no desire to urge us to accept. It is not here a question of scientific instruction, but of *our* present life in its subordination to God. It is in this way that the whole Biblical picture of the beginning of things (Gen. 1–11) must be read. The theme is always: man before God. Hence at bottom it is constantly concerned with ourselves.

Two distinct accounts speak to us about the creation: the first (Gen. 1—2:4a) belongs to the priestly document (fifth century), the second (Gen. 2:4b–25) to the Yahwistic (*circa* ninth century).

(*b*) *The first account* spans a wide curve from the world to man who is blessed by God. "Heaven and earth" stand first. Hence also the incomprehensible and, for ancient man, mysterious world of the heavens, the world of the stars (which elsewhere are always considered as gods), are the creation of God. What is here attested and affirmed is the loftiness and transcendence of God. This idea is majestically expressed in the statement that God uses merely His creative word: there is no wrestling with primaeval matter, no struggle against other divine beings (as there was according to the Babylonian myth), but here God stands forth as Lord and over against Him the world in its manifoldness is disclosed as His creation.

But the creative action of God is marked by the establishment of order. One thing follows on another and the stylistic repetitiveness which strikes us in the description of the six days of creation is a most effective expression of the thought that God acts according to His sovereign plan. What He thus creates is *good*: the Creator says "yes" to the creation. Again, all this living interconnexion of creatures created in goodness and due succession has as its aim and meaning the creation of man, who is made in the image of God. And once again, man is called to subdue the earth unto himself: he is endowed by his Creator with a privilege and a commission. At the same time a limit is set to this: here not the animals but only the plants are given to man for food. The whole account reaches its crown and culmination in the "rest" of God on the seventh day: the Creator is free from the officious business of evil man and the aim of the creative process is peace. The Sabbath, the epitome and symbol of the divine peace and the expression of the divine attitude, must become also the ideal attitude of man.

(*c*) *The second account* throws light not so much on the transcendence as on the inexhaustible goodness of the Creator. Here we move in the limited world of man. It is consonant with the concreteness of the narrative that the divine name Yahweh is used. "In the day that the Lord God made the earth and the heavens" . . . the account begins. The earth stands first here. And this earth, prepared by Yahweh, awaits man to till it (and hence, in contrast to a widespread stupid opinion, man is destined to work and not to laziness). God takes man from the earth ("you are dust", we read in 3:19). It is God Himself who grants man life from the fountain of His own divine life—"He breathed into his nostrils the breath of life" is the vivid description. But at once Yahweh shows His care for man. He gives him a garden, a sphere in which to live and work ("paradise" has nothing to do with Lubberland); and, in virtue of the waters which stream forth from it, this garden becomes the navel of the earth: the great rivers of Mesopotamia, the Euphrates (Phrat) and the Tigris (Hiddekel) flow from this home of man. In the Old Testament the river is largely used as a symbol of blessing.

But this man, thus richly endowed, remains wholly dependent on his Creator; his life is not derived from within himself and he does not live for himself. This is revealed to him inasmuch as he is allowed to eat of all the trees of the garden except of the tree of life (or the tree of the knowledge of good and evil). The ultimate thing, life itself and the *independent* power to distinguish between good and evil, belongs to God alone. By his own resources man has no life and he knows good and evil only through the wisdom of God. Were he to try to gain an independent control of life, he would succeed only in drawing death upon himself. Were he to try to be able to distinguish independently between good and evil (Gen. 3) he would succumb to evil. Hence his Creator wills to save him from the possibility of transgressing his limits. The command is therefore a kindness.

Man however must not stand over against his God in solitude. He is called to be God's partner and for this purpose he needs a human partner. The animals cannot fulfil this role; man is indeed their lord (and this is implied in his giving them names) but he cannot have real fellowship with them. This can come to him only through someone like himself. The likeness of woman to man is suggested by the fact that she is taken from man's flesh; in the creature of another sex adjoined to him man finds the more emphatically a mirror of himself; thus the Creator has ordered it. Hence in this connexion, before the fall, there is no room for shame.

(*d*) *The world.* Two points are here of special importance. Firstly the Old Testament knows nothing of dualism, no enmity between the world and God, no cleavage in reality; and secondly it knows nothing of a world left to itself, and living from within itself. This remains true also in the New Testament.

Hence first: "The earth is the Lord's and the fulness thereof" (Ps. 24, cf. also Pss. 66; 96; 97). The Bible knows nothing of a piety which negates the world, in order to be able to enjoy God. The world which is rejected[1] is the world which "is in the power of the evil one",[2] man's world resulting from man's revolt against God and corruption of the things which were subordinated to his use. There is no question of a withdrawal into the sphere of the "purely spiritual". Sin—with which we shall be concerned later—lies not in the worldly and the bodily but precisely in the realm of the spirit. Hence it is that the Old Testament is so concrete and speaks in such world-affirming terms. It is significant that what stands at the centre of the Old Testament is a land. Earthly life is here directed and promised. The hope of the Bible too is not without a this-worldly emphasis. It is fixed not on the beyond of the soul, but on the rule of the Creator over the world which He has made. At the end of history stands not merely the new heavens but also the new earth.[3]

But secondly, this world-affirmation so characteristic of the Bible is not made for the sake of the world itself but on behalf of the Creator. The world, the earth, nature, is good because He has fashioned this created order. Its goodness and life are not

[1] "Do not love the world or the things in the world . . . for all that is in the world, the lust of the flesh and the lust of the eyes and the pride of life, is not of the Father but is of the world. And the world passes away, and the lust of it. . . ." 1 Jn. 2:15–17.

[2] "We know that we are of God, and the whole world is in the power of the evil one." 1 Jn. 5:19.

[3] "Then I saw a new heaven and a new earth; for the first heaven and the first earth had passed away." Rev. 21:1.

contained within itself and do not arise from its own matrix, but consist in God: in God is the "source of life" and "in His light we see light" (Ps. 36:9). The Bible is well aware of how dangerous the world can be when man turns away from his Creator. It gives intimation of terrible catastrophes, and the prophetic books are full of such descriptions. Also it speaks emphatically enough of daemonic powers, under whose control falls a world subjected to the wrath of God. But from its first page to its last, it is filled with the conviction that this world has a sovereign Lord. Man may misuse and devastate the world, daemonic powers may be unleashed within it. But the Lordship of God stands at the end of things as at the beginning. To believe in the Creator always means to believe in the sovereignty of God over the world.

(*e*) *Man*. First of all it is true of man that he is a creature among other creatures and interlinked with the rest of the creation. But to this is added a second feature: man stands in a special relation to his Creator; he is made in the image of God and called to fellowship with God.

What is the meaning of "the image of God"? It is well known that the Old Testament sternly forbids the worship of God through images or any attempt to represent God plastically.[1] And yet here we read of the image of God! This does not of course mean that man is the sole true image of God, for this would imply that man might be venerated as divine and it is just this thought which the Old Testament feels to be repulsive. The meaning is firstly that the dignity of man is not inherent to himself but is something that he receives from God. When God disappears from man's horizon, then the dignity of man is effaced and his humanity destroyed. But in what consists precisely this likeness to God? Formerly it was often thought that it resided in the soul of man. But there is no mention of this in Gen. 1, and the breath of life in Gen. 2:7 is not the soul in our sense. It should be observed that God speaks in the plural: "Let us make man", "in our image, after our likeness". This seems to suggest that God has as it were within Himself someone standing over against Himself: He is both I and Thou in one. The meaning of this personal relation within the Godhead only becomes clear in the New Testament where Jesus is spoken of as the Son of God. But let us notice that in 1:27, as though in one breath with the affirmation of man's similitude to God, the text continues: "And He made them male and female". Once more a personal relationship! Man is not only I: he is always also Thou. In this relation-

[1] Second commandment of the decalogue: "You shall not make yourself a graven image or any likeness of anything . . . you shall not bow down to them or serve them; for I the Lord your God am a jealous God." Exod. 20:4,5.

ship to the other, of man to woman, we must see the essence of man's likeness to God. Consonantly with this, God's relation to His people linked to Him by the covenant is often compared with the marriage bond.[1]

We must consider later what became of the image of God after the fall of man. By anticipation we must simply point out that a disturbance of man's relation to God would have as its inevitable consequence a disturbance of men's relations with each other.

(*f*) *The Creator*. The most important point is first that God in no way belongs to the world but confronts it in His sovereign freedom, and secondly that He nevertheless comes forth in freedom out of His hidden being in order to draw man into communion with Himself.

Myths, sagas, theories, surmises about the origin of the world (i.e. cosmogonies) abound. But always their characteristic feature is that the gods or the forces of nature, to which the genesis of our world is referred, are in some sense component parts of this world. There is nowhere in all this any hint of what the Bible affirms in its first word: the beginning. For it is impossible for us men to picture to ourselves a real beginning which did not also imply the end of something previous. Everywhere we meet something which has arisen—but which has arisen out of something else, whether it be a god or force of nature. As long as we must view things in this way our world is left to itself and so has no support or stay. It can only have such support when somewhere within it something emerges which is not itself "the world". And this is something which we simply cannot imagine. For this reason, all the gods of all the peoples are somehow involved in the world, they are as it were the epitome of what we mean when we speak to-day of "nature" or the "powers of nature". But the God to whom the Bible bears witness is "in the beginning"; He stands outside the world of becoming and decay. Therefore in Him we can trust and rest. The word for "create" which we find in the first verse of the Bible always connotes a divine activity. Whatever man creates is only a process of change. But God creates in freedom, "out of nothing". He alone is in truth Creator, He does not merely refashion, and because He has created us—in whatever way—our existence has meaning.

If this is so, then the world is completely robbed of its deities. In place of the countless gods and powers of which man is afraid and which he must propitiate or render innocuous (whether it be the primitive fetish or one of the substitute deities of modern times, as for example economics with its intrinsic laws, or race or

[1] Cf. esp. "I will betroth you to me for ever; I will betroth you to me in righteousness and in justice, in steadfast love, and in mercy. I will betroth you to me in faithfulness; and you shall know the Lord." Hos. 2:19,20.

nation or state or capital, etc.) God stands forth alone and sovereign. None is to be feared, none is to be trusted, except God. It is from this viewpoint that in the course of centuries it has proved possible to survey the world soberly and factually. The world-view proper to natural science has grown up on the soil of a Western world orientated by the Christian faith, and it was able to do so because this faith in the Creator-God deprived the world of its divinity. It is only when we believe in the Creator that the world is really a world for us. If we do not believe in the Creator then we must either deify the world or mystically transform it or—as so often happens to-day—regard it as a meaningless chaos in which man cannot truly exist as a human being.

God is the free Lord of the world. That was our first point. But the second is inseparably involved with it: this same God who does not need the world, nor man, has yet come forth out of His inscrutable being. The world is in fact a something positive outside God. The Bible knows nothing of those fantastic opinions according to which the world is simply so to speak a garment of God, a radiance or emanation from His being. In virtue of the divine creative will, the world is something in its own right. It is only so, to be sure, because it is grounded in God. With man it is likewise. But of man it is further true that God enters into communion with him. He wills to be God for man. He draws man into the covenantal relationship.

It is clear that such thoughts cannot be of man's own devising. They cannot be inferred from observation of the world or of man. That we know about the Creator at all is due solely to the fact that He has revealed Himself to us. In other words: that God is our God and that we are to be in communion with Him through His covenant of grace, is revealed to us in the Person of Jesus Christ. This is latent even in the creation stories. Thus the gospel of St. John (ch. 1) has seen the matter, and the epistle to the Colossians expresses the same thing: "For in Him all things were created, in heaven and on earth, visible and invisible" (Col. 1:16).

2. *The Fall of Man*
(Genesis 3,4:1–16; 6:1–3; 9:1–7; 1:11–9)

(*a*) *Sin as Disturbance*. It is not said that sin was "in the beginning". It is something secondary. It represents a disturbance of order, a corruption. The Bible declares that it is not pristine. It is not as though from the deep origin of things God had in opposition to Himself a counter-god, evil or the devil. This would be dualism (a division in ultimate reality). In that case we men would stand poised between God and the devil; we should belong wholly to neither. The Bible knows nothing of this. According to it, man and his world belong wholly and integrally to the Creator. Evil has no part in man. What he yields to evil, of that he robs God.

(*b*) Whence sin springs, no one can explain. Nor does the Bible attempt to do so. It narrates how man and woman *become guilty* of sin. The Bible does not engage in a theoretical discussion of it, but tells of it in narrative form. The story of the fall, like the second account of creation, belongs to the Yahwist. This story too may from a literary point of view be considered a saga. But how terribly real it is, every attentive reader must recognize; it is like a mirror in which we see our own face reflected.

The encounter between the woman and the subtle serpent is something of a mystery. Who or what speaks through the creature's voice? The serpent asks a cunning question, which according to the facts can only be answered negatively: the Lord God by no means forbade them to eat of "any" tree. But his interest is aroused by the correct answer which the woman gives. Really, why this inexplicable exception? What is there about the tree in the midst of the garden? The command of God can no longer be taken for granted. With the suggestion: "Should God have said?" we see sin at work, here and ever afresh. The serpent is quick to develop his point: your God is not a good God; He does not grant you the highest; He wishes to keep you down, and stupid; hence this limit. You could have more than you have; there is the tree and if you enjoy its enticing fruits (you have only to stretch forth your hand) then you can be more than men; you can be as gods: then God will no longer be able to tell you what you shall do and what you shall not do, what is good and evil; you will know that yourselves, you will thus be yourselves the masters.

Then the woman surveys the precious fruit and yields to the promise of the serpent (3:6)—and the eating of it and giving of it to her husband has the effect of something almost accessory, an inevitable consequence: the decisive thing has already taken place.

And now there does in fact occur something like a "becoming wise": these two persons look at themselves and are ashamed. Now they know something about evil. Nothing has changed in the outer world; they were naked before this happened. Now they are no longer able to live with each other unembarrassed, they have a bad conscience: the natural has become the painful. But even if now—and always—they can conceal themselves from each other, they cannot conceal themselves from God. They try to do so at first by hiding among the trees. Then they try prevarication: one transfers the guilt to the other. That then is the nobility which man has acquired, his constant assertion that "it was not his fault". But God takes man at his word. It was the serpent, says man. The serpent receives his condemnation. It was the woman, says the male. The woman is judged: she is no longer free *vis-à-vis* her husband but dependent on his will, and childbirth, the supreme fulfilment of her life, is now both torment and peril for her. But the man who thus attempted to excuse himself does not after all go free. The land which his God had prepared for his use is subjected because of man to the curse, and the work for which man was created (2:5,15) shall no longer bear its proper fruit in spite of toil and trouble, while death casts its shadow over all.

Man had wished to become a god, now he is wholly relegated to the earthly. Dust thou art and to dust shalt thou return! But is not death itself a favour granted to man who has now become the victim of sorrow and pain? In any event, if now man were to put forth his hand in self-will and take of the tree of life (3:22), of the fruit of the other forbidden tree, he would perish miserably beyond hope of salvation. Therefore God expels man from the garden, driving him forth into the world of hard toil, which however does not cease to be God's world.

(*c*) *Sinful man.* The penetrating psychological insight disclosed in this story has often been praised. It springs from the fact that the Biblical witnesses, just because they have a vision of God, are also able to sound the heart of man. For what is here depicted goes to the roots of man's being. Temptation does not flow from outward things, not even from the nudity of bodies or the precious beauty of untouched fruits. All that has its intrinsic worth and splendour. But man! He allows himself to be persuaded and clearly only too willingly (at all times) that he might be more than man—and in so doing he sinks below the human, losing his nobility because he loses his God. Here he would so much like to be as God—hence not to live grounded in God and in the presence of God, but to confront God on equal terms. Here lies the heart of sin. The manifestation, the particular transgression, whether it be the taking of forbidden fruit (how trivial this might seem in itself) or robbery or divorce or whatever else, is but a consequence, fruit borne of a corrupt tree. In this account the Bible does not use the word sin. But it secretly governs the whole narrative. And now we understand why the Bible takes sin with such deadly seriousness: it is the spiritual suicide of man, whereby man separates himself from God.

The Old Testament never refers back to this story of the fall. Does it wish to prevent man from referring his own sinfulness to Adam and Eve and thus once again trying to relieve himself of guilt? In any case from now on the Bible declares to sinful man what the prophet Nathan declared to his king with knife-sharp reproachfulness: "Thou art the man!" (2 Sam. 12:7). Adam means man simply. There is no page of the Bible where the sin of man is not presupposed. The Bible does not flatter us; henceforth it depicts the history of man as the history of a sinner. It tells how God is not set aside through sin or banished to a remote distance, how God fights against sin and finally overcomes it. The great enmity between man and the serpent which is in question in 3:15 mirrors a yet deeper opposition, essential to the theme of saving history and to the "finale" of which the New Testament bears witness.

(*d*) *God's attitude to sinful man.* It is usual to group the stories of chs. 4–11 of Genesis with chs. 1–3 under the general heading: "primal history of man according to the Bible". In them we see this clash of which we have been speaking powerfully at work.

The whole begins with a murder committed from motives of religious envy (Cain and Abel) and deeds of violence (see 4:23,24), transgression of the limits ordained by God (6:1–4), sin and wrongdoing spread further. But a more important point is that sinful man is not left to himself. This is shown in the first place by the fact that God holds judgment: He confronts the murderer Cain and makes him a wanderer on the earth, in the flood He brings to an end a corrupt generation (chs. 7 and 8). He shows Himself still more powerful and glorious by the fact that He exercises grace, chooses men who in spite of everything lead a life according to His will (Enoch 5:21–24 and especially Noah, 6:8ff.) and excepts them from the general condemnation. Henceforth judgment and grace are constantly interacting. And the symbol of grace is the covenant. In 8:20ff. the theme is the conclusion of a covenant with Noah and it is treated in a very concrete, earthly way. To the covenant however is allied the law, which is as it were a covenantal ordination. The first law in the Bible is found in 9:1–7. It is striking that now on the shattered earth man is permitted to enjoy the flesh of animals: peace is no more (9:2–4). But Noah, on whom Yahweh had showered his grace, is a sinful man too (9:20,21) and his descendants are still more so.

It is important to notice what a great part is played in this section of the Bible by the family and its history. In chs. 5 and 10 we meet long family registers: a hint that man is not an isolated individual in the sight of God but a link in a chain, and that sin and grace are not confined in their effects to individuals but operate powerfully on the children and the children's children. In the table of the races given in ch. 10 the totality of ancient humanity is traced back to Noah and his three sons: it is placed under the protection of the covenant made with Noah, but equally it shares in the guilt of Noah and his family. In any case the Bible surveys mankind as a whole. The unity of mankind is presupposed in the unity of God, whereas conversely nationalism is always allied to polytheism (belief in many gods). But this very unity becomes for man the motive of sin: the story of the tower of Babel shows how men by the arrogance of their cultural ambition desire to make a name for themselves and to erect a protecting sign of their unity—and how then Yahweh shatters the tower and the unity. If the primal thing and the will of God (for so we must understand it) was unity, there arises now under a divine judgment of wrath the multiplicity of peoples and languages; very soon, clash and conflict and war. The developing process of sin makes inroads into human existence that grow ever wider.

But the subsequent chapters of Genesis show that the gracious deed of God also takes a wider sweep: separate peoples now exist and the gracious choice of Yahweh, which in Noah turned to humanity as a whole, now fixes on a single people: in Abraham, Isaac and Jacob.

Chapter 5

ISRAEL

(Genesis 12:1–9; 15; 22; 28; 32:22–33; Exodus 3–4; 19; 20–23; 32; 33; Deuteronomy 4; 6; 7)

1. *The Patriarchs*

(*a*) *The position of the patriarchal stories.* We have maintained that the heart of the Old Testament is Yahweh's covenant with Israel. But according to Biblical tradition this covenant is not the first work of God. Certainly the God who calls the world into being is none other than Yahweh, the God of Israel. The God who establishes His covenant with Noah is Yahweh. But Israel is not yet the theme: the covenant with Noah applies to collective humanity, which is traced back to him. Not until we reach the figures of Abraham, Isaac and Jacob do we as it were reach the preparation for the covenant concluded with Israel. But even then only the preparation; for the fathers or patriarchs are involved not only with Israel but equally with other peoples. Abraham is also the father of the Ishmaelites (Gen. 16), Isaac is also the father of the Edomites (who are traced back to Esau; Gen. 25:30); both of these peoples were many times the enemies of Israel. But it is more important to notice that the fathers stand in a covenantal relation with Yahweh, that they live by faith and experience the faithfulness of God, although as yet that law did not exist in which Israel later was to see the summary of the divine covenant. Hence Yahweh's covenant precedes the law, and faith is exercised before the emergence of the law. This point was strongly underlined by Paul (Rom. 4). His argument is that the goodness of God is not the outcome of the fulfilling of the law, but conversely that the law rests on the goodness of God.

The pastoral stories have been woven together from various strands of tradition. Not only the priestly source which we found in Gen. 1 and the Yahwistic which we encountered in Gen. 2 and 3 have been utilized, but there now springs to view a third, the Elohistic. Thus reminiscences of the patriarchs were kept alive in wide circles. Whether we should think of the fathers as historical personages is a matter of dispute. They have often been interpreted as personifications of tribes: what is here narrated of individual men is thus in essence meant to cover whole peoples. In any case this type of thought is characteristic of the Old Testament where as often as not individual persons and the tribes or families to which they belong are confused together in thought, just as we embrace parents and children in one family unity.

(*b*) *Abraham.* We are not concerned here with particular narratives. The point is what these narratives as a whole in all their multifariousness aim at saying. Abraham[1] has often been regarded as the "father of faith", and in fact we can learn from him what the Bible understands by faith. That this man should abandon the well-protected form of life in his tribe to obey the call of an alien God[2] in a foreign country, where he would enjoy no protection, and (according to the custom of the time) have no rights, that he obeys and dares—such is the essence of faith. That in the teeth of all appearances he should believe the promise of his God to give him an heir and a rich posterity, is described here by the Bible itself in the terms: "he believed in the Lord."[3] And the summit of this faith is attained when the patriarch is bidden by his own hands to sacrifice the heir, the pledge of the divine blessing (Gen. 22) and thus as it were to destroy the very symbol of his relation with God. Faith as obedience, courage, trust, self-surrender—all this is to be seen in Abraham. And in Gen. 15:6 it is added: "the Lord reckoned it to him as righteousness", which implies that God requires just this, nothing more and nothing less; that man should allow Him to be his God. When this happens, man is right with God. Thus the figure of Abraham towers above the centuries. The Bible depicts him as no more faultless than any other great witness: he is in truth a witness and not a moral pattern.

(*c*) *Isaac and Jacob.* The figure of Isaac is reflected in the Abraham stories rather than in the little we learn about the man himself. The most important thing about him is his position as an heir; the promises Abraham received—and the stories are full of this—are related directly or indirectly at any rate to the heir; for all these promises are aimed at the later time. Abraham has little enough for himself and his own share in the promised land is merely a grave (Gen. 25).

Much more strongly characterized is the figure of Jacob (Gen. 25 and 27–50). He is indeed represented as the direct tribal father of Israel,[4] the

[1] As far as Gen. 17 the name is spelt consistently as "Abram". The meaning is not quite certain (exalted father, my father is exalted). With regard to the name Abraham: "Your name shall be Abraham; for I have made you the father of a multitude of nations." Gen. 17:5.

[2] "Your fathers lived of old beyond the Euphrates . . . and they served other gods." Josh. 24:2.

[3] "And he believed in the Lord, and He reckoned it to him as righteousness." Gen. 15:6. Cf. Rom. 4.

[4] Israel is said to be the second name of Jacob: "Your name shall no more be called Jacob, but Israel, for you have striven with God and with men, and have prevailed", Gen. 32:28. Israel might be rendered: one who strives with God. But the meaning is not certain.

people of the covenant. But this fact has not led to the idealization of his character. What calculating deceit we find in his attitude towards his stupid brother Esau and his dishonest father-in-law Laban! And how he himself endeavours to approach his God as a bargainer![1] Yet this man who is to have ample experience of the consequences of his actions (flight from his father's house, danger and dependence, trouble with his children) is in spite of everything a man whom divine grace has found: "I am not worthy of the least of all the steadfast love and all the faithfulness which thou hast shown to thy servant" (Gen. 32:10) he prays in a crisis of his life. The election of God comes to him without any merit on his part, as indeed is always the way of God fundamentally.

For the understanding of the later history of Israel it is important to notice the names of his sons, and also the fact that they came from two wives (Leah and Rachel) and two slaves (taking the place of wives); the later tribes were from their very sources quite unequal. Finally it should be observed that according to Gen. 48 the sons of Joseph (Ephraim and Manasseh) are adopted by Jacob: later a Joseph tribe is mentioned less often than these two: Ephraim becomes the focal point of the northern kingdom. We will not concern ourselves with the Joseph stories in more detail here. Trial in a foreign land, fidelity to brothers in spite of their conduct—such is the inner theme of the Joseph stories, which moreover count among the finest parts of the Old Testament from a literary point of view.

2. *The Covenant with Israel*

(*a*) *The foreign land.* "Out of Egypt I called my son"; thus Hosea begins his survey of the past of his people (Hos. 11:1). The history of Israel as a people begins with their sojourn in an alien land. This alien culture has so much influence over them that Moses[2] hardly expects them to realize who the God of their fathers really is. In any event it is not the case that the Israelite tribes earnestly sought their God during their stay in Egypt. According to our available data they were sunk in heathendom. Just as the patriarchs[3] were called forth from their idolatrous worship, so Israel as a people is delivered from degradation. But it is the aim of the Bible to show that this people, who are concerned in His promise to the patriarchs, are not abandoned by Yahweh Himself: while they are still held in the bonds of servitude He is preparing the emergence of a de-

[1] "If God will be with me and will keep me . . . and will give me bread to eat and clothing to wear, so that I come again to my father's house in peace, then the Lord shall be my God." Gen. 28:20,21.

[2] "If I come to the people of Israel and say to them: 'The God of your fathers has sent me to you' and they ask me 'What is his name?' what shall I say to them?" Exod. 3:13.

[3] "Your fathers lived of old beyond the Euphrates . . . they served other gods. Then I took your father Abraham from beyond the River and led him . . ." Josh. 24:2,3.

liverer and even a daughter of the Pharaohs must become contributory to this: Moses bears an Egyptian name ("son") because an Egyptian princess draws him forth out of the waters and adopts him as her son.

(*b*) *Moses.* The figure of Moses is so bound up with the formation of the Israelite covenant people that he has been described plainly as the "founder of the Israelite religion". In any case the divine covenant of Sinai differs from previous covenants in that it has not merely a human recipient—the people—but also a mediator. Moses represents his people before God and God before his people. This task in its dual aspect foreshadows the task of the later prophets. Thus the weapon in Moses' hands is essentially the word; the other instruments of power at his disposal (e.g. the rod) are of subordinate significance. Moses is called as a prophet: in Exod. 3–4 we have before us something in the nature of an account of a prophetic call.[1] Moses flees and stays with a Midianite priest whom he serves as a shepherd. Then Yahweh appears to him on Horeb (Sinai), the mount of God (which in the thought of later times is regarded as the dwelling-place of Yahweh). Moses rebels against the charge which is laid upon him.[2] It is very striking that the two prophets who are most absorbed by the conviction of their prophetic vocation seek instinctively at first to resist it: they are Moses and Jeremiah. But finally Moses obeys.

In fulfilling his mission he encounters resistance not only from the Pharaoh but also from his own people, whose inner rebellion persists to the end. At the close of the Egyptian period stands the terrible Passover night: ruthless judgment on the sons of Egypt, a gracious sparing of Israel, which from now onwards is to celebrate every year the passover meal in recollection of their deliverance and in token of God's gracious care for them. The wandering in the desert (at first with the goal of Sinai in view) consists in a sequence of divine help and human refusal. Decisive for the future are the events on the mount of God (Sinai, Horeb); Moses declares Yahweh's will to make covenant with His people; He has borne His people on eagles' wings to His dwelling-place ("to myself") and wills to have them as His own possession, as a kingdom of priests and a holy nation,[3] if they do but keep His covenant.

[1] Read especially the accounts of the call of Jeremiah (Jer. 1) and Isaiah (6).

[2] "Who am I that I should go to Pharaoh and bring the sons of Israel out of Egypt?" ... "But behold, they will not believe me" ... "Oh, my Lord, I am not eloquent, either heretofore or since Thou hast spoken to Thy servant." Exod. 3:11; 4:1,10. Cf. "Ah Lord God! I do not know how to speak, for I am only a youth." Jer. 1:6.

[3] "You have seen what I did to the Egyptians, and how I bore you on eagles' wings and brought you to myself. Now therefore if you will obey my voice and keep my covenant, you shall be my own possession among all peoples; for all the earth is mine, and you shall be to me a kingdom of priests and a holy nation." Exod. 19:4–6.

The encounter with God, which the people are permitted to experience only from a distance, arouses awe and dread: this God who comes to them in gracious condescension is at the same time terrible in His majesty, and remains so through the whole testimony of the Bible. But this unapproachable God, who may not be represented by any image or any earthly human likeness,[1] wills eternally to be the God of this people and does not abandon them however many times they break faith with Him. This duality, the awful holiness and the tender mercy of God, is the heart of the Old Testament message and in fact of the message of the Bible as a whole.

Moses, mediator of the covenant, messenger of the holiness and condescension of his God, becomes also the mediator of the law. But this people so richly favoured, who have found in God their unity as a people, who have a promised land before them and slavery behind them, persist mysteriously in an attitude of perversity: "You have been rebellious against the Lord from the day that I knew you" (Deut. 9:24) are the words which the Book of Deuteronomy puts into the mouth of Moses. In fact, Moses has to put up with wicked taunts from his closest associates (according to the text a brother and sister, Num. 12). Finally impatience seizes the man himself (Num. 20.1–13) and he, the mediator of the covenant, is not allowed to enter the promised land which as he dies he views from afar (Deut. 34). The people however must atone for their ingratitude by the fact that a generation has to pass before the land in reality stands open to them. Thus the story of Moses' achievement ends painfully enough, although certainly a sunset glow irradiates his death.

[1] Cf. in the N.T.: "The blessed and only Sovereign, the King of kings and Lord of lords, who alone has immortality and dwells in unapproachable light, whom no man has ever seen or can see. To Him be honour and eternal dominion. Amen." 1 Tim. 6:15,16.

3. *The Law*

(*a*) *The law as living.* Old Testament tradition combines especially with the work of Moses the institution of the law. Of course, as it is hardly possible at this date to extract with any degree of certainty the historic kernel from the Moses traditions (such does exist), neither is it possible to say to what extent the tradition of the law goes back in reality to Moses himself. The law was handed down during the course of centuries, interpreted, adapted to new circumstances, expounded from new points of view, in short it was alive; it was only very much later petrified into a dead letter. But this whole corpus of tradition was coupled with the name of Moses: later bearers and moulders of the tradition did not feel themselves to be independent creators, but continuers of a work which had reached them from the most ancient times.

Thus on close investigation the law is analysable into a number of quite distinct strands.

(*b*) *Basic idea of the law*. Looked at as a whole, the law embraces every department of life. For in Israel there is no sphere of life withdrawn from the divine will. Because this is so, there stands alongside the law of the cultus (the rules for divine worship, for sacrifice and the priesthood, etc.) with quite equal justification the law concerning punishments or regulations about property or questions of inheritance. Here there is no distinction between "secular" and "sacred"; for the people even in its secular existence is still the covenant people of Yahweh.

Since the decalogue (the ten commandments) may be presumed to be known, we may emphasize here as a specially instructive example of the law the Book of the Covenant; as we have said, it is specially old and furthermore shows the influence of Babylonian law. If we study this body of law, which also from a historical point of view is very informative, we get a strong impression not only of the wide scope of the law (from injury by a vicious ox to the feasts of the community) but also of specific points of view characteristic of the Old Testament conception of law. Thus it is significant that, in this ancient period, a transgression is punished even when it was not caused by the conscious will of man (21:28); it is as though a heavily charged electric circuit were placed around human life; if an animal touches it the latter must die too and its flesh, devoted to Yahweh, must not be eaten. Hence it is not merely the evil will but the action in itself which renders liable to punishment. Old Testament law from its origins has a pronounced *social* character (cf. also 23:9,11,12; 22:20; 24–26). The much discussed "eye for an eye, tooth for a tooth" (21:24), the so-called *jus talionis*, lies in the last resort at the basis of every law: the demand for equivalent compensation. It has also been justly pointed out that in general man is inclined to knock out two teeth for one: thus the law not only requires retribution but forbids inordinate vengeance. However, we must not forget that Jesus lays down quite a different rule (Matt. 5:38ff.).

(*c*) *The law and the New Testament*. If we know anything of the New Testament, or in particular of Paul, we can hardly resist the impression that the law in Israel was a sort of strait-jacket. But such an impression does not appear in the Old Testament itself. Israel is proud of its law: "And what great nation is there which has statutes and ordinances so righteous as all this law which I set before you this day?" says Moses according to Deut. 4:8. The long Psalm 119 has as its one theme thankfulness and praise for the law of Yahweh, and it does not stand alone.[1]

[1] Esp. "The law of the Lord is perfect, reviving the soul; the testimony of the Lord is sure,

But we must not overlook the fact that Jesus Himself rejects the imputation of changing the law in the slightest degree,[1] and that Paul calls the law "holy and just and good" (Rom. 7:12).

The gospel is not a critique of the law but its fulfilment.[2] The failure lies with man, who does not fulfil the one law of love[3] which is all-embracing and which challenges his whole personality because there God turns wholly to him. Instead he cleaves to the multiple and particular and expects salvation from the following of rules. When this happens, then the law operates either to bring about the ruinous arrogance of those who think that they can fulfil all obligations by adherence to particular precepts,[4] or to induce the despair of those whose energies are dissipated in the struggle to obey multiple prescriptions. Jesus has something to say about both these groups of men: there are on the one hand the Pharisees (whose zeal in itself is extremely praiseworthy) and on the other the "weary and heavy laden". He confronts them both with the sovereignty of One who consummates the law and thus removes the yoke and forestalls arrogance. Paul too understands the matter in this light.

In Christ's fulfilling of the law, however, another development takes place: all that is provisional and transient now falls away. In this category belongs the whole sacrificial cultus, the rules for ritual cleanliness, in fact everything which limited salvation to Israel and separated Israel from the nations; above all, circumcision.[5] The gate is now flung wide open and this tremendous event is symbolized by the fact that when Jesus dies the veil of the temple, which hid Yahweh from the whole world, is rent in twain (Matt. 27:51). After the true essence of the law has been manifested and fulfilled in the work of Jesus, all that is secondary disappears: the true meaning of the law now stands revealed as freedom.[6] The law has reached its goal.

making wise the simple; the precepts of the Lord are right, rejoicing the heart; the commandment of the Lord is pure, enlightening the eyes." Ps. 19:7,8.

[1] "Think not that I have come to abolish the law and the prophets; I have come not to abolish them but to fulfil them." Matt. 5:17.

[2] Apart from Matt. 5:17, esp.: "Do we then overthrow the law by this faith? On the contrary, we uphold the law." Rom. 3:31.

[3] "You shall love the Lord your God with all your heart and with all your soul and with all your might." Deut. 6:5. "You shall love your neighbour as yourself." Lev. 19:18. "When a stranger sojourns with you in your land, you shall not do him wrong. The stranger who sojourns with you shall be to you as the native among you, and you shall love him as yourself; for you were strangers in the land of Egypt." Lev. 19:33,34.

[4] The rich young man: "All these I have observed: what do I still lack?" Matt. 19:20. "Woe to you, scribes and Pharisees! for you tithe mint and dill and cummin, and have neglected the weightier matters of the law, justice and mercy and faith." Matt. 23:23.

[5] "If you receive circumcision, Christ will be of no advantage to you." Gal. 5:2.

[6] "But he who looks into the perfect law, the law of liberty . . ." Jas. 1:25.

Chapter 6

THEOCRACY AND THE EMERGENCE OF THE PROPHETIC MOVEMENT

(Judges 8:22,23; 1 Samuel 8–12; 2 Samuel 7:1–16; 12:1–12; 1 Kings 12; 21; 22)

1. *Theocracy and the Kingship*

(*a*) *The rule of Yahweh.* When, according to the narrative of Judges 8:22, a delegation came to Gideon, the liberator of his people, and suggested to him that he should become a ruler over Israel, his answer was: "I will not rule over you and my son will not rule over you; the Lord will rule over you." These words are a classical formulation of the idea of theocracy: there is only one governmental authority, namely that of God. In the opinion of Gideon this excludes every human authority and rule; and in fact Gideon declines to exercise the power of a king. The same thing happened again, as we see in the case of Samuel.[1] Nevertheless, a monarchy was eventually established in Israel and Judah. How did this come about and what did it imply? The answer to this question reveals an important characteristic of the Old Testament message.

(*b*) *The period before Saul.* The period of the wanderings and the conquest of the land does not yet disclose any attempt to set up monarchical authority. It is true that Moses does not wield a merely religious leadership, but is considered also as the supreme bearer of juridical authority: on the other hand he is not also a military chief. Joshua rather appears in the light of a warrior. We may say that both Moses and Joshua are *charismatic* leaders (i.e. endowed by Yahweh with a special gift and commission).

The same thing applies to the "judges" in the Book of Judges. These are not princes, still less anything in the nature of what we mean by judges. Rather they strike us as men who, in the special crises occasioned by the invasion of Canaan and the early stages of consolidation, rallied one or more tribes either to resistance or attack and that—as is several times stressed—in consequence of an ecstatic excitement by the Spirit of Yahweh which rapt them beyond themselves.[2] Hence

[1] The people pray (1 Sam. 8:1–9): "Appoint for us a king to govern us like all the nations." "The thing displeased Samuel . . ." Yahweh's command: "Hearken to the voice of the people . . . for they have not rejected you but they have rejected me from being king over them."

[2] E.g. the judge Othniel: "The Spirit of the Lord came upon him and he judged Israel; he went out to war." Jdg. 3:10.

these men do not act by their own resources and initiative but by the command of Yahweh—theocracy! But the offer of rule to Gideon (see above), and still more the setting up of a short-lived kingship under his violent son Abimelech (Jdg. 9), show how easily monarchy could develop out of the rule of judges. In this process it is certain that the example of the Canaanites, who of course were still in control of the land, played an important part.[1] According to the oldest account the kingship of Saul arose out of a sudden crisis which flared up in war.[2] As in the case of the judges here too the really decisive thing is the intervention of the Spirit of Yahweh.[3] Saul is a "charismatic" military ruler: this first Israelite kingship is understood in thoroughly theocratic terms: it rests on the working of the Spirit of God.

We have further of course two other accounts of the genesis of the monarchy:[4] the first of these is sceptical towards the institution but it too shows that the choice of the king, who is admitted in spite of everything by Yahweh, depends on divine guidance.[5] This is still more true of the second account, the whole spirit and content of which shows how this decisive matter was determined by the guidance of God. It is clear from the very fact that we have reports how much the minds of men were agitated by this question of the monarchy. We may also assume that from the very first there were circles which rejected the monarchy because it did not seem consonant with theocracy and set up the rule of men in place of the rule of God.[6]

(*c*) *David*. Saul was able only in part and at times to assert his kingly rule. The Bible explains this by reference to his disobedience towards Yahweh. After much confusion his successor David emerges.

The Old Testament sees in the figure of David the theocratic ruler *par excellence*. The picture given of the king is certainly not that of an impeccable character; in 2 Sam. 11–20 we have a very old account of the serious troubles over Absalom in which the king was guiltily involved and it lashes the sinful monarch without flinching.[7] But this did not prevent him from being pictured up to the latest times in an aureole of splendour, nor from being thus idealized also by the most important advocates of theocracy, namely the prophets. In his figure the twin ideas of kingship and theocracy are made

[1] Cf. 1 Sam. 8:5: "Set now a king over us . . . as all the nations have."

[2] The oldest historical report is contained in 1 Sam. 11.

[3] "And the spirit of God came mightily upon Saul." 1 Sam. 11:6.

[4] On the one hand 1 Sam. 8 and 10:17ff.; on the other, 1 Sam. 9:1–10, 16.

[5] Samuel after the choice of the king: "Do you see him whom the Lord has chosen?" 1 Sam. 10:24.

[6] Cf. esp. the farewell words of Samuel, 1 Sam. 12.

[7] Nathan in the story of the cruel rich man: "You are the man . . . You have smitten Uriah the Hittite with the sword . . . and have taken his wife to be your wife." 2 Sam. 12:7ff.

one. David too is a military chief, but his kingship is not based on military control; the Second Book of Samuel gives a detailed account of the elaborate structure of his administration. With him monarchy becomes a form of government.

(*d*) *The penetration of oriental influences.* People are fond of asserting to-day by means of a current quotation that the world is ruled "by the providence of God and the confusion of man". Everywhere the Bible is sober enough to attest not only the providence of God but also the confusion of man. The monarchy too stands under this judgment. The very discrepancy of the reports of its beginnings under Saul (see above) shows this. In its further history too there are mingled in the highest degree traits that are both human and all too human, in fact downright pagan. Nothing brings this out more clearly than the figure of Solomon.

He is the builder of the temple, by which he crowns the work of his father. He is a teacher and a poet.[1] But he is also, out of consideration for his many wives, an idolater.[2] And he is not merely the king but unfortunately also already the oppressor of a part of his people, namely the tribes of the north.[3] Thus to the traits of the theocratic kingship are now added those of oriental monarchy; perhaps we should say, despotism. In the further elaboration of the pattern of monarchy both these traits remain visible. But after the death of Solomon, in addition to the dynasty of David, which now controls only the south and Jerusalem, there springs up the unstable succession of the changing dynasties in the north, beginning with Jeroboam I, who from political motives and as a counterblast to the sanctuary in Jerusalem specially fosters the essentially old sanctuaries at Beth-el and Dan. The fact that, in the south, the house of David remained in control to the very end is certainly due to the religious splendour which played around this house in spite of all turmoil and in spite of all the unconcealed weaknesses of which the dynasty was guilty. In the north the monarchy was preponderantly built up on the basis of actual *power*, whereas in the south it lived on the contrary in virtue of a *dignity* which was stronger than either human power or weakness. In a certain sense we may say that the temple sustained the monarchy.

(*e*) *The people.* But the monarchy was never either in Israel or Judah the only theocratic power. The rule of Yahweh was not committed solely and indivisibly to the hands of the

[1] "He was wiser than all other men . . . and his fame was in all the nations. . . . He also uttered three thousand proverbs: and his songs were a thousand and five." 1 Kgs. 4:31,32.

[2] "For when Solomon was old his wives turned away his heart after other gods, and his heart was not wholly true to the Lord his God." 1 Kgs. 11:4.

[3] "Solomon raised a levy of forced labour out of all Israel." 1 Kgs. 5:13.

kings. Here we must first speak of the *people*.

We recall that the people is a confederacy centring in Yahweh, that it is "a holy people". In accordance with this fundamental conception we find that the kings do not attain their power apart from the concurrence of the people. Quite late we see that the people in the land are capable of acting as an independent political factor.[1] One of the main reasons for Elijah's condemnation of Ahab of Israel was his tyrannical conduct towards a man of the people.[2] Likewise in matters of justice the people played its part until quite late in history.[3] In Israel-Judah theocracy could never mean elimination or undervaluing of the people. But it is equally unquestionable that, both in the north and the south, certain kings cared nothing about the people.

But in addition to the people and the priests (whose role was fluctuating) there stood forth as a theocratic authority, above all, the prophets. In later times—and the person of Elijah already shows this—they are the inspired representatives of the sovereign rule of Yahweh over against a monarchy which grows absolutist and arrogant (Elijah and later especially Hosea), over against a priesthood careless of its duties and half-heathen, and in championship of the poor and underprivileged (thus already Elijah, and later above all Amos, Isaiah, Micah). Thereby again they expressed the theocratic idea. The prophets are the living witnesses of the fact that this people is never abandoned by its God. They are the attorneys acting on its behalf, and attesting its origins.

2. *The beginnings of the prophetic movement*

(*a*) *Ecstasy and the Word.* The Old Testament derives prophecy from very ancient sources. Abraham himself is counted a prophet.[4] Moses, like his sister Miriam, is called a prophet. Prophetic speakers come forward in the tent during the period of Israel's wanderings. In the time of the judges, we find a prophet and poetess (Jdg. 5, Song of Deborah) who is the author of one of the most valuable and inspired of ancient songs. Men seized by prophetic rapture ("ecstatics") cast their spell on the young Saul.[5] Samuel too is a prophet. It is noteworthy that some of these prophets mentioned in early times do not speak specific words but are simply described as being in a state of ecstasy (so the prophets around Saul). On the other hand a prophet

[1] After the murder of King Amon: "But the people of the land slew all those who had conspired against King Amon, and the people of the land made Josiah his son king in his stead." 2 Kgs. 21:24.

[2] The murder of Naboth at the command of the king or rather queen, 1 Kgs. 21.

[3] Jeremiah is judged by "the priests, prophets and all the people". Jer. 26:7,8,11,12,16.

[4] To Pharaoh: "Now then restore the man's wife, for he is a prophet; and he will pray for you and you shall live." Gen. 20:7.

[5] Samuel tells Saul: "You will meet a band of prophets coming down from the high place with harp, tambourine, flute, and lyre before them, prophesying." 1 Sam. 10:5.

like Nathan (2 Sam. 7 and 12) is the bearer of a special message. Later the pure ecstatics fade out completely. For in the Old Testament it is the *word* which is the chosen way of God's self-communication to men.

The Old Testament implies that there are also prophets outside the borders of Israel. Thus we are introduced to a foreign prophet of the name of Balaam. Also well known are the 450 prophets of Baal with whom Elijah has such a mighty contest. The religions of the East had—and still have—a strongly ecstatic emphasis. The Bible too, both in the Old and the New Testaments, describes ecstatic phenomena. We must always bear in mind that a soberly rational relation to God is something alien to the Bible. He who has to do with God falls into a state of emotional disturbance. The only point to decide is whether such emotional or ecstatic excitement really points to God as its source. Prophetic inspiration of an ecstatic nature in and for itself does not prove the possession of divine revelation. Thus Deut. 13:2ff. reckons with the possibility that a prophet or dreamer may give signs or wonders which do come to pass and yet may urge defection from the worship of Yahweh. Hence the psychological form of behaviour, ecstasy and even the working of miracles, do not in themselves prove anything.

(*b*) *Prophet against prophet.* We are not therefore surprised when in the Old Testament a highly dramatic struggle arises between the prophets. Most impressive is the scene depicted for us in 1 Kings 22. We notice here that Yahwistic prophets are maintained in great numbers (22:6). The aim of such is to prophesy success to the one who maintains them (*ibid.*). We would suppose that such prophecy could be of service to no one; but in the ancient world the word spoken in ecstasy was considered to have magical efficacy. Prophet against prophet! We see that even in the Old Testament faith was not supported by obvious proof; even the prophetic word could be deceitful. The sole valid criterion arose from the inquiry whether the prophet was seeking his own advantage or the sovereign command of Yahweh.

It is significant that the prophets of the word for the most part announced extremely unwelcome tidings. At least in the later period Samuel stands against Saul, Nathan must at least twice oppose David: oppose his plan to build a temple (2 Sam. 7) and his crime towards Uriah (2 Sam. 12). Solomon too finds in a certain Ahijah a prophetic opponent. Thus it goes on. These men warn, summon, admonish, like the alarm clock which interrupts sleep. What men want to hear, they can readily enough convince themselves of. And the false prophets are magicians whose instrument is the word. Genuine prophecy is one emphatic warning that Israel is the people of Yahweh and that the structure of their life should be theocratic. In the early period this is clearest in the work of Elijah. He is the fiery-hearted radical opponent of the proliferation of the Baal cults in the land; he is a fighter for the honour and majesty of Yahweh, the only Lord.

(*c*) *Israel and idolatry*. We must now inquire what are the implications of the Baal against whom the prophets struggle. The word Baal in itself means master. The Canaanites and neighbouring peoples venerated a large number of such Baals, which were not seldom the particular gods of specific towns. Their feasts were celebrated as uproarious revels, for the Baals were essentially gods of fertility and to their cult belonged both the copious enjoyment of wine and sexual excesses. Into this world penetrated the Israelites, those sons of a tribe whose God was austerely ethical, lofty in majesty, who, as was usually supposed, had His dwelling at a remote distance on the mount of revelation. We can readily imagine how alluring to the Israelites were these feasts of the Baalim. We may also assume that the Israelite peasants, while believing Yahweh to be their national God and their deliverer from Egypt, considered the local venerated Baalim to be competent for ensuring the fertility of the soil and the flocks. Thus at a very ancient period, probably during the desert wanderings and the early conquest of the land, an extensive mixture of religions arose, which is described as "syncretism". Yahweh was honoured together with "other" gods (just because Yahweh was believed to be one among many gods whose propitiation was supposed to be compatible with loyalty to Him).

But at an early period the development took place by which Yahweh was honoured in those very sanctuaries which had formerly served for the cult of the Baalim, and moreover He was worshipped in exactly the same way as the latter. This can be very plainly seen in the well-known story of the golden calf. It was certainly not the intention of the Israelites to fall away to the service of another god; but they wish to make of Yahweh Himself an idol, they wish to have something material to handle as do other peoples.[1] Thus they *make of Yahweh an idol*! And thus it is throughout the whole history of the old covenant (and of the Church); when man devises for himself a tangible god in whom he does not need first to believe, whom he has merely to contemplate and worship by sacrifice, then God becomes an idol. The word-magicians (the false prophets) also made of Yahweh an idol. The priests made of Yahweh an idol when they supposed that He was firmly tied to His temple and in fact utterly dependent on the

[1] Exod. 32:1–8 must be read in this connexion; only in vv. 1, 4, 8 instead of gods we should read God; as v. 5 shows Yahweh is meant.

bringing of sacrifices. Thus the belief developed that between God and man there was a sort of bargain: if man performed the ritual which was prescribed, then the idol too must do his part. People came to believe that they owed to Yahweh merely the performance of a cult, but not that they must give their lives to His service. Sacrifice took the place of obedience.[1]

(*d*) *The writing Prophets*. In what precedes we have described the arena of the struggle into which the first writing prophets entered, i.e. those whose words have come down to us in written oracles, not seldom on the basis of still recognizable notes. In this way the word of the prophet is not merely effective for its own time and place, but goes forth to the ends of the world and to foreign peoples and future generations. Thus the written word becomes a sort of primary source of information: the prophet gives as it were a written guarantee of the reliability of his words and the truth of his prophecies.

With the emergence of the writing prophets the movement of prophecy reaches its full scope and characteristic expression. The law, the writing prophets and the psalms may in truth be regarded as the cardinal points on which the entire Old Testament turns. For the purposes of historical dating we may add that Amos, Hosea, Isaiah and Micah followed each other in the course of the eighth century, Jeremiah, Nahum and Zephaniah about the end of the seventh century, Ezekiel at the beginning and Deutero-Isaiah (Isa. 40–55) about the middle of the sixth century, Haggai and Zechariah towards its close. The books of Habakkuk, Joel, Obadiah and Malachi, as also inserted sections of other books, can be only tentatively dated. The Book of Daniel belongs to the second century, and among the Jews themselves is classed not among the prophets but among the "writings".

[1] "To obey is better than sacrifice, and to hearken than the fat of rams." 1 Sam. 15:22. "I desire steadfast love and not sacrifice." Hos. 6:6.

Chapter 7

THE FIRST WRITING PROPHETS

(Amos 3; 4; 5; 7:10–17; 8:4–14; 9:7–10; Hosea 1; 2; 6:1–6; 11; Isaiah 1; 2:2–4; 3; 5; 6; 7; 8:11–22; 9:1–6; 10:5–19; 11:1–9; 28)

1. *Amos*

(*a*) *Circumstances of the time.* One of the most successful kings of the northern kingdom was Jeroboam II (of the dynasty of Jehu, which had then been almost a century in power). The political heavens around the year 762 B.C. were almost unclouded. There were indeed some terrifying natural catastrophes, earthquake and famine, and also at times critical military situations. But on the whole peace and victory prevailed. The northern kingdom was at that time in the first phase of an economically successful development; the original predominantly agricultural mode of life was being increasingly overlaid by prosperous commercial trading (which in Israel had first been carried on by foreigners). The consequence was that if people had money they could exploit the poor peasants as much as they pleased; enormous capital accumulated in the hands of the rich and was either employed in luxury building or squandered riotously (cf. Amos 3:12; 6:1–6,11; 8:5,6). In Judah things were not otherwise (in Isa. 5:8–25 we have a very fierce description). Abundance and poverty stood side by side in relentless and cruel contrast.

(*b*) *The reluctant prophet.* Then, shortly before the year 762 B.C. there emerges on the scene a man who tears down this appearance of things because he has been gripped by the reality of Yahweh. Who he is, we can read in 7:10ff. Amos is a man of Judah, a shepherd and a dresser of sycamore trees from the extreme south of that country (1:1). He does not wish to be a prophet; at no cost does he want to belong to bands of easy-going prophets of success and magicians of the word. Now he stands in Beth-el and it is a truly disquieting message which the high priest of the sanctuary sends to the king about him. Nevertheless the priest is afraid to expel him forcibly (one never knows what such a man can say dangerously against oneself): he advises him to go back to Judah and his home and to eat bread there by his prophetic trade. But Amos at once replies that he is not a paid prophet. Something very different from what is known to the "prophets" has been experienced by him: it is Yahweh Himself who has gripped him, has torn him away from his pastoral occupation and sent him with this message to the northern kingdom. Amos does not attempt to describe how this happened; the fact in itself, inexplicable and mysterious, suffices for him. To what an extent he was a man overwhelmed by his God is reflected again in 3:3–8. Here are simple pictures: no cause without its effect, no phenomenon without its cause. And the whole passage leads up to the exclamation: "The lion has roared; who will not fear? the Lord God has spoken, who can but prophesy?" (3:8). His God stands behind him with compelling power; he cannot evade God and remain silent. A prophet against his will! What he says, is certainly not his own thought.

(c) *Against the people.* But what does he say? We have from him a number of terse sayings and songs contained in his book. They are clumsy in expression and inartistic in the use of images, but everything is said clearly and convincingly. In one essential Amos agrees with the popular opinion: namely that Yahweh has known Israel (i.e. loved or chosen her) alone of all the peoples of the earth (3:2). This faith in the election of Israel was an inevitable consequence of the covenantal idea. But Amos draws from it a most disturbing conclusion: "Therefore I will punish you for all your iniquities" (3:2). For Israel, Yahweh's election is a matter of course. Amos says: it is dangerous to have dealings with Yahweh; just because you belong to Him, He will judge you! The choice of Israel is for Amos a miracle: Yahweh equally controls the destinies of other nations (9:7,8 is important) and holds them in His grasp. If He has turned to this one people with particular love, the fact implies a claim which Israel cannot evade. But Israel merely thinks that it implies a privilege to be enjoyed; it has transformed Yahweh into a nationalistic idol who must be complaisant towards the wishes of men.

The same situation recurs in regard to expectations of the future. In Israel also such expectations had been cherished from the earliest times: the work of Yahweh at some time will be consummated to the good of His people. But since Yahweh had been transformed into an idol, this hope had quickly changed into something in the nature of a future golden age in which at last earthly happiness would be complete. It was in this sense that the people "desired" to see the "day of the Lord" (5:18). But Amos is aware of something quite different: the day of the Lord, the coming great event, will be darkness and not light (5:18). How terrible in His holiness and austerity is this God whom Amos proclaims! Thus Amos threateningly warns this people who are living in careless ease: "Prepare to meet your God, O Israel!" (4:12). Where God is at work, man is not calmed but disturbed, startled, challenged. All that Amos says must be seen in the light of his vision of God.

(*d*) *Yahweh's demand.* But what is Israel to do? Now, Israel is already doing all sorts of things. Not only is it living from day to day in luxury or poverty. It has its piety, expressed especially in its sacrificial feasts with their pomp and pageantry (5:21ff.). People go to Beth-el and other sanctuaries and think that by accumulating sacrifices they can be sure of the favour of Yahweh. Amos tells them it would be better to leave such things alone. The will of Yahweh is something quite different: He desires not cultic performances, but righteousness (5:24).

The prophet is a divinely-sent disturber of the peace—Amos and all his successors. It is best to read the whole of chapter 5 in sequence. It is a summary of the total message of this prophet.

2. *Hosea*

(*a*) *The love of God.* Hosea was active about a decade later than Amos. He is the only native Israelite among our writing prophets. We can easily realize the difference between Hosea and Amos if we compare Hosea 6:4–6 with Amos 5:4–7: where Amos demands righteousness, Hosea desires love. For it is love which Israel has received from its God; the original relation between Yahweh and the people is thought of as a marriage bond, and Israel has shamefully broken this marriage (cf. especially Hos. 2:4–15): it has become preoccupied with idols in the supposition that it will obtain fertility from them, and it will be in the event bitterly deceived. But Hosea visualizes the future state of salvation which Yahweh will bring to pass after a period of judgment and punishment, in terms of a marriage likewise: 2:20,21. Thus love stands at the centre of the message of Hosea. The judgment of Yahweh too is that of a deceived husband and lord, and for that very reason it will not be final and destructive: 11:8,9. It is remarkable that the prophet has to experience in his own life and as it were symbolically what has happened in the relations between Israel and Yahweh: his wife is an adulteress, and his children are children of harlotry (ch. 1). Thus his whole personal existence is interpenetrated with the force of his prophetic message.

(*b*) *Protest against the kings.* A specially prominent characteristic of the work of Hosea is his attitude to the monarchy. Amos too prophesied ruin to Jeroboam.[1] But Hosea, who lived through all the confusion which arose after the end of the dynasty, became a far more radical opponent of kings. The house of Jehu (i.e. the

[1] "I will rise against the house of Jeroboam with the sword." Am. 7:9. "For thus Amos has said: Jeroboam shall die by the sword, and Israel must go into exile away from his land." Am. 7:11. The dynasty actually broke up under the son of Jeroboam II.

dynasty to which Jeroboam II belonged) came to the throne by bloodguiltiness, and therefore it will be destroyed.[1] But even the monarchy of Saul is rejected:[2] Hosea thinks that by its essential character and origin the monarchy spells rebellion against Yahweh; it contradicts the theocratic idea. And we must remember that at least the earliest of these utterances are from the prosperous days of Jeroboam II. Only he can speak in this manner whose aim it is not to please men but to be the messenger of the God who is never mocked by men.

(*c*) *The interpretation of history.* Both Amos and Hosea from the midst of their present evils take a retrospective glance at the past. Amos recollects that in the desert there were no sacrifices,[3] he remembers the deliverance from Egypt (9:7) and the basic event of election (3:2). Hosea's historical survey goes much deeper, for he is the first prophet who is able to grasp the developments of past history in one comprehensive view: the election and call of the people,[4] the time of first love in the desert, and the later unfaithfulness. In fact the sweep of his vision takes in the figures of Jacob and Moses (ch. 12). In the work of Hosea we can see how in ancient Israel a sense of history and its meaning could develop: the mighty acts of Yahweh were exalted, and the defection of the people was confessed in penitential submission. But Hosea with his vision of the past was a solitary figure and even his call to renounce the corruptions of the present evil time and to break up fallow ground (10:12) went unheeded. Israel plunged headlong into its ruin, not unwarned but without perception. Perhaps Hosea experienced the bitterness of the end. It was only later that he won influence: then it was seen how, a century after his time, a still greater prophet had learned something from his message. But Israel had already perished long before.

3. *Isaiah*

(*a*) *Call.* Amos and Hosea had both prophesied in the northern kingdom. In Judah written prophecy begins at once with its climax: Isaiah is rightly styled "the king of the prophets". His characteristic vision is at once clear in the story of his call (Isa. 6). We are in the year

[1] "Yet a little while and I will punish the house of Jehu for the blood of Jezreel" (Jehu came to power by the murder of a king). Hos. 1:4.

[2] "From the days of Gibeah you have sinned, O Israel." Hos. 10:9. Gibeah was the home of Saul.

[3] "Did you bring to me sacrifices and offerings the forty years in the wilderness, O house of Israel?" Am. 5:25. Later Jeremiah said much the same: "For in the day that I brought them out of the land of Egypt I did not speak to your fathers or command them concerning burnt offerings and sacrifices." Jer. 7:22.

[4] "When Israel was a child, I loved him, and out of Egypt I called my son. The more I called them, the more they went from me . . ." Hos. 11:1,2. "Like grapes in the wilderness I found Israel." Hos. 9:10.

of King Uzziah's death (739 B.C.). The grave crises of the northern kingdom have hardly as yet begun. Both north and south are still unmenaced from without. At such a moment Isaiah, who moreover was a prophet by vocation, has a soul-subduing vision. He beholds Yahweh in the temple, surrounded by angelic winged beings who praise His glory: "Holy, holy, holy is the Lord of hosts; the whole earth is full of His glory" (6:3). Yahweh does not remain self-contained, He comes forth out of His hidden being and makes His sovereign power known on earth. These two factors determine the declarations of Isaiah: Yahweh is holy and Yahweh is near to man.

But first the prophet is moved in his deepest being with awe and dread. To behold Yahweh spells death to sinful man. Then the prophet experiences Yahweh's power to efface sin: a seraph touches his lips with a live coal from the altar. Only then, turning to the cleansed soul, Yahweh is heard to speak: "Whom shall I send?" Isaiah answers without hesitation: "Here I am; send me." Here there is no lack of confidence (how differently Moses and later Jeremiah behave!) Likewise in all that follows we see Isaiah unshaken in his confidence. Yet his message is almost doomed to failure, and crushing in its effects: no success is promised him, but he must face the prospect of preaching to deaf ears (6:9,10). His prophecy will not deliver and heal, but harden: it will bring to light the evil will, and burden the people with the guilt of rejection. And this will go on until judgment overtakes them! Only a faint glimmer of hope shines at the end—but it is a hope which can only be realized after the process of judgment and ruin (6:13). This Isaiah is stern and relentless and the bearer of a stern and relentless message. Of course he had also a word of comfort and promise and spoke also of a salvation that would one day come. But the people heeded neither his "yes" nor his "no".

(*b*) *Judah's self-security*. The earliest oracles of Isaiah preserved for us in chs. 2–5 remind us very strongly of Amos. Once again it is the stillness which precedes the storm. And Judah is equally unmoved, living comfortably for its own pleasure as did Israel in the time of Amos. Isaiah however, like Amos, foretells the day of the Lord which, like a hurricane, will sweep away all that is proud and lofty (2:5–22), and, like Hosea, he foresees the imminent overthrow of all present arrangements (3:1–7). He calls down a terrible punishment on all the inhabitants of Judah who have forgotten the Lord and for that very reason neglect the rights of the poor (especially important is 5:8f). The form of his oracles is often artistically moulded. Thus (5:1ff.) he appears among the people as a wandering minstrel and begins in the style of folklore a lament of love about an unfruitful vineyard on which its owner has lavished every care and which nevertheless refuses to bear fruit. The people of Judah liked to hear such songs. But then in a lightning flash the prophet and his message come out: "It is you to whom I am alluding" (we may recall Nathan's "Thou art the man", 2 Sam. 12:7). You are the vineyard of the Lord which cheats God of its fruit! At the close there is a subtle play on words which may be imitated thus: "He looked for the declaration of justice and behold the lament of injustice, He looked for the reign of good, and behold the reign of blood" (5:7). Thus the messenger of Yahweh assails the self-security of the people. But in vain.

(*c*) *The faintheartedness of Judah.* But no less vain is the message of good cheer which Isaiah had to deliver shortly afterwards. A few years after his call the horizon became suddenly clouded. Assyria threatened those northern neighbours, Damascus and Israel. They formed an alliance and attempted to coerce Judah into a league with them. Jerusalem was threatened and all sense of security and self-confidence vanished (7:2). With anxious care King Ahaz went to inspect the fortifications of the town. Just then he was confronted by Isaiah, the very prophet who for long had been threatening doom. But at this moment he does not say: you see, the catastrophe I prophesied has now come upon you. He is not a pessimist on principle and even the coming catastrophe is not a fixed idea with him. He holds a small son by the hand, whose name is both threatening and comforting: "*shear-jashub*", "a remnant will return"—only a remnant,[1] but still a remnant! All is not lost. And the prophet beseeches the king to number himself among those who return and are saved. But this means: believe! For the essence of the remnant is that it consists of believers. Thus we understand, in the light of this severely critical situation, the meaning of the message: "If you will not believe surely you shall not be established" (7:9). Isaiah had issued threats against the mood of self-security; now he meets faintheartedness with a call to believe. Both messages failed of their effect; King Ahaz did not believe but took the way of apparent wisdom. He cast himself into the arms of the Assyrians and incited the stronger enemy against the weaker. Thus he prepared the way for the direst peril to his country, which he himself did not live to see realized.

(*d*) *The future.* The idea of the "remnant" moved Isaiah strongly and especially in these years of the first great crisis. It appears that he temporarily withdrew from public life; in ch. 8 we find words which were addressed to a narrower circle of disciples (8:11f. and 8:16ff.) in whom no doubt he saw the nucleus of the remnant. Judah went its way

[1] According to 6:13 there remains of Judah only a stump. But: "The holy seed is its stump," Isa. 6:13.

undeterred, still entertaining the idea of various pacts. But those who belong to Yahweh must enter into covenant with Him alone (so probably the text of 8:13), neither must they be interpreters of signs and inquirers of wizards who are so popular in times of catastrophe. They must heed the will of Yahweh alone (8:19,20).

Thus for Isaiah a new community is moulded out of the ruined collective of the people: it is the community of the future. If already the bounds of the covenant had constantly narrowed, from humanity to Abraham, from Abraham to Israel, the circle was now to become still narrower: there was being prepared that community which in the exile was to be refashioned until in New Testament times its gates would be thrown wide open to the world of the heathen. At the centre of this future community, whose outlines Isaiah was the first to discern, there stands a mysterious figure, that of a child! God begins all over again, with a child. But this child is not merely a human child, nor merely a royal child; it is a child of quite a special character. The first allusion is already found in 7:14. Once more the prophet confronts the king. He urges him: demand a sign! Ahaz is evasive and finds a pious excuse (7:12). Then the prophet boldly speaks out: Yahweh Himself will give you a sign, menacing enough for the existing monarchy; a child will be born bearing the name Emmanuel ("God with us")—a symbol of the divine presence with believers.

Isaiah can hardly have imagined that his word was not to find fulfilment for many a century, until at last it could be applied to the one who transformed the earthly theocracy of Israel into an eternal and universal one.[1] But the picture of the future is already here. We call this expectation "Messianic" (Messiah means the anointed one). In Isa. 9:6ff. the figure of the future divine child takes on firmer outlines and gives us the best-known of all Messianic promises (the Old Testament does not yet employ the word Messiah in this sense, in contrast with the New where the Greek translation of "Messiah" is "Christ"). Thus there arises before the vision of Isaiah the outline of a great hope hovering over the ruins of Judah. In ch. 11:1–9 and also ch. 2: 2–4 it expands into a mighty picture of the kingdom of peace which will be established by the coming king, the perfecter of the theocratic idea: to us it appears utopian and Isaiah himself does not of course think of it as a human possibility, but as the very deed of God. It is the unique characteristic of Israel that in its moment of collapse it points over the waste of the centuries to the sovereign and exclusive rule of God.

(*e*) *The last phase of Isaiah.* The menacing words of Isaiah received in the event a strange vindication. After

[1] Matt. 1:23 refers Isa. 7:14 to Jesus Christ.

a time of unparalleled political intrigue, the Assyrians, who, as we have said, destroyed the northern kingdom in 722 B.C., decided that matters had gone too far: they made a severe assault and occupied almost the whole of Judah, laying siege to Jerusalem. How terrible things seemed just then and what Isaiah had to say in the situation is disclosed in ch. 1 of his book, which may be read as a summary of his prophetic message. Yet matters did not come to the direst extremity; at the last moment (one cannot say exactly how it happened in detail) Jerusalem was torn from the lion's maw and Isaiah himself during the time of distress had constantly an enheartening influence on King Hezekiah. Must he have pictured Jerusalem to himself as the locus of the new community for him to be able to expect so confidently the preservation of the city? We do not know, but the short section, 2:2–4, especially supports such a surmise. This great crisis took place in 701. After that Isaiah disappears from the ken of the historian. His figure towers up over the lapse of centuries as that of a lonely witness to the holiness of God and a summoner to have faith as the only right basis of a true relation with God.

One of the contemporaries of Isaiah was the prophet Micah. If not exactly a pupil of Isaiah he was at any rate an associate of his and had the same dispositions of mind. This can be immediately seen if we consider ch. 2 and ch. 6:1–9 of his book; it is the same demand which Micah makes and the same point of view from which he attacks the people. In addition, as the well-known prophecy of ch. 5:2 shows, he shared the hope of Isaiah.

Chapter 8

JEREMIAH

(Jeremiah 1; 2; 7; 14:1; 15:4; 23; 27–29; 31; 32)

1. *The prophet and his time*

(*a*) *The time.* Decades have passed since the end of the activity of Isaiah. Judah passed through difficult times; it had bad rulers and was no doubt continuously subject to Assyria. But the power of this great military state gradually crumbled. Soon the smaller states of the Near East were astir with new hopes. Very soon too the heirs of the Assyrian power loomed up: Egypt and the neo-Babylonian kingdom. Also wild and barbarous hordes from the north were soon making incursions into the decaying Assyrian empire, spreading terror wherever they went: such were the Scythians who no doubt plundered Palestine also. The destinies of the Near East are again being shaken up. And the tiny state of Judah was a participant in all this without being able to play a part worthy of mention.

Just at this time there arises in Judah the figure of a prophet who shows by his oracles that he is aware of the One who is the real Protagonist in this drama. About the year 626, Jeremiah, the young son of a priest in the village of Anathoth, is called to a task which from the very first was too hard for him and from which he was thenceforth to suffer deeply. He is distinguished from Isaiah and others by the fact that he must himself live through the disastrous events of which he speaks. He becomes a witness to the capture of Jerusalem.

(*b*) *Man and Prophet.* None of the prophets is known to us as a man so thoroughly as Jeremiah. Apart from his oracles we have not only his account of his call, but a curious collection of "confessions" in which this man over the centuries permits us to take a glimpse into his very heart. He not only rebels against his overmastering call (1:6), but during the period of his activity as a prophet, which lasted for decades, he was constantly wrestling with his sense of mission. This is the more remarkable because in his visionary experience of his call he is given the certitude of being chosen as a prophet before his conception in his mother's womb (1:5). None of the prophets was more filled with the sense of his mission than Jeremiah, and yet none has felt so tormentingly the difference between his personal being and the word of his God.

Thus the whole book is governed by an acute tension. At times the prophet can hardly bear it. His office causes him an almost bodily pain,[1] it is as if he were a vessel filled to overflowing with the fierce anger of Yahweh,[2] and the distress which he must announce tears at the roots of his being.[3] The striking fact about this man is that, while he must stand against his people, in his heart he stands on their side and with personal sympathy suffers the guilt they must bear and the trials of judgment they must undergo. Thus in ch. 14:1—15:4 we become acquainted with him as a real intercessor on Judah's behalf, as reflected in a most moving poem which was occasioned by a severe drought. Again this prophet who is so utterly one with his people in sympathy is hated by the people because of his message, is repelled by his own family, threatened by his village associates, and compelled to call on Yahweh to defend his cause against the oppressors. It is no wonder that he has to struggle with his own despair[4] and feels tempted to cast aside his mission, even curses the day of his birth.[5] All these expressions of his mind can be understood only when we realize that he expounds a message which has by no means been devised in his own head, but which he feels as a charge which has been laid upon him, indeed as a burden which he finds at times too heavy to bear. In every respect he is the most personal of the prophets.

2. *The message of Jeremiah*

(*a*) *The guilt of Judah.* In order to get to know the message of Jeremiah we start from ch. 2. Right at the beginning he reminds us of Hosea: Jeremiah also interprets the relation between Yahweh and Israel as a marriage bond, implying that it was established by Yahweh out of the depths of his love. But the people have cast to the winds the blessings of Yahweh (2:5–7) and have forgotten their God. The stupidity of such conduct tears the heart of the prophet. Not even do the heathen peoples change their gods so wantonly and these are not even gods (Jeremiah believes in Yahweh as the one and only God radically and consistently, ch. 2:10,11). What Israel is

[1] "My anguish, my anguish! I writhe in pain! Oh, the walls of my heart! My heart is beating wildly; I cannot keep silent." Jer. 4:19.

[2] "I am full of the wrath of the Lord, I am weary of holding it in." Jer. 6:11.

[3] "My grief is beyond healing, my heart is sick within me." Jer. 8:18.

[4] "Woe is me, my mother, that you bore me, a man of strife and contention to the whole land!" Jer. 15:10. "Lord, thou hast deceived me and I was deceived; Thou art stronger than I, and Thou hast prevailed . . . For the word of the Lord has become for me a reproach and derision all day long. If I say: 'I will not mention Him or speak any more in His name', there is in my heart as it were a burning fire, shut up in my bones." Jer. 20:7ff.

[5] "Cursed be the day on which I was born . . . because he did not kill me in the womb . . . Why did I come forth from the womb to see toil and sorrow, and spend my days in shame?" Jer. 20:14ff.

doing is madness: it is cutting for itself the very threads of life (2:13 specially important). But this betrayal is not of recent date: Jeremiah, like Hosea, surveys the past and finds there the same apostasy; this people is ripe for destruction; it has, as we would say, played fast and loose with its historical mission (2:20–37). The coming judgment of Yahweh is the necessary consequence of this contempt for the love of God (as is shown in this chapter 2). Jeremiah hammers home to his people this recognition of his with monotonous insistence in a large number of oracles. It is necessary enough to do this: if disaster is now imminent, Judah must realize that this is not because the great world powers are at work with their incalculable machinations, but because Yahweh Himself is taking action against His people.

(*b*) *Protest against the idolatrous worship of Yahweh.* How terrible this action of Yahweh can be is seen in ch. 7, which is about 15 years later than ch. 2. In order to be able to set it in its right context we must make a short digression.

A few years after the early emergence of Jeremiah, Jerusalem and all Judah became very agitated by a sweeping reform of worship carried out by King Josiah. This cultic reform of Josiah had the effect of sternly concentrating the worship of Yahweh in the temple at Jerusalem. A by-product of this was that all the hopes of the people were likewise now concentrated on the temple. People thought that they had now finally stopped up the source of so many evils, that they had finally obeyed the will of Yahweh and done all that was necessary and that in consequence no further disaster could overtake them. It is possible that Josiah himself was influenced by such ideas when in the year 609 he dared to engage in the really unequal battle with Pharaoh Necho who was moving northwards. But Josiah fell in the hopeless fight. For a few years Judah became subject to Egyptian domination.

Chapter 7 introduces us to this black year 609, and ch. 26 offers us valuable and historically important additions. In its great distress the nation takes refuge in temple worship; that seems its last stronghold. Then Jeremiah appears. He has one requirement to make as a means of measuring up to the severity of the crisis: amend your ways and your manner of life (7:3). And the fulfilment of this is the condition on which Yahweh will dwell in this place! Hence he implies that Yahweh must not be assumed to dwell in the sanctuary anyhow. On the contrary, it is false when it is said and affirmed so simply and played as a trump card: "This is the temple of the Lord" (7:4). These deceptive words are dangerous: they harden the heart; men come to the temple without in the least changing their way of life—and think they can find there a refuge which is not there to be had; for the house of Yahweh is desecrated when it is made a den of robbers (7:11). Such a desecrated temple can even be destroyed by Yahweh Himself. The prophet points to the ancient sanctuary in Shiloh: it lies in ruins although once Yahweh had His seat there. So also will it be with the temple at Jerusalem (7:14,15). A God who shatters His own temple! No external enemies will devastate it, but Yahweh Himself! For truly He is no idol dependent on man's worship: He is no nationalistic god who must cease to be when his people perish. There is only one way in which the people can prove themselves to be the people of this God: by doing the right, by obedience. And just this Judah has declined to do, as northern Israel aforetime.

But the prophet did not limit his struggle against idolatry to the question of the temple. Likewise the emphasis on holy books, on the ancient tradition of the Torah (the instruction book of the law) could be false and lead astray. Thus we read in ch. 8:8–13. Clearly Jeremiah supported the ancient traditions of the law, but this meant for him at the same time that he must oppose the scribes, who comforted the people with the idea that after all the ancient rolls of the law were there and by so doing hindered any real attention and obedience, prevented a real conversion.

(c) *Protest against the prophets of good.* The same meaning must be attached to Jeremiah's struggle against the prophets of good who flourished in his time. In this connexion should be read ch. 23:9–32 and the dramatic picture given of his conflict with Hananiah in ch. 28. Again it is unquestionable that Jeremiah is completely convinced of the high importance of the prophetic office. But he knows very well that some prophets make a business of their ecstatic experiences, and for every possible statement invoke the authority of their dreams (23:25–29), that in a spirit of self-will they say whatever comes into their heads and what people wish to hear—instead of speaking the word of Yahweh, being His true messengers (23:16–24). Such prophets must of course prophesy success: who otherwise would wish to hear them and to pay them? Apart from such hireling prophets there are also cult prophets pledged to the service of the temple, and apparently sincerely convinced that the sanctuary of Yahweh can never perish. Such a one is no doubt Hananiah.

Fifteen years have passed since the events of chapter 7. The Egyptian domination begun in 609 proved to be of short duration, since Egypt quickly succumbed to the Babylonians (Chaldeans). There followed a short breathing space, after which the Chaldeans made their power felt; under Nebuchadnezzar Jerusalem was captured in 597 and part of the aristocracy was driven into exile. The Chaldeans also plundered the temple of some of its wealth and holy things. They set up as king in place of Jeconiah, whom they deported, the latter's uncle to whom they gave the name Zedekiah and who was the last king of the dynasty of David. But Jerusalem still contained people who refused to accept the situation. There were people enough who set their wild hopes on Egypt and even on smaller neighbours, expecting much from their manœuvres. It is understandable that such people nourished their unbridled fanatical patriotism with the idea that Yahweh Himself would avenge the plundering of His temple and drive off the Chaldeans. It is this view which Jeremiah opposed (ch. 27): no, Yahweh Himself has rather brought the Chaldeans into the land, has appointed Nebuchadnezzar as His "servant" and made him lord of the peoples! (We shall later see how little this signified a glorification of the Chaldeans: they too will perish; ch. 29.)

Jeremiah symbolized the subjection of the nations to the might of Babylon by appearing with a yoke around his neck among the ambassadors of neighbouring peoples in order to distribute yoke-bars among them. But Hananiah stops this; as the cult prophet he comes forward with the exactly opposite message: the plundered vessels of the temple and King Jeconiah will be brought back within two years: "I [Yahweh] have broken the yoke of the king of Babylon" (28:2). Hence this prophet too, like our Biblical messengers of God, speaks in the name of Yahweh and with the "I" of Yahweh; but his message is a facile prophecy of good. Jeremiah says "Amen" to these words, for he too loves his people and what could he desire more than that they should prosper? (28:6). But for Jeremiah, the prophet of good stands outside the genuine prophetic tradition: for the genuine prophet does not say what people would like to hear. But Hananiah remains unmoved. He materially enforces his message by publicly breaking Jeremiah's wooden yoke: thus will Yahweh do! But Jeremiah knows that Yahweh has decided otherwise and he receives a word of Yahweh to the effect that the yoke of Babylon is now to be still harder, a yoke of iron (28:12ff.).

(*d*) *Grace through the fires of judgment*. Is there then no hope? We must reply at once that Jeremiah never expressed the hope of Yahweh's turning judgment aside. But it is so much the clearer that Yahweh through the process of judgment will build a way to grace and salvation. Jeremiah turns his attention to the fate of the northern kingdom, which had lain so long in ruins: it has judgment behind it and therefore Jeremiah can promise it the coming of divine grace.[1] *A fortiori* Jeremiah sees in the Jews of the deporta-

[1] "Return, faithless Israel, says the Lord. I will not look on you in anger, for I am merciful, says the Lord; I will not be angry for ever." Jer. 3:12.

tion of 597, who have already experienced the judgment of Yahweh, the starting-point for a new Israel. This comes out very impressively in the letter which the prophet addressed to the exiles themselves (ch. 29). Much that we read there may not have sounded very comforting in the ears of the recipients: they are to build houses, to work, to marry, and to pray for the alien (hostile) town in which they must live, since their own prosperity depends on its well-being (29:4–7). How disillusioning! For there were naturally many exiles not without the hope that their exile would soon come to an end, and there were also among them prophets of good who strengthened them in their vain hope. Jeremiah has to undeceive them; he tells them to settle down in their exile, for they themselves will never return; seventy years must pass before any Jew can return home.

But this disillusioning message has behind it a bracing inspiration. We have seen that he tells them to pray. Is then Yahweh not far removed, in Jerusalem itself? Jeremiah clearly implies that He is not and that He can be found in a foreign land too. And he then says specifically: the great hope for the future lies with the exiles above all. Not only the expectation that some time the might of Babylon, like all human power, will come to an end (29:10) but especially the certainty that the thoughts and plans of Yahweh are concerned particularly with these rejected ones. These plans, he suggests, are plans of salvation (improbable as it sounds) and Yahweh wills to be sought and found of them even in exile. The decisive thing, he says, is not in what land they are nor whether the temple is near or far, but whether they seek the Lord with all their hearts (29:11–14). Thus Jeremiah is not merely a prophet of judgment but also a messenger of the salvation (not success) which springs from a real return to God.

(*e*) *The end of Jerusalem.* This letter was written a few years before the final destruction and capture of Jerusalem by the Chaldeans. Jeremiah was compelled to suffer in these last days of Jerusalem much torment and persecution. He was arrested and escaped death only through the courageous intervention of a foreign court official. In chapters 37–45 his disciple Baruch gives a sort of history of his master's martyrdom. But even in imprisonment he is permitted to have, about the end of the time of siege, a remarkable experience. At this time a relative penetrates the ring of the siege in order to propose to him the purchase of a field, which in fact he is by law obliged to effect (in Israel land remains within the family). The prophet completes the purchase with all due form and ceremony described in detail for us (the account gives us an interesting glimpse of domestic customs then prevailing). For Yahweh gave him the realization that defeat and destruction were not to be the final thing: "Houses and fields and vineyards shall again be bought in this land" (32:15). This minor occurrence is for the prophet a pledge that not only has the people a future (ch. 29) but also the devastated land has a future. Thus here again judgment is not the final word of Yahweh. The freedom of Jeremiah was restored as a result of the entry of the Chaldeans into the city, and he chose to remain among the Jews who were left in the land; but later when bloody strife broke out he was forced by his own compatriots to flee with them to Egypt. There he must have died: but we hear nothing of it. The collapse and ruin of the nation engulfed his own personal life. But he was able to see beyond the ruins. In fact he saw, beyond the destruction of the old covenant, the new one which God would establish. Jer. 31:31ff. lays the foundation for the hope of the new covenant.

Chapter 9

THE LATE JUDAISTIC COMMUNITY

(Psalm 137; Ezekiel 3; 18; 36; 37; Isaiah 40–43; 49; 50; 53; 55; 63:15—64:11)

1. *The exile*

(*a*) *The situation of the exiles.* Jeremiah (29:10) had expected the exile, which had begun in 597 and 586 B.C., to last seventy years: that is, as we should say, an epoch. If we reckon from 586, it did not last even half a century. The disposition of the exiles is disclosed in Psalm 137: they experienced grief, longing for their lost homeland, fierce hatred for the related Edomites who had meanly taken advantage of the collapse of their brother people. The exiles enjoyed a limited degree of political liberty: we must not picture them as prisoners (cf. the counsel of Jeremiah, 29:4–7). Even economically they do not seem to have suffered any great distress. Nevertheless they were homeless men without rights. Their situation gave rise to a double danger. On the one hand it was tempting for them in their own interests to enter into close relations with their alien environment in which foreign gods were worshipped (the temple of Yahweh lay in ruins and even the ruins were inaccessible), and finally to assimilate themselves completely to that alien world. On the other hand there were certainly many who lived on their memories, no doubt also cherished their ancient traditions, which during the exile were circulated both in speech and writing and also expounded. These would take part in communal prayer and worship, though later, and above all in the second generation, they succumbed to weariness and despair.

(*b*) *Faith during the exile.* The fact that in such a situation faith in Yahweh remained alive at all was due to the effects of prophetic activity. In consequence of the work of the prophets the popular linking of Yahweh with the temple and the sacrificial cultus had for long been loosened among large sections of the Jews. The cultus was now at an end. The temple was devastated. There could be no sacrifices on unholy and heathen territory. But there were many who had for some time realized that Yahweh was God, and therefore not inextricably involved in temple, cultus or nation. He could be called upon even in a foreign land. Then too the word of scripture which was cherished was also an important influence with the exiles. We can imagine what enormous importance must have been attained during this time by those men who knew and could expound the holy traditions. The religious salvation of exiled Judah was above all the work of the scribes, who now took over the task which once the priests had discharged. But this involved a certain danger: in the absence of all other tangible pledges of the divine mercy many thought that they should now cling to scriptural traditions, and the sacred rolls became a substitute for the living God. It was also and above all the prophets who were witnesses to the continued living presence of God with His exiled people. We may hardly suppose that they entered into debate with the scribes; but by their very existence they drew attention to the truth that Yahweh was not confined to the past, which was the theme of the traditions cherished by the scribes, but that He was also the living Lord and Protector and Helper in the bitterness of the present and even more in the expectation of the future.

2. *Ezekiel*

(*a*) *A Pastor of the exiles.* At this point we must first mention Ezekiel, who was called before the destruction of Jerusalem and probably worked at first in Jerusalem itself. He is sterner than Jeremiah and is filled with a sense of the overmastering majesty of his God. In one essential, however, he is fully in accord with Jeremiah; he too, up to the time of the destruction of the holy city, is a relentless prophet of judgment, and only after the disaster has taken place may he become the messenger of a great hope. His work, especially after the catastrophe, is that of a pastor. Not that he loses sight of the large outlines of events, of the past history of his people, their guilt, and later their permissible hope. To all this he testifies. But in the people his attention is concentrated on the individual. He is made a watchman (3:16ff.; 33:1–20); he is to warn the impious but also to exhort the pious (the "just"). And, what is more important, the individual will receive his deserts—everything depends on the individual's obedience or disobedience. Even if the people as a whole are hopelessly lost, the individual life stands under the promise of Yahweh that he does not desire the death of the wicked but rather that the latter may return and be saved (18:23; 33:11). No one can excuse himself by saying that he is merely bearing the consequences of the sins which past generations have loaded upon him (18:1ff.). How often this excuse must have been made in Judah and during the exile: people had the paralysing feeling that they were the doomed heirs of an evil past. This attitude gave rise to what amounted to a reproach against Yahweh Himself: "The fathers have eaten sour grapes and the children's teeth are set on edge" (18:2). No, says Ezekiel, the individual is always fully responsible. He did not overlook the burden of past guilt; but such guilt cannot excuse any individual; each man can and must decide anew for himself, and even in the midst of judgment there is always the possibility of change of heart.

(*b*) *The renewed community*. Nevertheless the hope which Ezekiel has to formulate is concerned with the people as a whole. But not with the former people which had been rent asunder into Israel and Judah. It is something rather comparable with the integrated people of ancient times, and in one point at one with it: for Ezekiel expects a return of David. But such a return is an unthinkable miracle and the prophet refers to the Spirit of Yahweh as the power which will achieve such a marvel. The Spirit by its life-giving power will make of the rigid dead bones scattered in the valley (which the exiles resemble) a new people (37:1–14). "It is the Spirit that quickeneth," says the evangelist John, and Paul strikes the same note of joy.[1] For the first time we hear in this passage of a resurrection of the dead.[2] As yet it is only an image of what the nation must experience. But it was just in this time of exile that the hope of resurrection seems to have strongly emerged for the first time—a new insight which God granted His people. The Spirit, which here creates life from the dead, is however also that power which will renew the heart of the people issuing from such a terrible disaster and weighed with so much guilt: a "new heart" and a "new spirit" take possession of men (36:22–32).

This expectation of a community renewed both outwardly and inwardly by the Spirit of Yahweh, i.e. of a community which is filled and governed by the living presence of God, is something which flows out from Ezekiel into the future. It is just this which the Christian Church felt to be fulfilled in its own being: here was the community in which the remnant of Isaiah found fulfilment and in which Jeremiah's new covenant began to be realized. Thus Ezekiel points forward to the New Testament. But at the same time he is still implicated in late Judaism: he is not only the prophet of an outpouring of the Spirit but also the bearer of the hope of a new temple, which he describes in every detail (chs. 40–48).

3. *Deutero-Isaiah*

(*a*) *The last phase of the exile*. A generation after Ezekiel the unknown prophet emerged whose oracles are preserved for us in chs. 40–55 of the Book of Isaiah: "Deutero-Isaiah"—and between him and Isaiah there are far deeper re-

[1] "The written code kills, but the Spirit gives life."

[2] We have in the Book of Isaiah: "Thy dead shall live, their bodies shall rise. O dwellers in the dust, awake and sing for joy." But the text (26:19) is an addition from a later period.

semblances than the mere fact that the prophecies of both are collected in the same book.

Time has passed and the dangers of the exile have disclosed themselves more acutely; apostasy from Yahweh and despair. The tiny remnant of Judah in the vast distances of Babylonia seems forgotten, both by the great world which has other problems and also by Yahweh. But: "Can a woman forget her sucking child, that she should have no compassion on the son of her womb?" (49:15). Deutero-Isaiah is not only the messenger of this promise but the living sign and token of it. For the prophets had always been the living witnesses to the truth that Yahweh was alive, however little the people realized it. The world in which Deutero-Isaiah emerged was in the grip of change. The empire of the Chaldeans was tottering. The Persians led by Cyrus and allied to other peoples were moving down from the north and soon the old world empire was to succumb to their heavy blows: Persia looked like becoming the master of the Orient for centuries. The master? To be sure, many of the exiles thought so: masters might change but the fetters remained. But Deutero-Isaiah is filled with the conviction that it is not really so: the master who controls Cyrus also, sending him not to judgment as He had sent the Chaldeans aforetime but to effect liberation, is the Lord of all that happens (of all history, as we would say); it is Yahweh alone! It is as though he would say to his compatriots: lift up your eyes, look not on earthly things, look not on your distress—look up towards your God, and then you will realize that there is no room for despair.

(*b*) *The message of Deutero-Isaiah.* The very first chapter of our little book which reflects the history of the call of the prophet directs our gaze aloft. The opening verses of ch. 40 are probably addressed to angelic powers: Comfort, comfort my people! Then the prophet hears the voice of a summoner: Yahweh Himself will come and will return to His desolate land; even the desert will not hinder this. Deutero-Isaiah then hears a word (v. 6) addressed to himself: "Cry!" (i.e. preach). But what? it appears to be no message of good which he now hears: it is a word about the transience of all flesh, of everything human, which is but as grass (which in the East so quickly withers). Such is reality. The exiles are not likely to quarrel with this idea. But do they realize the other aspect of reality? It may be expressed thus: "but the word of our God will stand for ever". The promise and the covenant of God does not participate in the perishability of all that is human. And who is this God? The sequence of the chapter directs our attention to the Creator and Ruler of the heavens and the earth (40:12ff.). The purpose of Deutero-Isaiah is to suggest that such a one is your God, you fainthearted people! In view of this how stupid is idolatry which attempts to confine God to a human image (40:18ff.). Thus this first chapter stands like some massive overture raising expectations of what is to follow. Attention is now drawn to the present (41:1ff.). A conqueror is now arising from the east. But does he drive onwards by his own initiative? It is Yahweh who has summoned him. The proof of this is that the prophet has foretold his coming beforehand (41:21ff.). The vocation of the prophet is to prove that God controls history! Cyrus is for our prophet in fact the "anointed" of Yahweh (45:1). But all this turmoil and change in the world does not take place for the honour of the Persians; it redounds to the honour and glory of Yahweh.[1] And in the midst of it all Yahweh has in view the saving of His exiled, apparently abandoned, and in any case unworthy, people.

(*c*) *Universalism.* In Deutero-Isaiah we find breadth and narrowness combined. The creator and the lord of the whole world is at the same time the God of this tiny despised people. This world-wide amplitude of the reality and action of God is called universalism. Yet this universalism is utterly concrete: it has its focal point in the chosen people, with whom God has made a covenant, that in all eternity shall not fail.[2] This does not spell nationalism. Deutero-Isaiah is quite free from any glorification of the nation. He calls his people "blind" (42:18–19) and "deaf", and he lashes its failings just as did the earlier prophets. The people did not call upon Yahweh, we are told in 43:22ff., and in general they have caused Him nothing but weariness and trouble with their sins and misdeeds. This nation is nothing else than a historical testimony to the fact that the mercy of God is utterly free grace. When God saves, He does so for His own sake: "For my name's sake I defer my anger . . . for my own sake . . ." (48:9–11). But because this God who has chosen His people and keeps faith with them is also the God of the whole world, He cannot remain confined to Israel. The prophet of universalism becomes the first great preacher of a mission: the divine covenant, which previously had constantly shrunk, now expands to embrace the ends of the earth. The symbol of this missionary idea is "the servant of the Lord".

(*d*) *The Servant of the Lord.* Mysteriously, fragmentarily scattered among the oracles of Deutero-Isaiah are certain songs, whose central theme is the figure of the "servant of Yahweh" (42:1–4; 49:1–6; 50:4–9;

[1] "To me every knee shall bow, every tongue shall swear. Only in the Lord, it shall be said of me, are righteousness and strength." Isa. 45:23,24.

[2] "For the mountains may depart and the hills be removed, but my steadfast love shall not depart from you, and my covenant of peace shall not be removed, says the Lord, who has compassion on you." Isa. 54:10.

and 52:13—53:12). The first two of these speak above all of the world-wide missionary task of this mysterious character. This servant, however, to whom Yahweh has entrusted such a comprehensive role, is described in the third (and still more in the fourth) song as being subjected to contempt, persecution and torment, and finally (fourth song) suffers the death of an outcast.

To whom do these songs allude?[1] Some critics are of the opinion that the servant is Israel itself. But in 49:3 the word Israel is an addition and in 49:6 the servant has a task to fulfil towards Israel. Perhaps after all an individual person is designated thus—a prophet and more than a prophet. A prophet and martyr who in his suffering and dying takes upon himself the sins of his people (53:4,5,6). We may recall that Jeremiah had suffered in his inmost being the terrible things which he had to declare: he, the prophet of Yahweh, was conscious of being at the same time in solidarity with the people. The same solidarity finds its expression in Hosea, for example; his marriage means that symbolically (and yet in reality) he has to bear in his own life-experience the guilt and punishment of his people. Yet in Isa. 53 this symbolical solidarity goes far deeper: the servant of Yahweh suffers death in fact and in such a way that in the process he bears the sin of the people.

[1] It is an ancient question: "About whom, pray, does the prophet say this, about himself or about someone else?" Acts 8:34.

Thus this figure (see especially the fourth song, a song of the community about the servant), towers in solitary eminence above the Old Testament and casts its shadow into the New. That the ambassador of Yahweh should exercise power and mastery was in accordance with popular feeling. But that he should have to suffer rejection and death for the sake of the nation and of humanity was an unheard-of idea, and in it the Old Testament unlocks its deepest secret to us. At this point the Gospel of Christ radiates from the Old Testament.

4. *The post-exilic community*

(*a*) *Its foundation.* Soon after his victory Cyrus made a decree granting the Jews liberty to return home. They availed themselves of the permission with some hesitation. They were of course sons and grandsons of the first exiles. And their homeland had not much inducement to offer them; those who set out assuredly acted from religious motives. But the work of Ezekiel and Deutero-Isaiah had borne fruit in some circles. We must note in particular two distinct groups of returning exiles. The achievement of the first group was the very necessary rebuilding of the temple, with the consecration of which (516) a new period of Judah's existence began. The second group undertook the reorganization of the structure of the state. This was above all the work of Ezra the scribe. Judah did not regain its political independence, it remained a Persian province. More important is the fact that henceforth a large and, very soon, a larger section of the old Jewish people no longer lived in Palestine: there arose a widely scattered Jewish diaspora, the origins of which date from before the exile. The small community in Judea was a strictly religious community. It was very conscious of being the heir of the traditions and promises and it lived more in the past and the future than in the present.

(*b*) *The prophets.* That this community had in its midst not a remote but a near God, was attested not only by the temple and written tradition but also by prophetic men who emerged within it. On the very threshold of this new period stand two prophets who felt their mission to consist especially in exhorting their brethren to build the temple and in resisting both the weariness and the selfishness which stood in the way; such were Haggai and Zechariah.

The collection of prophetic oracles which stand at the end of the Book of Isaiah (chs. 56–66) belong wholly or in part to a later time. Some critics consider that they are the work of a single author whom they call Trito-Isaiah. Here again Zion, the holy temple on the sacred mountain, plays a great part. But it is striking that in the last chapter of this collection there stands a sharp warning against superstition and the idea that Yahweh is bound up with the temple (66:1–2). It is also striking that an overvaluation of fasting is criticized: rather than fasting it is righteousness and mercy which should be exercised (58:6–8). But the most moving portion of this collection is the plea which the prophet makes for his brethren who are so severely oppressed; this is one of the most tender petitions that can be read in the Old Testament. It is especially important to see how the prophet, moved by the distresses of his time, soars aloft beyond all tradition to the God who is the father of Israel: "For thou art our Father, though Abraham does not know us and Israel does not acknowledge us; thou, O Lord, art our Father, our Redeemer from of old is thy name" (63:16). Here we see how in this community which is so readily condemned as petrified it was possible to wrestle with God and to pray to Him with earnest supplication.

(*c*) *Piety.* The piety of the post-exilic community is chiefly characterized by the zeal and the fidelity with which it clung to the treasures of the past. As we have seen, this temper was expressed in literary form: this is the period of the final maturing of that editorial, collecting, completing, expository work which has led to the definitive form of our Old Testament. The life of the community too was deeply fashioned by fidelity to tradition. Yet at the same time it was quickened by the hope of a future which would fulfil the promises of the prophets. All hope was concentrated on the great time of salvation which God purposed to bring about—such expectation of a mighty act of God bringing to an end the previous course of history is called "eschatological". It could hardly be expected that in such eschatological hopes there were not also mingled very earthly and self-seeking traits; when the new covenant brought fulfilment of these hopes at the same time it shattered a picture of the future which was "fleshly" and not "spiritual". Where it was desired to adapt God to the measure of human wishes, to bind Him to the temple or the law, there very easily arose a separation from the greater world which was not in harmony with the glory of the Creator. Late Judaism shows that kind of decadent tendency. Nevertheless how the faith of the fathers continued to live on in it, to what an extent it could still pour out its heart, how intensely and sincerely it could still praise and worship God, express its sorrows and wrestle in prayer, is shown by the Psalms and other examples of the Old Testament's poetry.

Chapter 10

THE PSALMS AND THE WISDOM LITERATURE

(Psalms 1; 3; 6; 23; 27; 32; 42–43; 46; 51; 63; 73; 84; 90; 93; 99; 103; 118; 121; 143; 146; Proverbs 1; 8; 14; Job 1–3; 14; 16; 19; 38–42; Ecclesiastes 1–3; 7; 12)

1. *The Psalms*

(*a*) *The Psalms as a hymnbook.* The Psalms have been rightly called "the hymnbook of the post-exilic Church". Like our own hymnbooks, this book contains songs from very varied periods of the nation's history. The authors are unknown to us; the fact that David is so frequently mentioned as a contributor is due to his well-accredited skill as a poet and musician; thus he became as it were the patron of the psalmists, and later poets honoured him by placing themselves under his protection. Neither are tunes given us; yet there are some musical indications (among which is the frequently occurring "Selah", and occasionally we find an indication about the mode of singing[1] or the instrument to be used as an accompaniment).[2] Many psalms are intended for specific choirs; whole guilds of singers existed in the community, among whom, for example, are the Sons of Korah (e.g. Ps. 84). Also certain psalms were destined for use on special occasions (e.g. 92); others were written for the pilgrimages to Jerusalem (120–134). Thus we can to some extent picture what conditions were like in the singing Church. The Psalms however were not only songs; they also served the purposes of private edification: the psalter is also a prayer book. We can get a general idea of how the people understood the divine covenant and what it meant for them in public worship and private prayer. To use an expression of Luther, we can here "look into the heart of all the saints", and with justice Christianity has read no other book of the Old Testament so eagerly and devoutly, nor so abundantly assimilated the contents of any other for church worship.

(*b*) *Amplitude of the subject-matter.* If it is asked what may be read in the Psalms, the answer must be: everything which we find elsewhere in the Old Testament has been precipitated into this book. If the reader were to go through the previous chapters once more, he would find that the theme of each has an echo in the Psalms. But it is so much the more important to notice which elements

[1] "To the choirmaster according to The Hind of Dawn." Ps. 22 (Kittel).

[2] "With stringed instruments." Ps. 54.

of the Old Testament message are most forcibly articulated here. And in this connexion we must make at once an important observation. We have tried to clarify the outlines and the nature of the post-exilic Church. We have spoken of the law which lies at its heart, of the temple and the cultus and the effort to preserve strictly the treasures of tradition. All this is expressed in the Psalms too. We need only to call to mind Ps. 119 or the better known Ps. 1, in order to find an impressive example of the pious man's joy in the law. Again, we need only mention Ps. 84 or Pss. 42 and 43 or even 24, to show how the longing for the temple and its services ruled the minds and hearts of the pious. And yet there can be no suggestion that this element alone is in supreme control of the psalter. For the psalter reveals that the piety of the post-exilic Church was far richer than is commonly supposed, that in it the totality of the Old Testament message remained alive and furnished insurmountable obstacles to any hardening or deadening tendencies.

(*c*) *The Individual.* It is important to realize that in the Psalms the pious individual also speaks to us. The Old Testament is no mere collective, in which the individual is engulfed, just as conversely the individual does not live an insulated existence. We see both factors beautifully expressed in Ps. 42, which originally formed one poem with Ps. 43; a poem whose theme is the yearning for God and which strikes home forcibly to our hearts. The poet dwells far from Jerusalem, far in the mountainous north (42:6). And he is surrounded by men who taunt him because of his belief in Yahweh. He has no sort of tangible guarantee for his faith. "Where is now thy God?" (42:3). It may also have been the case that he was ill or in some other distress—hence the more pointed was the question: if the faith of the pious man corresponds to the reality of God, why is he now left in the lurch? In this situation, in the midst of these crushing waves of temptation and trial (42:7) he too eventually feels oppressed by the problem as to whether God who has promised so much (42:8) may not at present have forgotten him (42:9; 43:2). The only consolation which might help him in this deep and confusing distress is that he might go to Jerusalem with other pilgrims, in order there to behold the face of God (42:2,4; 43:3,4). But just this is denied him. And yet in the midst of all trial one hope remains alive in him; that hope is focused not on the temple, which is far away, but on God alone (expressed in the repeated refrain: 42:5,11; 43:5). Thus the pious individual, while being utterly rooted in the ancestral soil of the Church, and distressed when circumstances separate him from it, still retains the strength of his individual personality since even in his solitariness he feels God to be his strength and stay. It is instructive in this connexion to compare Pss. 23 or 63 as impressive further examples. In both cases the certitude of the pious is that they are securely hidden in God. This conviction blossoms forth in rejoicing when the pious is really allowed to enter the sanctuary and take part in its worship: convincing examples and testimonies to this are Ps. 27:1–6 or Ps. 84 or Ps. 121.

(*d*) *Psalms of trial and sorrow*. But in contrast to these testimonies to the sense of joyful security in Yahweh and at the heart of the Church stand quite a number of other songs in which is reflected the acute distress of pious individuals. There are three types of trouble in particular which find their echo constantly in the Psalms: sickness, unjustified reproach, and sin. Not seldom they merge into each other. Thus it is, for example, in Ps. 6, the author of which is terrified by the anger of God and prays for the help of divine grace. He is sick unto death, and to his sense death signifies an absolute limit, beyond which there is no possibility of communion with God (v. 5). And, as we must infer from vv. 8–10, this very sickness becomes the occasion for every possible reproach on the part of his adversaries, in face of whom however he is certain that Yahweh is saving and justifying him. Thus the sick man is assailed from two sides. Piety in those days lived largely on the idea that God rewarded the pious with prosperity and punished the wicked with misfortune. Such a view finds its clearest expression in the well-known Ps. 1. From this the converse may easily be deduced; if any one is enjoying good fortune then he must have been pious, if any one is afflicted or above all ill, then he must have been very godless. This opinion may be called the doctrine of retribution. In consequence of it, God becomes a sort of impersonal law: He reacts almost mechanically to the conduct of men. This is what really lies behind the many cases in the Psalms where a sick man is at the same time accused, persecuted, despised.

It is remarkable however that these very sick people who cannot deny their illness find nevertheless, in the Psalms, that God is their refuge and strength. This means that they clearly do not share the belief in the doctrine of retribution; for if they did they would merely pray for healing. Their sickness of course convinces them of the frailty of their existence and also of their sin, but in spite of all they wait for Yahweh to justify them and make clear their innocence. Thus at times the poets who confess their sins to Yahweh sharply reject the accusations of their adversaries. This can be seen, for instance, in Ps. 143. From the same point of view moreover we may endeavour to understand the so-called psalms of vengeance, e.g. Ps. 55. They are throughout spoken from the standpoint of the accused, and, as the parties to a lawsuit await the verdict, they cherish the hope that Yahweh will vindicate the innocence of the accused by publicly branding the injustice and falseness of the adversary.

This is not of course in harmony with the spirit of the New Testament, where we see how Jesus suffers death while praying for His executioners (Lk. 23:34) and how He rebukes His disciples when they thirst for an open vindication. "You do not know what manner of spirit you are of", Lk. 9:55. But let us remember that Jesus is the incarnate "Yes" of God to man, and the Christian must not desire any other kind of vindication. In the old covenant and dispensation, however, this final "yes" spoken once for all has not yet been uttered to the universe, and therefore the pious desire a personal and public vindication. The New Testament community itself does not expect a universal declaration of the "yes" of God to His own until the end of all things: it contents itself with the "yes" spoken in Christ. We must return to this question briefly later in connexion with the Book of Job.

(*e*) *Man before God.* However much it may be the case that the righteous man of the Old Testament asserts his righteousness in the face of men and prays to his God for the public vindication of that righteousness, yet in the presence of God he knows himself to be a sinner even when he is in health and free from trouble. There are certain psalms which suggest this in the most striking way. In Ps. 25 this particular aspect of the religious consciousness is strongly emphasized as against all others. It becomes fully dominant in the three best-known penitential psalms: 32, 51 and 130. Here man before God becomes the central issue, and the petitioner of Ps. 51, who puts himself in the place of the deeply guilty David and sees his own situation in the same light, expresses this directly: "Against Thee only have I sinned and done this evil in thy sight" (51:4). Because in these psalms the mind of the psalmist is so utterly concentrated on God, sin is most deeply realized: it is seen as something which does not come to man from outside but is rather an overmastering tendency to corruption innate in him (51:5) and thus nothing external can be of any use, not even sacrifice, only the forgiveness of God and the creation of a completely new man through the Spirit of Yahweh (51:10,16). These three Psalms have been perhaps most of all beloved of Christians, for they express the very convictions of the believer in Christ.

But another problem is set in a new light when the attention is directed not to the world but to God alone; namely the distress to which we have referred above, and which arises from the fact that to all appearances the pious by no means prosper nor do the wicked suffer. In practice this doctrine of retribution turns out to be reversed by life. The problem has received the deepest consideration in Ps. 73. The poet is oppressed by the prosperity of those who impudently mock God; he no longer understands God nor the world. Then he goes into "the sanctuary", i.e. the place where God is revealed. There it becomes plain to him—and this he can never know from common experience—that the reality which we perceive is not the whole of reality. It is possible that he still imagined the "terrible end" prepared for the ungodly (73:19) to be something earthly. But how little this is really so he shows himself by the very fact that after this reflection he returns to his original complaint and feeling of distress (73:21,22). To be sure, God has means of helping the righteous to attain victory and justification—but where do we see this? He gives no answer to this torturing problem. Nevertheless he experiences a complete change in the whole character of his life, for in the midst of the problems which torment his mind he can still say: "Nevertheless I am continually with Thee . . . Whom have I in heaven but Thee? and there is nothing on earth that I desire besides Thee" (73:23–26). To live thus is not a solution, but a transformation of the problem. Here the believer no longer is concerned to inquire about "heaven and earth"; he understands as little about the world as any one else, but he has found his one sure standing ground in the certainty that God is for him.

This psalm too remains within the framework of the Old Testament, but it points far beyond it. It suggests that the righteousness which the pious man can claim for himself is nothing other than the righteousness which God grants us.

(*f*) *The praises of the community.* So far we have been speaking of the pious individual and of his sorrows and joys in the presence of God. But the individual does not stand alone in the Old Testament, and so little is that the case that in many psalms it is hard to decide whether it is the individual or the community which is speaking. This is true of the well-known Ps. 103, for example, that hymn of praise to the God of grace and mercy. Here "I" and "we" are constantly merging with each other. He who experiences the mercies of God, who with His everlasting love sustains and enfolds us frail creatures who are subject to the menace of death (103:14–18) is by implication speaking about the covenant which God has established with His people in the Old Testament (v. 18) as well as in the New. The hardly less well known Ps. 118 is the result of a mingling of praises flowing from the heart of the individual with the praise of the Church. But the individual many a time fades into the background completely. We hear then the song of praise of the people as a whole, and it is important on such occasions that the vision of the community should embrace the universal aspect of the glory of God. There was no doubt in the later period a special feast in which Yahweh was honoured as King, who had set up His throne in Israel and would set it up in the whole world (accession Psalms of Yahweh). In this connexion Pss. 93, 97 and 99 should be read; songs of a small community, with no political independence and subservient to the great powers, and yet filled with confidence and rejoicing through their vision of the Lord, and turning their thoughts to the whole round earth. When we recall Deutero-Isaiah we find here clear echoes of his teaching.

(*g*) *Disposition reflected in the Psalms.* Most of the Psalms, whether as prayers, songs or hymns, are addressed immediately or mediately to Yahweh Himself. It is either the individual or the worshipping community whose laments or whose thanksgiving and praise we hear, and this is addressed to God Himself. But here and there prayer gives way to meditation before God. It is in Ps. 90 that we have the most impressive example of such meditation. This is a prayer, but it is also a prolonged meditation on the theme of the frailty, transience and nothingness of human life. Yet because this meditation is made not with a feeling of God as remote (which would have resulted in pessimism and nihilism) but with the sense of the intimate presence of God, this most searching of the Psalms has in spite of everything a ground tone of confidence; for the God who is free from human perishability is just the God whose mind is turned towards the seeker after Him and who will again and again turn to His own. It is advisable to read the whole psalm with this in view. Other psalms offer us a meditation which is not carried on in the form of prayer; we then get pure wisdom literature. In this category we may mention Ps. 91 and also Ps. 1 and perhaps Ps. 119. Such poems take us already to the borders of the last type of Old Testament literature with which we must now briefly concern ourselves.

2. *The Proverbs*

(*a*) *Wisdom in Israel.* In Israel there is no separation between "religion" and "life" or between "Church" and "State", between the outer and the inner. Thus the Old Testament also offers us books which show us the very same men who in the Psalms allowed us to share their life of prayer and wrestling with God and human existence, now engaged in the daily round of life and domestic concerns, in eating and drinking, in trade and occupation. But from the heart of this daily routine there again emerge a number of searching questions. We have found such questions arising already in the literature of the Psalms—the problem of sickness and the reproaches of enemies. Such problems however are not confined to the Psalms. All that in this dual way is connected with daily existence, is the special object of the wisdom books of the Old Testament; of Proverbs and Ecclesiastes and the Book of Job.

The cult of wisdom is extremely ancient in Israel. From very early times it was the especial concern of a particular class of men: the wise. The latter exercised influence as the teachers and educators of youth, and as the mentors of the great. This was so everywhere and the content of wisdom teaching is to a large extent international. Solomon was regarded as its patron. Our "Proverbs" which stand under his name are in fact a collection of various groups of proverbs proceeding from different times; individual proverbs are often rooted in hoary antiquity.

(*b*) *Wisdom and success in life*. For the theology of the Old Testament it is first of all important to notice what is understood by wisdom. To this a twofold answer is given. On the one hand, wisdom has its roots in the fear of Yahweh (very well known are Prov. 1:7; 9:10); if one does not rightly take God into account, one cannot have good success in life, and if one does not fear God one must become the victim of fear in the daily concerns of life. Thus in our common parlance we should say that Old Testament wisdom has religious roots. In essence it is not at all a possession of man but the property of God Himself: we are told in ch. 8 that it "was set up at the first, before the beginning of the earth" (8:23); it stands at the side of the Creator and was with Him when He created the earth. Hence man cannot find in himself the real solution to the problems of life, but in God alone. But on the other hand if a man really trusts in God and is pious and righteous then he is *ipso facto* wise also; piety is wisdom and impiety folly. Whoever in daily life waits upon God, he alone in the last resort is able to act sensibly; the despiser of God destroys his life. This principle is tirelessly insisted on in Proverbs. Again and again the pious and the impious stand over against each other in stark contrast.

The question nevertheless may be asked: is this view justified? Is piety really the means of attaining success in life, and is the contrary also true? In this connexion we must first of all bear in mind the purpose of the Proverbs: they are intended to be of service in the education of the people. In a rightly ordered public and social life it ought always to be the case that the just man is defended and protected while the wrongdoer is punished: even according to the New Testament the State exists in order to protect the good and punish the evil (Rom. 13:3,4). As the Proverbs put it: "Righteousness exalts a nation but sin is a reproach to any people" (Prov. 14:34). It is obvious that in this context "good" and "godless" are not used in their truest and deepest sense, as implying the state of the soul in the eyes of God, but in the sense of earthly and material rightness.

But, secondly, do the authors of the Proverbs not realize that life does not to a large extent shape itself according to their rule, even in a well-governed State? We have discussed above the "dogma of retribution" and have already noticed how sharply it is at times contradicted in the Psalms. Even in the Proverbs the doctrine is in control only in the foreground of the scene. This is suggested by the way in which the poor are spoken of. The idea of retribution would necessarily suggest that poverty and hence ill-success in earthly life is the consequence of sin; had a man been pious he would inevitably have been successful. Hence it is so much the more significant that the Old Testament again and again vigorously champions the cause of the poor. This is a contradiction of the doctrine of retribution which is fruitful in consequences. We have seen something of this already in regard to the law (read, for example, Exod. 23:6,9,11,12; Lev. 19:9,10,13; Deut. 15:1ff.). We have come to know the prophets as the passionate defenders of the poor. In the language of the Psalms it seems often to be the case that the words "poor" and "in misery" are used almost in one breath with the notion of pious. And in the Proverbs too we find Yahweh again and again on the side of the poor. "He who oppresses a poor man insults his Maker" we read in 14:31, and the same tone is heard in many contexts. Much as the Proverbs otherwise condemn idleness as leading to poverty,[1] their authors are certain also that there is innocent poverty, and for this reason success in life and piety do not always and necessarily go together.

But of course the Proverbs do not speak the last word on this question. They remain confined within the sphere of the earthly and material which they wish to regulate and serve by their counsel. The truth that all our righteousness is no righteousness in the sight of God remains neglected. The further truth that a man must suffer just because he conforms to the Will of God is also neglected. This latter truth does not remain outside the ken of the Old Testament, as we have seen from the example of the suffering servant of Deutero-Isaiah. But the Proverbs do not plumb these depths.

3. *Job*

In the Book of Job we see a man whose life in every respect is going well. But then Satan appears before God with the accusation that he is pious only because his piety is profitable to him and that if his prosperity were to collapse he would curse God (1:9–11). God disputes this but allows the matter to be put to the test. Everything that is dear to Job is now snatched away from him. He does not complain, but says rather:

[1] "Go to the ant, O sluggard; consider her ways, and be wise . . . A little sleep, a little slumber, a little folding of the hands to rest, and poverty will come upon you like a vagabond, and want like an armed man." Prov. 6:6,10,11.

"The Lord gave, and the Lord has taken away; blessed be the name of the Lord" (1:21). The test is then made sharper: Job himself is smitten with a repulsive illness. This again he at first withstands. Then, however, his powers fail. Satan appears to be justified, for Job now bursts out into heart-rending lamentation. Did this prove that God was wrong in His expectation? God would only be justified if it were shown that Job was not pious merely for success in life, but out of unselfish devotion to God. Thus a sharp opposition to the dogma of retribution emerges. But much travail of experience has to be traversed before Job himself comes to realize that God is right even in the face of his misfortunes.

A dramatic framework to the struggle is provided by the appearance of the friends of Job, who maintain the thesis that Job must have done something wicked, otherwise he would not be in such adversity, and who urge him to repent so that things may go better with him. It is quite clear that the friends represent the dogma of retribution. Without knowing it they are on the side of Satan and not on the side of God. If we compare the remark of Satan in 1:9–11 with the word of the friend in 22:2 we see the point at issue. In argument with his friends Job keenly defends his innocence; while recognizing the general sinfulness of mankind, he is aware of no particular guilt which could explain such bitter suffering. And yet he is continually tormented by the question: why does God take sides against me? He demands that God should procure him his right, and in fact plainly challenges God to a judicial procedure.[1] Only—before what bar of judgment? Job realizes that for God there is no higher court of judgment; one might almost say that he challenges God to appear at His own divine judgment-seat. And he is convinced that there he will receive righteous judgment—in the presence of God and against God. For him, the tormented one, God Himself becomes an advocate. "My witness is in heaven," he says in 16:19. In the depths of his misery he knows no other way of escape than to seek refuge with the very God who has smitten him. And even though he must suffer death, he is aware that "My Redeemer lives and at last he will stand upon the earth" (19:25). He is certain that he will "see God" after death (19:26) and that not as an enemy (19:27).

We may indeed say that seldom does the religion of the Old Testament penetrate so deeply into the story of man's wrestling with God. But Job is scarcely able to hold firmly to the hope that thus soars up in him; these words of believing trust are followed by others which disclose the depth of his despair. How is it possible to sustain the thought that

[1] E.g. "Oh, that I had one to hear me! (Here is my signature! let the Almighty answer me!) Oh, that I had the indictment written by my adversary!" Job 31:35.

against God there is no other advocate but God Himself? Job attains a solution of the conflict, not through a new thought but through an action on the part of God. God reveals Himself in the whirlwind and what He says to Job is a string of questions merely; these show that in creation things are by no means controlled by the petty rule of human "reason"; no law stands above God (chs. 38 and 39). If someone realizes that he has to do with God, he must also understand that he is not confronted by a rigid law, by "fate" as we say, or by a dogma of retribution, but by the Transcendent and Unfathomable. But—and this is the conclusion of the book—where man does justice to this God (40:1–5) because he does not simply think thoughts about Him, but is aware of God in the realm of the spirit (42:5), then God justifies such a man (42:7ff.). Job is vindicated as righteous after he has condemned himself as guilty (42:6). However tortuous the path, he has at last finally proved that it is God he has in view and not his own happiness, and at the same time God has thus refuted the complaint of Satan. By the same token the path is now free for the restoration of the lost happiness of life. "All these things shall be added," says Jesus, to the man who is "seeking first" the "righteousness" of God (Matt. 6:33).

4. *The Preacher*

Less boldly than the Book of Job, another wisdom book of the Old Testament pierces to the fundamental questions of human life: Ecclesiastes or The Preacher.

At first sight the book reads like an essay in scepticism. "All is vanity" (i.e. nothingness, the sphere of the perishable): so the book begins. And the proof of this is furnished by the most diverse regions of life. Everything has its own time, there is nothing new under the sun, and also nothing is permanent; all striving is "vexation of spirit" (1:14). Can this be considered the word of a preacher at all? But it is integral to the whole of the Biblical message that it tears down our illusions! "All flesh is grass"—such is the opening of the universalized theology of Isaiah (Isa. 40:6). It is necessary that man should recognize the limits of human life. That he refuses to admit them is the inner core of human sin (Gen. 3). And it is this very fact of limitation which the Preacher stresses: "God is in heaven and you upon earth" (5:2).

The essential message of this little book is that man can truly live only within his due limits and in modest affirmation of the limitedness of his life. For this reason he must not try to be too righteous or too wise (7:16); he must remain within the measure of the human. But at the same time he is permitted to remain in these bounds. This sober involvement in reality has its background in the fact that God is there and that He confronts man and challenges man's recognition. Where man does not take God into account, he lives in fear of reality or in idolatry of reality. But if he lives in the presence of God he can carry on the whole round of earthly activities with a certain modest cheerfulness: the Preacher encourages us in fact to enjoy life in moderation.[1] If man not only knows that he must die,[2] but also that God is his Judge,[3] and that the spirit of man is permitted to return home to God (12:7) such a life can truly be lived within its proper limits. There is of course more to be said than the Preacher declares. The New Testament also warns us against overstepping our limits by our own initiative; God alone is wise and God alone has immortality (1 Tim. 1:17; 6:16). But the New Testament goes on to say that God by His initiative has overcome the limits which we ourselves cannot overstep.

[1] "Rejoice, O young man, in your youth, and let your heart cheer you in the days of your youth; walk in the ways of your heart and the sight of your eyes. But know that for all these things God will bring you into judgment." Ecc. 11:9.

[2] "And the dust returns to the earth as it was, and the spirit returns to God who gave it." Ecc. 12:7.

[3] "For God will bring every deed into judgment, with every secret thing, whether good or evil." Ecc. 12:14.

THE NEW TESTAMENT

Chapter 11

THE SURROUNDING WORLD OF THE NEW TESTAMENT

1. *The Greeks*

(*a*) *The genesis of Hellenism.* It is well known that the New Testament is written in Greek. The messengers of primitive Christianity entered a world in which there was only one current language transcending the diversity of the nations, namely Hellenistic Greek, the late form of the language of Homer and Plato. A Greek translation of the Old Testament had already been made long since, and the apostles were able to use this translation. It needs no demonstration to say that the Christian mission was greatly promoted by the existence of one world language. But Hellenism was not only a language, it was a universal culture which had penetrated to all the border regions of the Mediterranean and had moulded their way of life. In fact, the culture which followed the Roman legions was that of Hellenism.

The cultural hegemony of the Greeks goes back essentially to the work of Alexander the Great. This opened up the realms of the Orient to the Greek way of life. But at the same time it permitted oriental influences to penetrate to the West. Hellenism was deeply fashioned by them, especially in the sphere of religion. The decay of Alexander's empire after his early death further promoted this interpenetration of Greek and oriental modes of life.

(*b*) *Philosophy and religion.* With the common speech which Hellenism gave to the Mediterranean world, there was also opened up to the Mediterranean peoples access to the thought of the Greeks. However, it was not primarily the "classical" systems of Plato and Aristotle which were now being spread abroad in the world, but new interpretations of reality by means of which the Greek mind sought ever more boldly to understand the totality of the universe and its underlying unity. We ought in particular to mention the Stoics. Their opinion was that a single ultimate reality was expressed in the laws governing all change and decay: that of the world soul. The effect of their type of thought was to render all that happened meaningful; even the facts of suffering and death. Man had only to fit himself into the course of nature and bow to the government of "providence" and he was happy. Of course the Stoics of a later time were not able to maintain this optimism. More and more a cleavage of reality (dualism) arose: the world of the bodily and that of the spiritual yawned asunder and the task of man was then felt to consist in preserving the soul untarnished by the material world, and thus assuring oneself of immortality.

We notice that the world-view of the Stoics was in a high degree religiously determined. It is true that in contrast to them stood groups of philosophers, especially the Epicureans, who rejected all religious attitudes and advised men to enjoy life in moderation, while not allowing themselves to become entangled in material things (it is only as a result of misunderstanding that they have become popularly known as advocates of unrestrained pleasure). But, broadly speaking, religious awareness tended to increase; it was favoured by the spirit of the time.

Of course the old Greek world of the gods had at this time completely vanished from the minds of many men. Oriental cults were abundantly pouring into the West. In many cases they became mingled together and also were mingled with the localized divinities (such mixture of religions is called "syncretism"). Above all, there came in from the East the "mysteries", secret cults by which men were (so to speak) transported into the sphere of the divine, and thus became sharers in the character and destiny of divine beings. The mystery gods were gods of whom it was told in the myth that they had suffered death and had subsequently risen again. Thus it was intended that man by his initiation into the mystery should participate both in the death and the life of the god, should become "deified". The aspiration of many in this age was to assimilate to themselves divine life. The influence of the mystery religions reached its climax in the later age of the emperors, when in addition the divine veneration of the emperor himself attained great significance.

2. *Rome*

(*a*) From a political point of view the world empire of Rome was the arena in which the life and death of Jesus and the evangelistic work of the apostles took place. The whole of the Mediterranean world was subject to the same political order, protected by the same military power, possessed a unified coinage and a powerful network of roads. It is true that the Romans respected the peculiarities of the peoples subject to them, that they did not interfere with their religion, and indeed often, as in the case of Palestine, allowed them to enjoy what remained of their political customs. They made no attempt to level things out. Nevertheless the tendency to unification existed and to a certain uniformity in the ways of life; the Romans did indeed take much from the inhabitants of their empire, giving them in exchange possibilities of trade and intercourse, of spiritual and cultural contacts, the like of which could not have been suspected before. All this uncommonly facilitated the spread of the Christian gospel. A further factor was that in consequence of the politics of Augustus universal peace reigned. On the other hand it was a severe and not seldom cruel government which the Roman officials exercised. Every slightest impulse of revolt met with the sternest repression. And this was felt not only by the Jews themselves: the death sentence on Jesus of Nazareth was carried out under Roman responsibility, and Paul was arrested and executed by the Romans.

(*b*) *The attitude of the Romans to the Jews.* After the break-up of the world empire of Alexander the province of Palestine fell after some confusion to the Seleucids. When in 168 B.C. the Seleucid Antiochus IV threatened the Jews with a cruel religious persecution, there took place a fierce rising from which developed, in consequence of a severe struggle for freedom, an independent Jewish state under the Maccabean or Hasmonean family. But in the year 63 quarrels in the Jewish royal family occasioned the intervention of the Romans. As a result the Jewish people also became a part of the Roman world empire. Yet after a time, direct power of government was given to a native dynasty (naturally under Roman supervision): in the year 40 B.C. Herod the Great became king —an upstart of Idumean origin. After his death (4 B.C.) his kingdom was first of all divided among his sons; soon however the Romans subjected Judea to their immediate control. During the ministry of Jesus, Pontius Pilate—a brutal man of evil repute—was procurator. The Romans interfered hardly at all in the religious affairs of the Jews; they merely reserved to themselves the right to choose the high priest, whom however they always selected from a priestly noble family qualified for this office. In the apostolic period the Jewish resistance to Rome became sharper, and there broke out in A.D. 66 a terrible revolt of the Jews which came to a cruel end with Titus' conquest of Jerusalem.

3. *The Jews*

(*a*) *Self-government.* As we have said, the Romans at times exercised their authority over Palestine only indirectly. Direct control was in the hands of Herod and his successors: among these we may mention Herod Antipas, to whom Galilee was subject and who was therefore the authority to whom Jesus owed obedience. In spite of their tactful government the Herods were disliked by the Jews: they were not considered to be fully Jewish and their despotic methods made them appear in serious Jewish circles in a more unfavourable light than the Romans themselves. The real government of the Jewish people —and this was recognized as a measure of self-government—lay with the high priest: he was the supreme authority in control over an area far more extensive than that of religious affairs. During the activity of Jesus, Caiaphas held this great office. Apart from the high priest there was the Sanhedrin, a council consisting of seventy-one members belonging to the ancient priestly aristocracy and numbering also some scribes. It represented a mixture of a supreme court of law and a parliament (a sort of "upper house"). The decisions of the Sanhedrin were recognized even by the greater Jewish diaspora.

(*b*) *Leading circles among the people.* Within the general framework of the Roman or royal jurisdiction the Jewish people remained a religious community with highly developed powers of self-government. Its religious bearing implied that the chief circles in control bore a religious stamp.

First must be mentioned the *priests*, who had their duties (often trivial enough) to fulfil in the temple at Jerusalem. As a body they had to belong to certain specific families and their numbers ran into many thousands. But among the people at large the influence of the *scribes* was far greater: they were the professional exponents of the law, and, as is known, the law embraced the whole life of the people. There was hardly a question even of the most trivial circumstances of daily life which was not submitted to their authoritative decision. The law itself both for them and the people was held to be inviolable and sacrosanct; the task of the scribes was merely to interpret it and apply it to the realities of life. In order to prevent any infringement of the prescriptions of the law they even forbade, in their expository technique, what might through its consequences lead to such an infringement—hence in their severity they went far beyond the letter of the law; this they called "setting a hedge about the law". The results of their expository work were later embodied in the Talmud.

The most radical group among the exponents of the law was that of the *Pharisees.* They were a very special class of men, numbering not more than about 6,000. But countless numbers everywhere paid heed to their teaching; they were considered as patterns of piety. By no means all the members of this special class were technically scribes; but both in their own estimation and that of the people they were all what may be described as a living embodiment of the law. Their name signifies that they were men "set apart", in opposition to the open sinners among the people, and the "publicans". But these "separated" men were not only the guardians of the great traditions of the past, they were also the bearers of their people's hopes for the future; in particular they expressed very vigorously the expectation of a future resurrection.

It was otherwise with the *Sadducees*, whose membership derived from the upper layers of society and also from the priesthood. They considered the hope of the resurrection, like some other views of the Pharisees, to be innovations; they considered the Pharisaic zeal for the fulfilment of the law to be exaggerated; in their own way they were "conservative", since they cherished the ancient privileges of the nobility and, generally speaking, even with regard to the law, emphasized the traditional rather than the living and progressive. It is understandable that the Sadducees got on more easily than the Pharisees with the rule of the Romans. Yet even the Pharisees were no friends to the idea of violence and revolution. It was otherwise with those circles included under the name *zealots*, who wished to compel the coming of the kingdom of God, showed a constant tendency to deeds of violence, and often had as their leaders men who gave themselves out to be Messiah. Eventually, in the great uprising in the year 66, they seized the reins of power.

(*c*) *Piety*. The piety of Judaism at this time is characterized above all by three traits: adherence to the law, otherworldliness, and expectation of the end. Such traits are by no means constantly found in combination; they are simply three focal points. Legalism had its most impressive representatives among the Pharisees, as we have already seen. But their attitude is something quite different from that joy in the law which we have to some extent found to be characteristic of the psalms. In many ways the law assumes the guise of a burden, and the pride of the pious man who keeps it does not conceal his unhappy consciousness of carrying a burden on his back. Yet the fact of taking up this burden serves above all the end of demanding from God, in acknowledgment of this achievement, a recompense either in this world or still more in the future life. But with this attitude anxiety creeps in: have I done enough? And in all piety the note of anxiety spells a certain tension; man makes ever more violent efforts; he constantly increases his demands both on himself and others, and more and more he comes to separate himself from those who do not think as he does.

This anxious element in Jewish piety also determined the way in which Yahweh was thought of. Here we see the element of preoccupation with the other world. The Jews began to fear to utter the name of God at all: instead of Yahweh they said "the Lord" or "heaven". The whole richness and breadth of the Old Testament disclosure of God thus shrank to this emphasis on the all-embracing, otherworldly, and inaccessible majesty of God. It was forgotten that God is the gracious and the ever living God whose gifts to man are prevenient to man's achievement. Only at one point was the living quality of the Old Testament message preserved: namely in the eschatological hopes which some circles cherished. Often these hopes were combined with Pharisaic legalism: it was supposed that if only for one day the law could be fulfilled in its true extent, the kingdom of God would certainly come. Often these hopes assumed a very earthy guise: in human fantasy the kingdom of God was transformed into a golden age. But there were also circles who in straightforward simplicity and inwardness of spirituality, and sometimes in flight from the world, waited for the great breaking in of God into the world, and lived by the assurance that their essential task was to prepare themselves for this event by cultivating the inner life of the spirit: these were called "the silent in the land".

The world into which Jesus of Nazareth entered was a world full of tensions. Its highly developed culture produced on the one hand a self-awareness of the human spirit, gave birth to optimism and a widespread this-worldly emphasis. But the reverse side of this was deep social misery: in the great towns of decaying antiquity the masses of a very decided proletariat conglomerated, and rootless wanderers from every race streamed into the famous centres of the world. Countless thousands were seized with the feeling that things could not go on thus much longer. A sort of world and life weariness began to show itself in many quarters; everywhere scepticism emerged, and a longing for redemption which was not satisfied by the traditional answers made itself felt. For many, the old gods of Greece and Rome counted no longer. Men turned in part to the most primitive forms of magic, others to the mystery religions, while others again respected and cherished a world-denying dualistic piety. The decay of public morality was a striking feature. It was a world in turmoil, filled with questionings. The Jewish mission found in it a rich measure of sympathy; it preached the one God, it spoke of the Creator, it brought to bear the most primitive testimonies, it expressed a serious morality. But its solutions were not yet fulfilled.

Jesus Himself cannot be understood entirely in the light of the circumstances of His time. But He entered into the midst of them and radically changed them as He changed man in general. That age has been compared to the crib in which the child Jesus was cradled. But the holy child Himself springs from the mysterious world of God and not from the historical situations of man.

Chapter 12

THE SON OF GOD

THE TESTIMONY TO CHRIST OF THE GOSPEL OF MARK

The gospel of Mark in sequence

Prefatory note. The word "gospel" in the New Testament has the meaning of "good news". The New Testament has one and only one piece of good news to announce: that of Jesus Christ Himself. Hence there can be no talk of a plurality of gospels. Nor of course can it be said that gospel is the work of any one man, of Matthew for example. It is rather the glad tidings given by God. Nevertheless Paul already—and he wrote before our evangelists—can say: "my gospel" (Rom. 2:16). This implies that gospel has acquired the meaning of "preaching of the good tidings". The gospel remains one and the same; but human testimony to it is manifold. Quite early there arises in the Churches the ministry of evangelists: they declare the gospel like the apostles but are of less authority than the latter. Thus from the one gospel, which excludes any other, there emerges a varied expression of it. But, as the New Testament states clearly, this is not an echo merely, it is the living personal witness of men who have experienced in their life the power of Jesus Christ. "That which we have seen and heard we proclaim also to you" (1 Jn. 1.3); this is true also of the varied testimony to the one gospel.

Since extra-Christian sources tell us practically nothing about Jesus, we are dependent for our knowledge of Him on the most primitive documents of Christianity, especially the gospels. And this means that we can learn to know Him as a historical figure only in proportion as we accept the testimony of believers. The gospels do not regard the Lord from the outside, in a detached, cool, and objective manner, but they speak of Him as the Lord of the Church; they are in fact confessions. Hence there is no means of access to Jesus except through the medium of such confessions. A second implication is this: there is access to Him only when at the same time we expose ourselves to the demand for an affirmation of faith—for our gospels have the intention not of enabling us to gain the information which the detached historian seeks, but of summoning us to believe.

1. *The appearance of Jesus in Galilee* (ch. 1)

The manner in which our gospels begin is significant for the character of their proclamation. With Matthew, Jesus springs from the Davidic line and from the divine miracle of His birth from a virgin, and thus enters the world of the Jews and of all peoples (Matt. 1–2). Luke offers us a detailed historical prologue of the broadest scope: even the emperor Augustus unconsciously contributes to the preparation of the work of Jesus, but those who consciously await His coming are silent pious people without name or rank (Lk. 1–2). John introduces the reader into the deeps of the eternity of God (1:1ff.). Mark begins with the brief and clear witness to the Son of God (1:1). But then in his terse way he says only a few words about John the Baptist and about Jesus' own baptism and temptation, in order to depict at once (1:14f.) an extremely impressive view of the appearance of Jesus in public. It is the *work* of Jesus which stands in the forefront of this gospel. But this work in its totality announces the coming of the kingdom of God (1:14,15) and so challenges the hearer to repentance and faith.

What the kingdom of God is, is not explained here in any detail; nor does the Bible give us elsewhere a definition. Kingdom of God means the kingly rule of God. In the Old Testament too it is often enough said that God *is* king. Yet in spite of this fact, the hope and expectation is expressed that He will set up His kingdom. Hence the kingly power of God is concealed: it is apparent that quite other powers reign on the earth. The coming of the kingdom of God means that these powers, which enslave men although and because men cleave to them, must give way to the power of God. The outward marks of the prevalence of these contrary forces are for Mark (and not only for him) sickness and the demons: man is subjugated and enslaved. But the real power which binds man and corrupts the world, is sin, unbelief, the devil. By announcing the imminence of the kingdom, Jesus takes up the fight against sin, the demons and sickness. This very fight is thus a declaration of the imminent coming of the kingdom and a preaching of the gospel.

Because the kingdom of God is thus near, it is a matter of urgency for men to repent (1:15). Repentance means a change of mind, a reorientation of outlook. It does not consist in the sentimental experience of remorse and dejection. On the contrary, in the gospel God offers Himself to man and opens to him the way for a re-direction of his life. Repentance means that in the light of the gospel man turns away from the old, from the dead past. He could not do so by his own resources. However deep his remorse, he could not effect a fundamental change in his life.

Hence in Mark repentance at once spells faith. Whoever in face of the gospel goes on living as before, simply does not believe. Belief does not mean primarily an assent to doctrines but saying "yes" to God, to Jesus of Nazareth, to the gospel. Or in other words, personally appropriating the "yes" of God which rings out in the gospel.

The baptism practised by John does not merely symbolize man's repentant turning away from his former paths, but it effects such conversion by the will and command of God. It is just baptism which proves that man repents not in his own name and initiative but through the action and power of God. Hence the baptism of John might be described as the sacrament of repentance.

Of repentance however! And it is of great significance that (according to the report of all the synoptics) Jesus Himself undergoes such baptism. Thereby He confesses His solidarity with sinful mankind. And this remains so up to the cross. But at the very moment when He does this, God accepts Him as His own: "Thou art my beloved son; with thee I am well pleased!" (1:11). Thus the divine sonship of Jesus is not an exaltation which removes Him from the rest of mankind but something which manifests itself in His turning towards sinners.

The ministry of Jesus begins in Galilee, in the north, far from Jerusalem. His first disciples are fishermen: the pairs of brothers, Peter and Andrew and James and John. (We must remember that fishermen did not enjoy a good reputation.) Accompanied by them, He teaches in the synagogue at Capernaum, thus doing what it was permitted to any Jew at that time to do, though of course not all were able to do. His teaching arouses attention by its note of authority (1:22). But the religious do not recognize who He is; this is first expressed by one who is possessed of a devil: "You are the Holy One of God" (1:24). And this man is the first to experience the liberating power of Jesus. The second is the mother-in-law of Peter and the third is a leper.

We meet the possessed or demon-controlled more frequently in the New Testament. It is often supposed that we have here to do merely with the sick in mind, and that their mental sickness is traced to the influence of evil spirits. In fact it was an idea of the time that many illnesses (not merely mental ones) were the effect of the agency of hidden dangerous powers, that there really are such abysses in the human psyche as have become terrifyingly plain to us moderns in some cases of mental sickness; the enslavement of the ego which we too notice in this respect is a special and extreme manifestation of the fact that we men have by no means a purely independent existence, but live within the sphere of influence of hidden powers. What demons are is perhaps still plainer to us when we consider the uncontrollably overwhelming power of the machine or of economic factors or even of political forces. But it is also seen in the mental or psychological subservience of one man to another or in the disintegration of a personality through succumbing to his dominant impulses or the pleasures of vice. The basic experience which men had from encounter with Jesus was that of the deepest liberation from the control of these forces—a liberation which had its repercussions in the sphere of the physical body. The New Testament bears witness to a personal attitude which is free from fear of the demons—and that not because man blinds himself to the abysses of reality, but because Jesus has demonstrated His victorious power over the daemonic world. The world outside the influence of Christ was then and is in a sense always either subject to the fear of the incalculable power of the demons, or was and is compelled to try to ignore their existence.

It is remarkable that the demons (1:24; 3:11; 5:7) testify to the special dignity of Jesus in virtue of their latent awareness: they say what the disciples will only dare to say at the turning point in the ministry of Jesus (8:27ff.). We should also notice however that Jesus does not allow the demons to speak (1:34). He wills to guard the secret of His person, and so it remains until He treads the way to the cross (cf. 8:30).

2. *The Ministry of Jesus to Israel* (ch. 2:1—8:26)

(*a*) 2:1—3:6. In this section a twofold truth is expressed: the welcoming affirmative of the Son of God to men, and especially to the abandoned and lost, and Israel's negative answer to Him. This is shown most impressively already in the entire second chapter. Bodily healing as proof of His power to heal the root disease of men (the story of the sick of the palsy)! The bringer of the kingdom of God sitting on a bench and in table fellowship with the outcast! (2:13ff.). The preacher of repentance (1:15) who does not compel His disciples to fast (2:18ff.) though fasting was the recognized sign of penitence and sorrow! The Son of God who does not adhere strictly to the Sabbath views of the pious (2:23ff. and 3:1ff.). Behind all this stands the "yes" which He declares to men. And this very "yes" is the manifestation of His high dignity: He can forgive sins (2:10), He is the physician (2:17), He is the Bridegroom (2:19), He is the Lord even of the Sabbath (2:28). Hence once more, as we have already suggested, His special dignity is disclosed in His gracious turning towards mankind. But the reverse side is visible at the same time; the "no" of the pious in Israel, the contradiction at every point (each single story shows this). They can only conceive of the coming of the kingdom of God when man brings his pious achievement to its supreme height and when the impious are finally separated from the pious; so long as sin prevails in the world, they know only the dejection and sorrow of fasting which again they understand as a pious meritorious exercise. In other words, in their opinion man must bring in the kingdom of God by his own efforts. But the action of Jesus moves in exactly the opposite direction; He, the Bearer of such unheard-of authority, comes from the heights to the depths, He goes to the lost, He bestows where others wish to acquire, He frees where others wish to bind!

Jesus frequently names Himself *the Son of man*. Perhaps the phrase was originally moulded in reference to Dan. 7:13. But it is more probably right to connect it with a late Judaic conception and to regard it as meaning "the man" in the sense of "true man", man as God wills him to be and as God in expressing His creator-will sends him at the end of days. If this is so, Jesus is not only the Son of God but also true man: Paul says "the second Adam".

How rudely emphatic is the "no" which Jesus encounters precisely in

His gracious turning towards the lost is shown in 3:6. The Pharisees and the Herodians (a party which in other respects are their opponents) plot to put Jesus to death. So early does the cross cast its shadow on this gospel. In fact we must wonder whether it was at all possible for Jesus to identify Himself so completely with lost humanity, so completely to negate the way of pious merit, without involving Himself in suffering and death. If He the Son of God truly stands where man stands, then by that very fact He takes upon Himself death, the final abandonment of man. From this point onwards the gospel of Mark becomes a passion narrative. Essentially all the gospels are nothing other than passion narratives with a long introduction. Hence the passion is not viewed as a catastrophe but as an end. From this point of view we can also understand why Jesus wishes to conceal His true dignity: He wishes as it were to remain in the depths and to meet men where they are to be found.

(*b*) 3:7—5:43. The ministry of Jesus, as described further from 3:7 onwards, has its focal point on the shores of Galilee and especially in Capernaum. From ch. 6 we find Jesus wandering to and fro, and His wanderings take Him even to his family town of Nazareth (6:1ff.).

At the head of this subsection is found a passage which marks the scope and the immensity of the action of Jesus (similarly already in 1:32ff.). He accords to His disciples a share in His action, and the names of the twelve are now given us (they are called after the decision of the enemies of Jesus to put Him to death; for in the conception of Mark they too stand under the shadow of the cross. 8:34–38). They have now become for Him His closest associates, while His own kin consider Him as mad (3:20ff.) and are disavowed by Himself (3:31ff.). In place of the natural bonds of kinship, which otherwise He carefully respects, there comes forward the new fellowship of mankind to which He is sent.

Mark hands down to us very few of the words of Jesus, still fewer of His discourses. In the whole of this section we find such only in chs. 4 and 7. In the former chapter there are merely parables, images and comparisons. Of these the best known are the parables of the sower and the mustard seed; the metaphor of the light which should not be hid under a bushel and the simile of the measure which a man applies and according to which he himself is measured (4:21ff.; 24ff.) appear also in the Sermon on the Mount in St. Matthew. On the other hand the parable of the seed growing secretly is found only in Mark (4:26ff.). It fits in with the whole tone and sense of this gospel: the kingdom of God cannot be coerced by man's effort, it springs up from the gospel word. According to the conception of Mark there is lacking in the words and works of Jesus any hint of impatience or haste. On the contrary, wherever He is, wherever He acts, the storms are smoothed, the demons depart, sickness and death itself are banished. This is shown in the stories of the stilling of the storm, the healing of the devil-possessed in the country of the Gadarenes (outside the area of Jewish settlement; hence the presence of a herd of swine), and of the woman with an issue of blood, as also in the story of the raising of Jairus' daughter. Such stories show furthermore how great is the delight of Mark in vivid description (compare the much more austere style of Matthew). It is also important to note that in the last two stories mentioned the faith of man plays a decisive part (5:34,36). It is further significant that in chapters 4 and 5 the opposition of the leaders of the people is left aside. Jesus does not seek a clash.

(*c*) 6:1—8:26. The final subdivision of this section is on the other hand once more heavy with tensions. It begins at once with the theme of the contempt which Jesus aroused in His home town of Nazareth: just as the Pharisees despise Him because He sits at the same table as the outcasts, so His village companions consider that He cannot be anything very extraordinary since He is so utterly one with other men; in both cases scandalization arises because of His lowliness and lack of pretensions. In the opinion of all these people, whoever is sent by God must as it were be quite obviously "from above", evincing a mysterious origin, and filled with a lofty scorn of the petty and vulgar and sinful. Because with their efforts and aspirations they strive upwards, the one whom God sends must emphatically be from above. How pressing the temptation must have been for Jesus to elude this contempt of Nazareth by the performance of a mighty miracle! But the performance of miracles never serves to preserve His dignity; on the contrary, where such a miracle is required as evidence of His mission He refuses it (8:10ff.).

As the choice of the disciples (3:13ff.) followed immediately on the mention of the plot against His life, so here—and this sequence is peculiar to Mark—the sending forth of the disciples is directly connected with Nazareth's rejection of Jesus (6:7ff.). The disciples and apostles must become aware of the heavy burden they are taking on themselves! But they must know also that their acceptance or rejection by others implies a decision of the greatest magnitude (6:11). At this point we can see how the most primitive Christianity was filled with the consciousness of a divine mission.

The ministry of Jesus is now affected by an event in which He has no immediate part: namely the murder of John the Baptist by Herod: this renders the tyrant the irreconcilable enemy of Jesus since he fears that the latter may be John risen again. We may recollect that already in 3:6 the Herodians appeared alongside the Pharisees as the opponents of Jesus. Powerless as He is, Jesus is repugnant not only to the pious but also to those who wield power. For their only means of defence against the weapon which He carries is sheer violence.

The disciples return from their mission (they are here first called apostles) (6:30) and Jesus seeks solitude with them (6:31; cf. 1:33); He needs silence and recollection and the disciples need it too. But the people throng after them without thinking of their necessary food. Jesus gives them food by a miracle (feeding of the 5,000; 6:35ff.). In this connexion we must bear in mind that Moses was reported to have given the people manna to eat; it was thought of as bread from heaven which no doubt the Messiah was expected to give, and Jesus grants men not merely His word but also bodily sustenance (6:34). Then He sends the disciples by boat to Bethsaida; but suddenly in the darkness and the storm He is with them and enters the boat—they are terrified; "for they did not understand about the loaves" (6:52); they have not yet perceived who their Master really is, they see wonderful things but they do not see the One who achieves them and who possesses divine authority!

How great this authority is, is seen in ch. 7. As in ch. 2, it is once again an emancipating authority which reveals itself not by an arbitrary and severe interpretation of the law, but by calling the attention of men from the external to the internal. Insistence on the strict observance of the Sabbath and ritual cleanliness were the two points at which the piety of the Pharisees was most prominently expressed; in both matters they went far beyond the law simply in order to ensure that they did not sin. Jesus also goes far beyond the law but not by the ramification of externals, rather by deepening interiority. The decision about men depends not on their hands but on their hearts; evil springs not from outward things but from within, and it is in the heart that it must be overcome. Such is the cleanliness to which the law refers (7:1–23). This does not make the law easier of observance: pure hands are easier to come by than a pure heart!

Jesus oversteps the limit which in the opinion of the Pharisees the law laid down; He breaks the hedge with which they surrounded the Sabbath, the prescriptions about cleanliness and the law generally. It is not through external attitudes, however important, that man is found to be on the wrong path but through his inner state, and in that realm of the spirit both the legalistically religious and the outcast are equally wrong and equally in need of help. In the last resort man is placed in confrontation with God; he stands at a point where he is not asked about what he does but about what he is. But it is just that question that the pious will not face.

But the final limit which the law marked for Israel—separation from the heathen—Jesus oversteps only under the pressure of necessity (7: 24f.). In the controversy about cleanliness His opponents come from Jerusalem (7:1); the ultimate authorities are casting their net wide! Yet His hour has not yet come. So He enters the territory of ancient Phoenicia. But this is not the true sphere of His ministry—He finally opened the way to the heathen world only through His death. A Gentile woman is told this (7:27). Nevertheless He helps her: she speaks a word which He had in vain awaited from Israel, a word of humble faith (7:28f.).

How the rumours about Him rapidly gather momentum! The miraculous feeding is reported a second time (8:1ff.; this time 4,000 men; the report is a doublet, a second version of the story). Then the Pharisees challenge Him with the decisive question about the "sign from heaven" (8:11). The Messiah must signalize Himself by an unheard-of miracle. And Jesus flatly refuses. In the feeding miracle He had done something which was essentially part of Messianic expectation: He repeats it in the circle of His disciples, but He declines to give a public demonstration. However, even the disciples understand nothing; they are infected with the "leaven of the Pharisees" and they too expect a momentous astounding happening to take place publicly. It is a question whether the story of the blind man (8:22ff.), which is peculiar to Mark, is dovetailed in just here in order to suggest that soon the eyes of the disciples will be opened as, according to this plastic narrative, the eyes of the physically blind have been opened.

This is the point at which to introduce a few reflections about the miracles of Jesus. The following points should be specially noted:

1. The world at this time had no inkling of the characteristically modern idea that all events take place in a closed circle governed by the laws of nature (an idea which has since become somewhat questionable). Hence it felt no contrast between miracle and natural happening. Rather it drew a contrast between explicable and inexplicable events: the latter were miraculous. Of course Israel believed that Yahweh was the Author even of explicable happenings; but His agency was more evident in the phenomenon of the mysterious. (We may rather exaggeratedly say that for the Old Testament "miracle" was an event marked out in some way as being due to the agency of Yahweh even though the form of its happening may not have been intrinsically inexplicable.) In any case in the times in which the Biblical authors wrote almost everyone considered miracle as both possible and real.

2. Hence the Bible does not confine the working of miracles to the agency of the living God and His messengers. Even the Egyptian magicians can perform miracles (Exod. 7:11,22; 8:7; but 8:14 etc.). Likewise a false prophet can effect a sign or wonder and it may come to

pass (Deut. 13:2,3). Or here in Mark; even false Messiahs and false prophets can "do signs and wonders" (13:22). With Paul too "the lawless one with the activity of Satan" achieves all sorts of deceptive miracles, i.e. real but misleading (2 Thess. 2:9–11).

3. Hence miracle in itself is never a plain proof of the fact that a man is working in the name of the living God. This is best seen in Deut. 13:2ff. But it is also implied in the fact that the enemies of Jesus, faced by His casting out of devils, merely suggest that He does so in virtue of the power of Beelzebub the prince of devils (Mk. 3:22); they do not dispute the factuality of the miracles but only their divine origin and basis. Conversely in Matthew Jesus counters with the question who then empowers the sons of the Pharisees to cast out devils (Matt. 12:27); here again the factuality of the miracles is not in question. Miracles and truth are not necessarily to be found together. Yet miracles are, as it were, a means of arousing attention, for they are evidence that a power which transcends humanity is at work. But whose power may not be inferred from the miracle itself, only from the preaching which accompanies it.

4. Almost all the miracles of Jesus are healing miracles; without exception they are performed in the service of mankind. No miracle of Jesus is wrought for self-glorification (cf. Matt. 4:5ff.) or in the interests of self-preservation (cf. Lk. 9: 51–56). Hence in the work of Jesus there is no display intended to arouse a sensation (as was the practice with the wonder-workers of the time) and in fact He not seldom commands secrecy (Mk. 1:44; 3:12; 5:43; 7:36).

5. The enemies of Jesus desired a "sign from heaven" in proof of His claims. This arose from their views concerning the Messiah whom God sent and anointed. As in general they regarded success as a confirmation of true piety, so the One who stood nearest to God must be able to show exceptional success, to perform deeds which would cast all else into the shade. In that event the daring venture of faith would not be necessary; tangible proof would be at hand. A sign of this nature Jesus radically refused to give: unbelief cannot accept a miracle. He rejected as a satanic temptation (Matt. 4:5ff.) the expectation that He would furnish such a spectacular miracle and replace faith by demonstration. Even in His passion He refuses to pray the Father to send "twelve legions of angels" (Matt. 26:53). And on the cross He has to expose Himself to the taunt that He should come down, since He was able to help others (Mk. 15:30,31). Miracle as a means of proof would be clean contrary to all that we have already seen of the work of Jesus and have yet to see.

6. There can be no doubt that as a matter of historical fact Jesus wrought miracles, and in particular that both for His contemporaries and us He healed in a mysterious way. We must however reckon with the possibility that fantasy has freely embroidered some themes: some miracle stories were no doubt from the start understood as parables for the one great miracle which Jesus did and still does for men (cf. the Cana marriage, Jn. 2). Quite another question is whether a more penetrating knowledge of nature and medicine would not explain for us some of the miracles of Jesus. This possibility cannot be excluded. The significance of an utterly superior mind and will for the healing of sickness is well known. But such a "natural" explanation of

miracle would change nothing in regard to the understanding of the miracles of Jesus: they would then be all the more manifest as signs arousing attention of which we have spoken. For the man who believes in God—and not in a deified nature—even the "natural" is a miracle. For fundamentally miracle is not a violation of the laws of nature (and it may be doubted whether we really know all about these) but a happening which makes manifest for faith the presence and the power of God. The real miracle is the presence of God Himself!

3. *The turning towards death* (ch. 8:27—10)

(*a*) 8:27—9:29. The section 8:27ff. is by common consent the central and crucial point in the exposition of our evangelist. So far we have seen how Jesus discloses and exercises His transcendence by establishing His solidarity with mankind and above all with the rejected and outcast. In this passage what is implied in this twofold factor is made clear. For the first time He Himself is now recognized as the Christ (by Peter) and without any contradiction on His part, and for the first time He speaks openly of His coming death. At the same time this implies what is to mark out the disciples: they are firstly the fellowship of those who confess Jesus as the Christ, and secondly this very fact means that they are destined to share in His passion and death. In these sentences we have outlined the core of the message of Mark.

Christ is not a name but a title denoting an office. The evangelists for this reason consistently put the article in front of it. It is therefore correct to say: the Christ. Christ is nothing other than the Greek translation of Messiah, which means "the anointed one". Hence the Christ is the promised and awaited King of the time of salvation which God wills to establish. But the word itself is not yet found in this meaning in the Old Testament. The Messianic expectation of late Judaism has partly legalistic features (the Messiah as the consummator of the righteousness of the law and so as the bearer of the kingdom of God—thus the Pharisees) partly political (the Messiah as the Saviour and the bringer of worldly power for Israel and the pious—so the zealots). Only much smaller circles awaited a suffering Messiah such as they found proclaimed in Isaiah 53. The proper conception of Jesus is to be seen in our gospel and especially in this passage.

There was also a widespread belief that before the coming of the Messiah one of the old prophets would rise again; this expectation was directed to Elijah (see the last words of the Book of Malachi). This should be noted for the understanding of 8:28.

It is significant that Jesus bids His disciples say nothing about His Messianic dignity (8:30). Before the crucifixion it is a secret which is several times broached but never wholly surrendered. We recollect that a similar injunction was several times given to those who were healed. Likewise the supernatural experience which they afterwards (9:2ff.) are allowed to share with their Master, must remain concealed (9:9). Jesus guards His "incognito":

He refuses to be a Messiah who arouses enthusiasm and only he must know of the exalted office of Jesus who also knows of His cross and is prepared to take up the cross. But the disciples are not straightaway prepared for this. The very same Peter who in the name of the others confessed the Messiahship of Jesus revolts against the Messiah's destiny of suffering (8:32) and must hear the rebuke: "Thou Satan!"—for this is the satanic temptation, to wish to be the Messiah without suffering. For in that case Messiah would be perhaps the most powerful of men, but not the one sent of God and bringing in true salvation which consists in forgiveness (8:33). Jesus also sees what may be so easily combined with the denial of His destiny of suffering; the disciples are enthusiasts who would gladly win the whole world for their Master (8:36), i.e. turn themselves into His propagandists and compel success; but they do not yet see that the true path lies through death and that what is at stake is true life, the soul, i.e. man as he stands confronted by God; that it is not a question of the maintenance of life in this world or of promotion and dignity. For them the kingdom of God consists in the fulfilment of their dreams. For Jesus it begins where the dreams of men cease.

In this connexion should be read Matt. 4:1ff. and also Dostoievsky's story of the Grand Inquisitor from *The Brothers Karamazov*. Here lies the key for the understanding of the Christian faith in general.

Almost immediately after the announcement of the suffering which Jesus must undergo and which the disciples must undergo after Him, Mark gives an account of the mysterious experience which three of the disciples share with their Lord on the mountain top (the "transfiguration"; 9:2ff.). The intention is to emphasize that He who is now entering the valley of suffering is truly the Son of God. He suffers the passion not under the compulsion of circumstances or under the pressure of human violence, but in free self-donation to men. Then at once there is added a healing miracle and a second announcement of the passion.

(*b*) 9:30—10:52. If the previous narratives of this section have already taken us away from the wider public of Israel into the narrower circle of the disciples, in what now follows it is essentially a question of the order which is to prevail among the disciples themselves. And we may say that the rule here is the exact reverse of what obtains in the world. In the circle of the disciples it is not the great who is first, but the least (9:33ff.), the little one, the despised (9:42), not the mature adult but the child (10:13ff.)—i.e. the child considered as the essentially receptive person—not the rich, but he who is freed from the lust of riches (10:17ff.); in this circle it is not the most powerful who rules, for here it is service which prevails and whoever wishes to be great must be the servant of all (10:35ff.). To sum up: over the whole earthly existence of the disciples stands the cross, which overthrows all pretensions to power and destroys man's need for security. In conclusion Jesus gives the reason for all this: "For the Son of man also came not to be served but to serve and to give his life as a ransom for many" (10:45). The connexion of this pregnant saying with the end of ch. 8 is obvious. What comes in between is, so to speak, the practical application of the message about cross-bearing.

The word about the man who in the name of Jesus cast out devils without being a disciple (9:38–41) belongs essentially to this whole line of thought. The disciples have certainly their high dignity (9:41). But they do not form a group which has to safeguard its own interests; like the individual, the disciples as a community should have no concern to maintain themselves as such (9:39–40). Here again we find the cross.

But what is the meaning of the saying about marriage? (10:1–12). Wherever the relation to God is built up on the achievement of man, we find a religious depreciation of woman. This applied to a large extent to the Judaism of that time (as it also applies to Islam, for example). Since there was no court of justice competent to adjudicate in the matter, the right of divorce lay with the husband, and even the Pharisees granted him the right to put away his wife with the greatest readiness (one permitted divorce if the wife had allowed the meal to spoil!). The male, who is the chief bearer of positive achievement in the world, the bearer of the active phase in human life, had exclusive privileges. But Jesus goes back behind the hardness of men to the primal purpose of creation where marriage was instituted as a bond of fellowship, not as the means by which the male exercises domination. Hence the male who divorces his wife in order to take another breaks the marriage bond just as much as would the female who did the same. Where man really has to do with the Creator once more—and this applies to the disciples—then human hardness of heart ceases to prevail; it is the will of the Creator which is aimed at.

It should be noted that the bill of divorce mentioned by Jesus was in fact a legal document which was designed to prevent the woman from being despoiled of her rights by the man: if she had such a document she could marry again and was not considered as an adulteress. Thus this ruling of the law was in reality permissive in effect (10:4); it was a protective measure, but not a prescription bidding the man put away his wife as he thought fit.

4. *Passion and Resurrection* (chs. 11–16)

(*a*) *Chs.* 11–13. The saying of 10:45 already mentioned connects the previous chapter with the story of the passion which now follows. The intention of Mark is to emphasize that events must inevitably turn out so. The work of Jesus is so shaped that no other issue is possible. Death is the seal set upon this work. The fearful tension which penetrates our passion narrative arises from the fact that in proportion as death draws nearer Jesus more and more lifts the veil of His secrecy. If it has already been the case that His self-giving to man was at the same time the manifestation of His exaltation, now the two aspects stand forth visibly. But at the same time the third factor becomes manifest which we have met from the opening of the gospel story: the negative pronounced by the people and its religious leaders against One who is as Jesus was! From this close interweaving of factors the death of Jesus develops with dread inevitability.

The passion opens with an authoritative declaration of the high dignity of Jesus: the entry into Jerusalem, which is without question a public proclamation of His Messiahship (11:1ff.). The cleansing of the temple has the same implication (11:15ff.). Likewise the acted judgment on the fig tree (11:11ff. and 11:20f.) expressing the rejection of Israel, is an act manifesting the divine authority of Jesus. Hence it is only in keeping with all this when He is asked by what authority He does these things; they attempt to challenge Him, but He challenges the inquirers (11:27f.).

The opposing forces are now lined up. This is shown at once by the debates which take up ch. 12. The parable of the wicked husbandmen, like the action on the fig tree, indicates the menace of judgment overshadowing Israel; because this people repels the One who brings it the very presence of God, it casts itself into the abyss and thus becomes the type and pattern of all human unbelief (12:1ff.). This rejection of Israel countering Israel's own rejection of its Messiah gives as it were the heading for what follows. Every time the intention is to set a trap for Jesus. And again and again He parries the blow aimed at Him in such a way that it turns back to pierce the heart of man. The meaning of the question about tribute (12:13ff.) is only too plain—the presence of the Herodians increases the danger of the situation —Jesus is meant either to declare Himself against the hated Roman tax or lose the favour of the people. But He is concerned to insist that God shall receive what belongs to Him and then the emperor is entitled to receive the money which bears his image!

The Sadducees, who otherwise appear rather seldom, are not to be missing in this lining up of the enemies of Jesus: they put before Him a question often in debate between themselves and the Pharisees (12:18f.). Might it be that they wish, now that the decision against Him has already essentially been taken, to brand Him as a Pharisee and so deal their own adversaries a sudden blow? However that may be, what determines Mark to introduce the controversy here is certainly the conclusion: neither the calculations of the Pharisees nor those of the Sadducees are correct; both parties take death too seriously because their attention is directed towards man and his destiny. But God is the God of the living! This affirmation is here made by Him who is moving towards death. Likewise the question which Jesus puts to His enemies, whether Messiah is the son or the Lord of David (12:35f.), belongs to this whole context: it is again a slight lifting of the curtain and the proof that these men have eyes which see not, see neither the One who stands before them nor understand the scriptures of which they are so proud. Nor is it otherwise with the question about the chief commandment (12:28f.). The fact that it is placed here obviously serves to clarify the meaning of the suffering of Jesus: He is going to be put to death because of His contempt for the law—but does not He fulfil the law whose whole life is lived out of love? When love is recognized as the content of the law, the meaning of the kingdom of God is also included; for in that kingdom God condescends to man, and the rule of God is the rule of love and self-giving. The cross looms before us!

But what is the purpose in our context (to mention only the most important and difficult points) of the discourse of Jesus about the imminent destruction of Jerusalem and the coming time of judgment and salvation (ch. 13)? Our point of departure is the saying about the fig tree and the parable of the wicked husbandmen (chs. 11 and 12): Israel is plunging itself into ruin by repudiating the One in whom God comes to it. As a consequence the cross, the sign of salvation for those who take it up and believe, becomes also the sign of judgment for those who reject it. There is thus in the most literal sense a cross-roads for humanity: the ways of men divide at the point of the cross. The way of Israel is the prototype for the way of all men who reject Jesus and thus themselves. Hence the grim expectation with which our text opens. On the other hand, the disciples themselves will be involved in this judgment on their people—and on humanity which rejects the Christ—they are granted no special privilege but rather are threatened with special suffering and the imperilling of their faith (13:5,6,9ff.). The cross would just not be the cross if believers were not also involved in what the rejecting and rejected man suffers, and in fact in deeper suffering also. But at the end stands not judgment, distress and temptation, but the second coming of the Son of Man in glory. As the resurrection follows His cross, so His return in unconcealed majesty follows judgment (13:24ff.). Thus all history that is to follow the Christ becomes the residue of history, the "last day", and all the life of believers becomes a waiting and watching. This attitude is "eschatological", i.e. an orientation of life to the ultimate end.

(*b*) *Chs.* 14–16. According to the report of Mark the passion now springs from the final decision of the Jewish authorities to execute Jesus (14:1,2) as also from the free will of Jesus which is most plainly declared in the words of the Last Supper (14: 22 f.). The new covenant is founded on the death of the Lord (v. 24). The negative of His enemies and the abiding and patient affirmative of Jesus both lead to the same goal.

The Last Supper is presented both by Mark and the other synoptics as a passover meal. Like so many pilgrims streaming into the holy city for the feast, Jesus has a special room prepared for Himself. On the afternoon of the day of preparation (the 14th of the spring month of Nisan) the passover lamb is slaughtered in the temple, and in the evening, which is according to the reckoning of that time the beginning of the 15th Nisan, the joyful fellowship meal begins. To the meal belong four beakers of wine to be drunk at specified points in the course of the feast, as also bitter herbs and unleavened bread. The singing of the hymn of praise was also part of the feast (14:26; i.e. Psalms 113–118). This formed the conclusion, while during the progress of the meal at certain points words were spoken reminding the partakers of the deliverance of Israel from servitude in Egypt. Hence the fact that on this occasion Jesus speaks certain words on the distribution of the bread and wine is part of traditional usage. Yet He speaks of His own body and blood, and the meal (which normally is the celebration of the old covenant, as once according to tradition it was sealed, and ever renewed) here becomes the celebration of the new covenant—a covenant which is sealed by the outpouring of the blood of Jesus and the breaking of His body. What will take place a few hours later—the crucifixion is not a whole day later—He now discloses as an event in which a new relationship to God, a new divinely based fellowship and a new freedom from slavery are to be grounded. As in His ministry Jesus disclosed His exalted state by giving Himself to His own, so now they learn that He gives His life for them in order to obtain for them fullness of life and freedom. The new covenant which is now established, however, finds its completion through the ultimate coming into the world of the kingdom of God (14:25).

There are notable divergences in detail between the words of the Last Supper as reported in the synoptics and in Paul (1 Cor. 11:23ff.). Paul does not plainly mention the passover even, and according to John, Jesus was not crucified, as seems to have been the case according to Mark, on the 15th Nisan but a day earlier. If this dating is correct then the meal may have conformed to the tradition of the passover meal without being a passover meal itself. Further questions are involved in this point which research has not yet succeeded in clearing up.

After speaking the solemn words of the Last Supper, Jesus goes out to die for the sake of His own. The disciples to whom He has pledged His love during the meal do indeed accompany Him into the night and swear their fidelity. But He knows that they will abandon Him and that Peter will deny Him. No ray of human faith and loyalty pierces this darkness. In fact, Jesus Himself has to wage a bitter struggle in order to follow this path unflinchingly to the very end. It is not the mere fact of dying which causes Him this agony, but the fact of dying *this* death: a death which to outward seeming spells a defeat of God, a defeat of One who had come forth into the world endowed with divine authority. The New Testament does not try to conceal the distress of Jesus on this account. It is not reporting the epic deeds of a hero. For Jesus dies the death of a *sinner*. He remains faithful to lost humanity—a humanity which now repulses Him.

The arrest of Jesus is made possible through the treachery of Judas. Jesus has up to now apparently been spending the nights in the neighbouring Bethany, and His enemies learn of His place of asylum in the immediate vicinity of the town solely through this traitor who at bottom was simply perhaps a disillusioned man. The fact that they do not dare to seize Jesus by the light of day suggests the continuing esteem in which He was held by the people. After the arrest Jesus is taken to the Sanhedrin (14:53f.). The chief ground of accusation is a word of Jesus which has a Johannine rather than a Marcan ring and according to which He declared that He would destroy the temple and rebuild it in three days (a saying which was Messianic in character and implied a fantastic pretension). Since Jesus maintains silence, the high priest proceeds to the decisive question: "Are you the Christ?" (14:61). Jesus affirms that He is, and thus the condemnation is sealed.

We may wonder why this Messianic pretension sufficed to secure the condemnation of Jesus. The law of course forbade blasphemy. But why do not the judges ask themselves whether this claim of Jesus might be justified? There was much known about Him in any case which had aroused sensational interest. It is clear that blasphemy is seen in the fact that it is precisely He who raised this claim, i.e. the One who had refused to give a demonstrative sign, who had associated with sinners and had violated the Pharisaic conception of the Sabbath. Jesus must die because in the opinion of His judges His claim to be the Messiah is palpably false. The fact which bears witness against Him is His complete solidarity with lost humanity, His lowliness and hiddenness, His refusal to acknowledge meritorious piety in any form. This amounts to saying that Jesus is condemned because He persists in His love for the lost. But at the same time that terrible thing happens—Israel finally affirms its adherence to the legalistic piety of man in the face of and in opposition to God.

It is remarkable that our evangelist now narrates the denial of Peter, for traditionally Mark is held to be a follower of Peter: just as he always faithfully reports the impetuous zeal of Peter (cf. 8:32f.; 14:29f.) so now he does not hide the most ignominious hour in the life of the apostle. The Master remains abidingly devoted to humanity—but there is no man, not even the foremost of the disciples, who remains faithful to Him.

From now onwards, the *silence of Jesus* hovers over all that happens. Hardly does He speak a word to Pilate to whom this victim is now surrendered (15:1f.). The powers of this world bluster and rage around Him. Unbridled hate vents its full fury on Him (15:29f.). The Roman legionaries' hatred and contempt for the Jews does its work (15.20f.). But the concern of Jesus is with God. "My God, my God, why hast Thou forsaken me?" Thus He prays, using the words of Ps. 22, which is the outpoured lament of a suffering and rejected soul. Jesus is now such a soul! His patient fidelity to man brings Him to this.

We must realize the significance of the fact that the earliest stage of the Christian tradition preserved this word of the Crucified and that in both Mark and Matthew it is the single word from the cross. They were certainly filled with the assurance of the complete sinlessness of Jesus. They were His disciples and believed in His exalted office and mission. And yet—this terrible word! Probably from the earliest time it was understood that Jesus suffered desolation and abandonment by God just because of His self-identification with lost humanity. He dies not His own death but the death of sinful man.

One person was deeply impressed by the dying of this man in stark loneliness, namely, the Roman centurion. He confesses Him to be the Son of God—and it is as though in this heathen man the whole of Gentile Christianity stoops at the cross in confession and adoration. Thus no doubt Mark meant it; for immediately before, he has spoken about the rending of the veil of the temple which guarded the innermost sanctuary from all approach—the way to God is now free and all barriers have fallen (cf. 15:38,39).

And then we find the women there—they have been able to do that which men could not (15:40ff.). Their jealous care and tenderness looks after the body of the Crucified (16:1f.).

The resurrection of Jesus as such is not described by any of our evangelists. This event falls completely outside what can be reported. All the gospels report merely occurrences at the empty tomb and appearances of the Risen One to His own. Thus Mark also. But the oldest form of the text available to us breaks off at 16:8. The disciples and Peter are told (through the women!) to go to Galilee where they would see their Lord. The women however are silent with terror. So utterly ungraspable is the resurrection.

We must regard the end of this gospel as lost. It is impossible to surmise what appearances it reported. Instead of the lost ending there follows in our traditional versions a section which also must have been written early and shows some resemblances to the ending of St. Matthew.

5. *The Evangelist*

Our gospel is ascribed to Mark in all the oldest tradition and there is no valid reason to doubt this. A remarkable passage right at the heart of the passion narrative seems to give us the very fingerprints of the narrator: this is the saying about the young man who was implicated in the arrest of Jesus and who was able to save himself only by surrendering his garment (14:51,52); this extraordinary note occurs only in Mark and may well be taken as a personal reminiscence of the evangelist.

John Mark was a nephew of the Barnabas who undertook a missionary journey with Paul which included Mark. Paul however refused to take Mark on a further journey because of a piece of non-co-operation (Acts 15:37–39). Yet later Mark is again found in the companionship of the apostle.

On the other hand the tradition very early arose that Mark was a fellow-worker with Peter and reproduced in his gospel the reminiscences of Peter. As a result the numerous—and especially the depreciatory—statements about Peter gain special weight.

We have tried to understand what it is the intention of Mark to say. His message is that of the all-powerful Son of God who embraces the cause of lost humanity, turns in mercy to those who pine in sickness and bondage to daemonic beings, and fulfils His Messianic mission through His solidarity with these rejected ones, to the bitter end.

For whom does he write? We can answer in complete confidence: Mark writes for Gentile Christians. This was most movingly apparent in the passages following the death of Jesus: the rent veil and the confession of the Roman centurion. Mark does not take up the cause of the Gentile world, but he expounds the work of Jesus of Nazareth as being undertaken both on behalf of the heathen and in face of the heathen. Hence it is understandable that discussion of specifically Jewish questions is narrowed down as far as possible. Also the fact that the words of Jesus (especially in the debate with His Jewish enemies) do not stand in the foreground and that the emphasis is rather on deeds, thus becomes more understandable. This also explains why, while liking to give Hebraic and Aramaic expressions, he usually translates them (cf. 5:41 or 7:34) and elucidates Jewish customs (e.g. 7:3,4 or 14:12); his readers have to be informed about all this. Moreover the connoisseur is able to note the striking occurrence of many Latin words, which strengthens the old supposition that this gospel was written in Rome.

Three-eighths of the text of this gospel are taken up by the passion narrative: this evangelist is concerned above all about the cross. The rest of his matter is in part very tersely presented, especially at the beginning. On the other hand the stories which he does offer us are to some extent narrated in more detail than their counterparts in the other synoptics (cf. Mk. 9:14f. with the parallels in Matthew and Luke). Mark likes to describe, his style is plastic and he emphasizes detailed traits (e.g. we find only in him the subtle observations of 10:21 or 10:16) and especially he suggests mood and feeling (e.g. 8:12). Of all the evangelists he is the best storyteller. His Greek is straightforward and without peculiarity; only the Latinized expressions are noteworthy.

His work is a testimony intended to awaken and strengthen faith—faith which lives on even in the midst of sorest temptation (e.g. peculiar to Mark is 9:24). Mark alone includes faith in the fundamental message of Jesus Himself (1:15). Compare also 4:40 and 5:36.

Whether an older form of the gospel lies behind our present Mark is a question we cannot discuss here. It is certain that the two other synoptics had before them a text of Mark closely related to our present gospel. We will now turn to a shorter survey of these two other gospels.

Chapter 13

ISRAEL'S REJECTED KING

THE MESSAGE OF THE GOSPEL OF MATTHEW

(chs. 1; 2; 5–7; 10–13)

1. *Peculiar features of the gospel of Matthew*

(*a*) *General structure.* As compared with the gospel of Mark that of Matthew does not reveal a basically different structure; we have already suggested that the fundamental pattern of Mark is reflected in the two other synoptics. Nevertheless even in general outline there are certain peculiarities here. In the first place there is the detailed introduction: Matthew gives us the ancestry of Jesus, tells the story of the wise men from the East, of the flight into Egypt, and Herod's slaughter of the innocents (all in chs. 1 and 2). Anything comparable to this is lacking in Mark. Further, at the first glance we recognize the wealth of material which Matthew has at his disposal in comparison with Mark (mostly in consequence of the "sayings-source") and it is also clear that Matthew likes to arrange the discourses of Jesus in lengthy units: the best known is the Sermon on the Mount (chs. 5–7). Yet in spite of all this the general pattern of Mark remains unchanged: here too the central and crucial point in the ministry is the confession of Peter at Caesarea Philippi (Matt. 16: 13 ff.), which, moreover, Matthew presents in his own characteristic and momentous way. Hence here too the work of Jesus begins in the north, in Galilee, and has its focal point on the shores of Lake Gennesareth, is repulsed by the Israelite pious (a clash which is rather more sharply described than in Mark), with the consequence that Jesus in part takes refuge in neighbouring territory. After the confession of Peter, Jesus here too turns rather to the narrower circle of His disciples whom He prepares for the end, the description of which once more falls into line with that of Mark. The Easter stories are far more detailed than in the case of Mark, whose account of course breaks off.

(*b*) What does Matthew intend to say? We have already observed in dealing with Mark that our evangelists do not put before us an objective detached account of historical events, but warm living testimonies of faith. If we wished to be critical we might say that they were tendentious. In modern speech this word, however, connotes the deliberate purpose of colouring the facts. Nothing of this kind is to be detected in the gospels. We can understand their procedure when we recollect that these writers are personally mastered by the Person of Jesus. And any one who describes a person for whom he has personally decided will never be able to give an objective picture of his hero. Would it be preferable for this reason to read cold, colourless accounts? But there is one final consideration: the truth is that even to-day it is impossible to adopt an objective and detached attitude to the Person of Jesus; just as Jesus compelled His contemporaries to say "yes" or "no" to Him, He does so still. Our evangelists reveal both the "yes" and the "no" and just in so far as they demand our own decision they are better historical sources than a detached exposition would be, which would certainly remove the very essence of Jesus.

The direction in which the special witness of Matthew moves can already be deduced by the reader of the first chapter. What is in question is Israel, and Judaism as it was at the time of Jesus, as also the history of the old covenant people. But the evangelist does not handle this theme in order to flatter Israel (if he did that Matthew would be a sorry disciple of Jesus and an unintelligent reader of the Old Testament). Rather he wishes to say two things: firstly that Jesus is the fulfiller of the Old Testament dispensation, that He is the King of Israel promised in the Old Testament, and secondly that Israel itself rejects Him and that for this reason He goes to the Gentiles. Hence in the person of the King rejected by Israel the promises of the old covenant are fulfilled in the life of the peoples of the world! Thus alongside the acceptance of the old covenant we have the repudiation of that Israel which rejects Jesus and in so doing plunges itself into an abyss of destruction.

Bearing these two factors in mind, Matthew turns both to the Jews and to the Christians within Judaism (Hebrew Christians). We must not forget that the conflict in which Jesus Himself was engaged developed further after the crucifixion. The Hebrew Christians were in a difficult position. They were always in danger either of dropping the traditions of the old covenant or of feeling themselves to be merely a minor variation within the synagogue. Matthew wishes to point out that both attitudes are false. Through Christ the Old Testament is confirmed because fulfilled—but really fulfilled and not simply continued.

The characteristic bent of Matthew is shown at the very beginning. The genealogy of Jesus begins with Abraham (not with Adam, Lk. 3:23f.) and leads through the whole Davidic line of kings (which in Luke is subordinate): the Lord is the son of David. On the other hand, of the four women mentioned among the ancestors of Jesus, three (Rahab, Ruth, and the wife of Uriah) are foreigners and the fourth is linked with a story of scandal (Gen. 38). Thus this Son of David has heathen women among His ancestors and hence is in some sense co-ordinated with the heathen world.

Further, it strikes every reader of this gospel that repeatedly Matthew explains particular traits of the story of Jesus by reference to Old Testament texts: all is presented as a fulfilment of the Old Testament (e.g. 1:22f., 2:5f., 15, 17, 18; 4:4f., etc.). The manner in which the Old Testament is thus used does not satisfy our modern historical attitude, but was in accordance with the custom of the time.

The discussion in which Jesus engaged with regard to the law, which as we know played a certain part in Mark, here receives far fuller attention. We shall have to go into this in commenting on the Sermon on the Mount. Jesus several times takes up a conscious and deliberate attitude to the law (cf. 5:17f.).

It is also striking that, unlike Mark, Matthew does not explain Jewish customs: his readers can be assumed to know what he means.

But on the other hand the conflict of Jesus with the Jews here assumes far harsher expression than in Mark or Luke. We should compare the story of the centurion at Capernaum in Matthew (8:5f.) and in Luke (7:1f.) and we shall see the difference. It is further characteristic of this gospel that Jesus the King of the Jews receives homage from foreigners, e.g. the wise men of the East (2:1f.) whereas from His own people He receives hatred and rejection. Even more in this connexion we should take into account the Sermon on the Mount and also ch. 23, that terrible and fierce indictment of the scribes and Pharisees.

We might ask: how are *we* concerned about this peculiarity of the message of Matthew? In point of fact this gospel is just as important for Gentile Christians as for Jewish Christians. For it is not a trifling accident that Jesus was born, lived—and died, as a member of the Jewish people. Whoever has to do with Jesus has inevitably to do with Israel, with the Old Testament, and the law. Jesus never called in question the truth that the election of God was primarily the election of Israel: it was to this people that God revealed Himself and concluded a covenant.

If that is so, then it is by no means a mere accident that Jesus was rejected precisely by this people. It is no doubt true elsewhere that great men have been misunderstood by their contemporaries and (like Socrates) even put to death. But that the Son of God was slain by the very people which God in such a unique way made the witness of His mighty acts—that is of special significance. By this act of rejection Israel casts Jesus and the gospel as it were away from itself out into the wide world of heathendom. From now on, Israel is the rejected people; not because God has changed His plan, but because Israel has cast out its own Messiah. The matter may also be put in this way: on the one hand, in the person of Jesus the divine covenant with Israel comes to its fulfilment as does also Israel's mission to the wider world, while on the other hand all the disobedience which the Old Testament reports about Israel now attains its climax through the rejection of Jesus.

(*c*) *The evangelist.* According to a very ancient tradition, which goes back to the first century, our gospel was written by the apostle Matthew and in fact first of all in Aramaic. This datum is probably justified to the extent that an underlying form of the gospel, or the sayings-source which is here capitalized, comes from Matthew himself. The latter is in the gospel identified with Levi the tax gatherer (cf. Matt. 9:9f. and parallels in Mark and Luke) whom Jesus calls away from the seat of custom and who at once, along with others of his ill-famed colleagues, gives a feast to the Master. Here is a Jew, but a Jew who is rejected by the pious. One who experiences at first hand the fundamentally new outlook which Jesus brought into the world!

2. *Certain elements in the content of the gospel*

(*a*) *Preliminary history*. What Mark sums up in the one word Jesus Christ (the Messiah), the Son of God (Mk. 1:1), Matthew explicates in a whole chapter (1). We have already spoken of the chain of ancestors; it is intended to show that, beyond His earthly father Joseph, Jesus is a member of the Davidic royal house. But is Jesus the son of Joseph? Yes and no. He is equally, by a miracle of the Holy Ghost, God's own Son (1:18f.). The father who takes care of Him is not His natural father but as it were a foster father. What Jesus is and does can only be understood as the very being and doing of God.

It is most probable that in 1:18ff. Matthew is countering the Jewish calumny that Jesus was the Son of Mary born out of wedlock. This very calumny implies that Christianity from the earliest times taught what is affirmed in the creed, "Born of the Virgin Mary". What Matthew emphasizes is something else: "Conceived by the Holy Ghost". It should not be overlooked that Mark with his phrase "Son of God" says essentially the same thing: the mystery of the person of Jesus cannot be grasped from within human connexions.

Jesus is born in Bethlehem (2:1)—though it is Luke who is able to tell in his Christmas story how this came about (Lk. 2). Matthew knows why it had to be thus: Bethlehem was the city of David and the promise was concentrated on the lineage and city of David (2:6). But it was not the case that Israel rightly received its King: in the person of its legal king Herod (Herod the Great, 40–4 B.C.) the shadow of hatred and persecution lay over the sucking child. The babe receives only from the Gentiles the homage which is His due.

Hence Jesus was born before the death of Herod, probably in the year 5 or 6 B.C.; thus our time reckoning is inexact. The indications of Luke (Lk. 2:1,2) also suggest this time.

As far as the star in the east is concerned, what was meant according to detailed research was a special constellation of Saturn, which in general was considered the star of the Jews (and so of their king). This story seems more legendary to us than it really is: such calculations by means of stars were very widespread in the ancient East.

(*b*) *The baptism of Jesus.* Matthew depicts for us the figure of the forerunner of Jesus in far greater detail than Mark. Above all we see manifested here already the opposition between those who are content to pride themselves on their descent from Abraham and the truly believing, i.e. penitent Judaism (3:7–9). Jesus confesses Himself as belonging to the latter group, since He too—despite the protest of the Baptist—is prepared to undergo the baptism of repentance: wherever the sinner ready to turn and repent is to be found, there is Jesus! The reason given for His willingness to be baptized takes us to the depths of the gospel: by establishing Himself in solidarity with the sinner, Jesus "fulfils all righteousness" (3:15). What God wills ("righteousness") is thus nothing other than this deliberate oneness of His Son with lost humanity. That in this attitude Jesus is conforming to the will of the Father is confirmed for Him by the fact that just at this moment the Father openly acknowledges Him (3:17). If we reflect on the matter we shall find foreshadowed in this narrative both the cross and the resurrection of Jesus.

(*c*) *The temptation.* This solidarity with humanity demands from Jesus a stern and life-long struggle. This struggle finds its most pointed expression in the experience of temptation. "Are you the Son of God?" so the tempter begins (4:3,6). Why do you not exploit your divine power and office? Why do you hunger, Son of God? Why do you not come forward with an open manifestation of your high estate? All mankind would then fall at your feet. Thus the first two temptations. But Jesus answers with Biblical texts, all of which emphasize just the distance between God and man, making it clear that He did not grasp at equality with God (Phil. 2:6). To the very end He remains at the side of man—in spite of the suggestions of the religious who challenge Him to show a sign (16:1f.), in spite of the efforts of Peter to turn Him aside from the way of the cross (16:23—"Satan"), in spite of everything that tried to tempt Him to disclose His Messiahship in tangible form. The third temptation shows that Jesus stands before the decision between the power of the world (i.e. the bondage of Satan) and—the cross (4:9). And He chooses the cross. Thus in this story Matthew gives a most comprehensive view of the implications of the work of Jesus. But by His decision, Jesus was affirming the harshest opposition to what the Jews expected of their Messiah; this we have already seen in Mark.

(*d*) *The sending forth of the disciples.* Matthew tells us more about the disciples than Mark. In the discourse relating to their mission (a conflation of several sources) he desires to show how in their activity the mighty works of Jesus are continued. The mission springs from the Lord's compassion with the harassed and helpless people (9:36). Just as He Himself —before the cross—confined His ministry to the "lost sheep of the house of Israel" (15:24) so the disciples too are enjoined to keep within these limits (10:5ff.). As His own teaching brings about a discrimination between men, so does theirs (10:11ff.). As in His own works of healing He identifies Himself with the cause of the sick and proves His authority by the casting out of demons, so must they do (10:8). As He found nothing but opposition, they too must reckon with it (10:16f.). Just as the Master "has nowhere to lay His head" (8:20) so the disciples are to be poor (10:9,10), wholly abandoned to God, and for that very reason fearless (10:26ff.). They belong utterly to Him, His honour is their honour (10:32f.), but also His cross is their cross (10:34ff., especially 10:38ff.). We see how all this forms the prototype for the coming Christian community. If the early believers are called "Christians" (Acts 11:26), this means that they participate fully and unreservedly in what Christ is and does.

(*e*) *John the Baptist and the people.* Matthew speaks more emphatically than the other synoptics about John the Baptist, whose work left a deep mark, and in this respect he is akin to the gospel of John. The question which the imprisoned John addresses to the Lord (11:2ff.) is characteristic. He does not mean it in the sense that this Jesus of Nazareth should be the one promised by him; what he is concerned about is that the great judgment of God which he expected (3:12) does not appear, and instead Jesus is engaging in acts of healing and in discussions, and furthermore is associating with notorious sinners! John wonders whether Jesus is not simply another forerunner of the Messiah. We notice that John is repelled by Jesus' association with the lost, very much as the pious are. The answer of Jesus is: what I am doing is in fact the work of Messiah, that is, I am healing and liberating (cf. Isa. 61:1 and 35:5f.). Here the true Messiah again clashes with the preconception of Messianic expectation, even in the case of John the Baptist. But let us not forget that Peter too tries to prevent his Master from treading the way of the cross (16:22f.). How solitary is Jesus! Matthew has added to the scene described here other sayings reflecting the judgment of Jesus about the Baptist: he is the greatest of men up to the present (Jesus is measuring with the criterion of the kingdom of God), nevertheless his work stands before the breaking in of the divine kingdom, in which the humblest will be greater than he (11:11): the fact is that the kingdom revolutionizes all values (19:30; 20:16; 20:26f.). Of course now is the decisive day of salvation: now has come the time of which it is (popularly) said that "men of violence take it by force" (11:12).

But what about the people? As Jesus shrewdly notes, the people entertain their private thoughts; they find fault with John because he was an ascetic and with Jesus because He was the reverse (11:16ff.), and thus they attempt to avoid a decision. Nevertheless a decision has been made. The temporizing neutrality which Jesus has met with in the towns where He has worked (in so far as He did not meet hatred and opposition) is in itself a negative which God will answer with a judgment of rejection (11:20f.).

(*f*) *The self-testimony of Jesus.* In the gospel of Mark, Jesus disclosed the ultimate secret of His being only to the disciples. Matthew offers us more of the sayings of the Lord to the disciples. He also offers us more of the words in which Jesus unveiled Himself. Among these belongs especially the tremendous and beautiful saying at the close of ch. 11. once again we see a connexion between the invitation to the "weary and heavy laden" and the declaration of the exalted status of Jesus (11:25ff.); as in Mark, so here, the glory of Jesus is shown just in the help He gives to the lost. Equally proud is the saying of 13:17; Jesus stands revealed as the One in whom all the hopes of the forefathers are fulfilled. To the same category belongs the saying which Jesus utters in reply to the confession of Peter (16:17ff.): the claim to build a new community of God, to found a new temple is typically Messianic (cf. 26:61). And in precisely the same circle of ideas is the promise that Jesus will be present with the smallest band of His followers (18:20). All these sayings point beyond the cross to the resurrection and foreshadow the final self-declaration of the exalted Lord in 28:18ff. If we consider such statements carefully we shall see how closely they accord with the tones of the gospel of John.

We may note further that Matthew gives more parables of the Lord than Mark. Let us indicate the best known: the leaven, the treasure in the field, the pearl of great price, the dragnet (all in ch. 13 which is composite), the unforgiving servant (ch. 18), the labourers in the vineyard (ch. 20), the marriage feast of the king (ch. 22), the ten virgins (ch. 25), the talents (ch. 25).

3. *The Sermon on the Mount*

The Sermon on the Mount is by far the most comprehensive body of teaching in Matthew and the New Testament generally. Its material is only in part peculiar to Matthew; the greater part of it is found also in Luke (in a partially divergent form, especially chs. 6 and 11), while scattered single sayings are found in Mark already. If we wished to summarize the content of this sermon in a heading, it would be best to choose the saying of 5:20 and paraphrase it as "the higher righteousness". But it must be said at once that it will have to be shown how this righteousness is not merely in excess of the righteousness of the scribes and Pharisees, but in point of fact represents something quite different—what, may be surmised if we recollect 3:15.

(*a*) *The Beatitudes.* The Sermon on the Mount is addressed to the disciples. It is a course of instruction (hence Jesus is seated: the teacher sits, and his audience stands). But most unusual instruction! If we examine more closely the particular statements with which Jesus begins, we find that the second part (beginning "for" . . .) always contains an element of surprise. In fact even in the first part there is something surprising: "Blessed are the poor (in spirit), the mourners, the hungry and thirsty . . ." A latent antithesis governs the whole structure of these pronouncements. The poor in spirit (i.e. poor in the Spirit of God), hence the publicans and sinners, are to be blessed, and that because the kingdom of heaven belongs to them *par excellence*! This point is illustrated by ch. 9:9ff. or 11:28ff. The poor in spirit are by no means blessed in themselves, but only because Jesus calls them to Himself and concerns Himself about their condition. And thus the discourse proceeds with unremitting insistence. It is obvious, for example, that the mourners are not blessed. It is not true that every mourner finds consolation. But Jesus means to say: blessed are you, you who now suffer and lament in this evil world—for *I* will give you the comfort of the kingdom of God. That the meek are blessed is clean contrary to common experience, and that they possess the Land (i.e. the promised land, a share in the kingdom of God) is by no means evident. This is only true when we consider *Who* says this. At the heart of each pronouncement stands the majesty of Jesus Christ, and only in consequence of that fact do the statements become meaningful. Such pronouncements express the good news of the kingdom of God, which subverts and transforms all earthly relationships, and in which the chief is not the powerful but the weak, not the Pharisee in the pride of his righteousness, but the humble.

Kingdom of heaven does not mean the better world to come, but is simply a variant of the kingdom of God.

It is important to note that already in these beatitudes Jesus emphasizes sharply His opposition to the exponents of the law; this is very evident in 5:12; cf. also 23:31,34ff.

In line with the beatitudes are the similes about the salt and light. Both are essential to the life of man. Thus the importance of the mission of the disciples is made clear. But both things can easily be rendered quite ineffective. Therefore take heed!

Salt was reckoned the symbol of wisdom; hence Jesus continues without image saying that the salt may become "stupid". Perhaps we should rather think of something saturated in salt which in course of time loses its salt content and so is spoiled and must be thrown away.

(*b*) *The righteousness of the disciples and the traditional law.* We do not correctly understand the Sermon on the Mount, especially the section beginning 5:17 (to the end of the chapter), if we read it as though it were a programme sketching out a new type of piety or ethics. Jesus Himself expressly disclaims (5:17–19) any intention of saying something new. He does not propose to cancel the past or to make innovations for the future. He desires to "fulfil", i.e. to bring out into fullest expression and to embody in actual achievement the underlying purpose of the law. And the law secretly aims at a righteousness which exceeds that of the professional pious. Hence Jesus does not go back behind it but carries it further forward!

But how? Why this authoritative "But I say unto you", point by point? Jesus extracts six examples, partly from the decalogue (vv. 21,27 and 33), partly indications which the law gives in other contexts (vv. 31, 38,43). They are in part quoted literally from the Old Testament, but also in part (vv. 21 and 43) with an immediate expansion such as was given by the scribes; in v. 43 this is very important, because in this instance anything at all similar is lacking from the Old Testament.

Now it is obvious that Jesus does not question any of the commandments as far as they go. He begins where the transgression has its root, in the heart of man. The law, as Jesus not merely expounds it but insists on its fulfilment, is aimed at the inner being of man. It does not merely forbid murder but also anger and contempt (which were common and unpunished), not merely adultery but also the impure thought, not merely the reckless casting out of the wife but in general the ignoring of the claims of others, not merely unbridled vengeance but harsh self-assertion generally, not merely lovelessness towards one's closest relations, but any and every kind of lovelessness. And still more, the law with its commands does not merely say "no" to the evil will, but positively requires the good will. And the good will—and this is the decisive point—consists in love, consists in what Jesus does, in His solidarity with others. Hence the law is concerned not primarily with the prohibition against killing but with the positive requirement of the limitlessly conciliatory disposition (v. 25), and Jesus scorns the wise who nicely calculate the various degrees of punishment due, by pointing to the judgment of *God* (vv. 25,26). The prohibition of adultery implies the decisive and self-sacrificial turning towards purity of heart, the prohibition of perjury, the straightforward declaration of the truth, and so on.

Envisaged from this point of view, the law concerns itself with the whole being of man. This gives it its ultimate gravity; for thus it cannot be evaded by compromise. But also as a result man is free; he is no longer lost in the thickets of innumerable attempts at exposition, no longer tries desperately to achieve this or that partial fulfilment, but stands naked and entire before God.

Much light has been shed on certain details of the Sermon on the Mount since we have become better acquainted with the views of the scribes in the time of Jesus. Thus it is now known how latitudinarian were even serious-minded scribes in their handling of divorce (vv. 27 ff.). One permitted divorce if the wife had allowed the meal to spoil, later another scribe permitted it if the husband found a more beautiful woman! Or (v. 43) it was really the case that the Pharisees thought it their duty to hate the impious. For here the enemy is not the enemy of the nation but one's religious opponent; it was a question of disunity within the people of God. As regards v. 39 it has been emphasized that it is a question of smiting the right cheek —hence a blow which must be dealt with the back of the hand: such a blow was common in the synagogue for the purpose of correcting a false teacher: hence it would not be correct to infer from this statement that as a general principle one should accept everything passively, the point is rather that the disciples should be prepared to be treated as heretics in the synagogue (cf. 10:17ff.; 24:9; Jn. 16:2). In general it cannot be sufficiently stressed that vv. 21ff. exactly like the beatitudes are addressed to the disciples and do not lay down universal rules—as also the law itself was not a universal thing but the covenantal law of Yahweh for His people. Hence Jesus intends to say: if you wish to enter into the coming kingdom of heaven, then your life must be contrary to that of others, you must be freed from self-concern and controlled by the spirit of love.

(*c*) *The practice of piety among the disciples*. With 6:1 there begins a new section but no new basic thought: it is only that other areas of life now come into view. As in 5:20ff. the theme is still "righteousness"—a word which means all that man does or does not do for the sake of God and in reference to the will of God. As in the previous section, so here, a general rule opens the passage. What is said in 6:1 about alms (i.e. works of mercy) applies exactly to the points that follow (6:5,16,18); true piety is not performed before others, not even before our own selves, its essence is self-surrender to God and hence it is done in the sight of God. The section continues up to 6:18.

What are we to think of the question of reward? Jesus speaks here (vv. 2,4,5, 16,18) and also many times elsewhere of this theme. Hence does the disciple of Jesus not serve God in pure disinterestedness? Our answer must be that it is proof of the mercy of God that He does not require from men a devotion to which He Himself makes no response. Man does not give himself to God in order to gain reward. But when he does say "yes" to God he may be sure that God also says "yes" to him. That this does not mean earthly success, is clear from the path that Jesus trod and from the thought of martyrdom which He holds out as the likely lot of the disciples. But after all some reward is in question. The boastful pride of man that "he does good for the sake of good alone" is a motive which does not occur in the Bible. Conduct of this kind is possible only to God who is goodness itself. But man lives by what he receives. He is not a free master, but a workman (this image is frequent; the best known example is Matt. 20:1ff.) who receives his reward. But we must remember that this reward does not by any means correspond to the degree of achievement (cf. Matt. 20:1ff. and 19:29); it is distributed by the free and boundless grace of God.

(*d*) *The prayer of the disciples.* Whoever practises his piety in order to win for himself a good position in the public esteem or in the eyes of God, whoso therefore lives not in the freedom of the child but in bondage to self-concern or in the spirit of religious officiousness, will submit his prayers to a hard yoke; he will feel that they must represent a considerable achievement if they are to be efficacious. For this reason many words must be spoken and the same prayer often repeated: it will be quantity that counts. The tension in which Jesus places His disciples to the piety of their time (and incidentally that of many another time) is in nothing clearer than in the matter of prayer. The prayer which Jesus teaches His disciples is probably not merely an example but a case of His teaching them to pray as children are taught (cf. Lk. 11:1), and in this prayer each individual word and phrase has its full weight (though it should not be abused in babbling). In the address "Our Father—who art in heaven" the whole gospel is essentially contained. To be able to say to God really and truly "Father", is the great privilege of the Christian (it implies so much more than receiving the information *that* God is Father). And in truth this is not something which goes without saying; for God is "in heaven": Jesus in no way derogates from the infinite majesty of God. Hence the petitions which concern the name, the kingdom, the will of God stand first. No one can be a disciple who is not first and foremost concerned about these things, and this prayer is therefore at the same time a credal confession. But whosoever prays thus may also freely come with his own requests, for it is the Father to whom he is speaking.

To be able to say *Father* is also in the eyes of Paul the supreme thing (Rom. 8:15; Gal. 4:5,6), for it is the gift which Jesus through the Holy Ghost grants to His own. It is significant that in both texts we find the Aramaic word *Abba* quoted; a sign that in the primitive community, even though normally Greek was the current language, the Lord's prayer was known in the language and probably also prayed in the language in which Jesus taught it to His disciples.

The "name" of God signifies the mode in which He reveals Himself. The New Testament witnesses to us that God discloses Himself to man in Jesus of Nazareth. Hence Acts 4:12 and 3:6,16; 4:7,10. But God must be reverenced in His revelation: He condescends wholly and graciously to man and yet He remains utterly Himself.

"Thy will be done." This petition no doubt means too the quality of resignation to the divine will (cf. Matt. 26:39.) But it is primarily meant actively: it is a prayer that ultimately the will of God as it is done in heaven so also will openly overcome on earth all the wills which oppose it. Thus this petition stands in closest connexion with the one about the coming of the kingdom of God.

The prayer for "daily bread" is, as contemporary parallels show, not simply a request for earthly sustenance. It is rather concerned in the first instance with the expected bread of heaven which the Messiah will distribute. But the request for earthly food is not excluded but included.

The conclusion of the Lord's prayer ("for Thine is the kingdom . . .") is not contained in the oldest manuscripts. It is a quotation from 1 Chron. 29:11–13.

(*e*) *False and true anxiety* (6:19–34). The whole Sermon on the Mount is largely concerned with life on this earth and in particular with the life of the disciple. Jesus did not promise His disciples an easy existence (cf. Matt. 10). They had already had occasion for anxiety: they were running into expulsion from the synagogue, general outlawry and material distress. Moreover they were mostly men from the lower classes of society. Man can have two attitudes in the main towards possessions: either he tries by the help of material goods to secure his life on this earth, or he frets because this form of security is denied him. In both cases he is bent on somehow making himself the master of his life. Jesus breaks down both attitudes. For in the first place they are simply foolish; wealth is in any case transient and chancy and carefulness avails nothing. But behind such considerations there are more fundamental ones: not only does your anxiety and hoarding avail nothing, but it actually destroys the one sure foundation of true life. "Where your treasure is, there will your heart be also." "You cannot serve God and mammon." And both the rich man and the poor man who worries are serving mammon. But we serve God when we enjoy the freedom of receiving everything from His hands (thus living like the flowers of the field) in the assurance that our life is of more abiding value than theirs. Again we are faced with the truth that was tirelessly insisted on in the previous sections—everything, all that the law requires, all the practices of piety, all prayer point to the fact that we belong to God and not to ourselves. Where this is realized, then anxiety and avarice are replaced by genuine trust. Whoever directs his aims and purposes to the kingdom of God and His righteousness (v. 33) has also the assurance that all other things will be added unto him.

We must further point out that Jesus is not a deluded dreamer and idealist. He knew also very well that the grass "today is alive and to-morrow is thrown into the oven" (v. 30) and He was certainly fully aware of the brutal struggle for existence which fills the world of nature. It should never be forgotten that He does not promise His disciples earthly happiness, but encourages them to await the free, pure gifts of God—only in that respect are they to be like the flowers and the birds.

(*f*) *Concerning the habit of judging* (7:1–6). In Israel at that time judgments were frequently made: day after day the law expert had to deliver his judgment on questions of human conduct and in this matter it was always understood that the teacher of the law knew the secrets of the will of God in his own life and mind; otherwise what was the use of all this erudition about the law? This whole attitude is forbidden to the disciples. Judgment rests with God alone, and whoever judges must be prepared for the condemnation that he has usurped the place of God. Moreover the one who judges constantly observes all the failings of others while not perceiving his own enormous and fundamental perversity (7:4,5). Of course the disciples will not therefore be without discrimination! (v. 6). "Dogs" were considered impure animals—the holy (i.e. what belongs to God) must be preserved inviolate.

(*g*) *Particular sayings* (7:7–23). To what a large extent the Sermon on the Mount is a mixed composition can best be observed towards its close; up to now there have been large unified passages; there now follows on the contrary a number of particular sayings which Jesus must have uttered on various occasions. The saying about petitions (7:7–11) might easily be considered a fantastic notion; how many requests are not granted! But Jesus has in mind the ultimate good which God will certainly not refuse (Luke says: the Holy Spirit, cf. Lk. 11:13; Matt. 7:11). And furthermore what is in question is praying in faith (cf. the bold saying of 17:20). Verse 12 is isolated: it is usually called the golden rule; it is noteworthy that in its negative form it occurs elsewhere proverbially. But how all-embracing is the positive form which Jesus gives it! Here the individual stands forth in full responsible existence.

The word about the "narrow gate" (7:13,14) leads us already to the several times repeated "either-or" with which the sermon closes: the narrow or wide gate, salvation or ruin, the tree bearing good or bad fruit, the word or the deed of obedience—up to the parable of the wise and foolish man, which stands at the close of the whole rich composition. In fact the Sermon on the Mount confronts the disciple of every age and time with a hard and ineluctable decision; for at this level of truth compromise is obviously not possible. And moreover the attitude of mere assent, assent to and admiration of the fine radicalism of the requirements of Jesus, is likewise of no use. What is necessary is sheer obedience, not the repetition of "Lord, Lord". This puts before man the question on what foundation he is going to build his life: will he find his security in the law, in the works of piety done for his own self-glory, will he make wealth—whether it be by amassing treasure or fretting about poverty—the basis of his life's security, or will he really come to the point at which he sees the law as the absolute claim of God on his whole existence, piety as his response to this claim of God and wealth as something which is essentially frail and incidental? The suggestion that the man who makes the latter decision is like one who builds his house on the rock is not immediately evident; for the man who does make this decision is in fact surrendering what the world means by security. But the message of Jesus is just this: that we have our own true security and, to go back to the beginning of the sermon, our own true blessedness in the fact that we cease to covet a security lying in ourselves or possessions that are our own, but rather determine to cast ourselves on God alone in His infinite mercy.

Thus the Sermon on the Mount does not project for us a lofty and utterly unattainable ideal, but in its wholeness it summons man to adopt an attitude which by the bent of his nature he resists. It is in fact a wide frontal attack on man as he naturally is. The disciple of Jesus is one who faces this challenge and exposes himself to this attack.

Chapter 14

THE SAVIOUR OF THE WORLD

THE TESTIMONY TO CHRIST OF THE GOSPEL OF LUKE
(chs. 1–2; 10; 12; 15; 18)

1. *The literary character of the gospel*

The opening verses (1:1–4) suggest two things: firstly that Luke has at his disposal and utilizes further reports about Jesus, and secondly that he has taken the initiative in instituting investigations of his own. His gospel is addressed to a man of high rank ("most excellent Theophilus" means in reality "my most powerful lord . . ." v. 3) and is intended to furnish him with the needed basis for the doctrine in which he has been instructed. Luke is the only evangelist who allows us such a glimpse into his manner of proceeding as an author; he has gone to work as though he were a historian of his epoch. If we glance through the gospel this is readily confirmed by many points. It is certainly true that in some chapters Luke follows Mark very closely (for example 4:31—6:19 or 8:22—9:50 or the passion narrative), and in this respect we have before us the one source from which he draws. But on the other hand he omits whole passages of Mark (e.g. Mk. 6:45—8:26) and considerably modifies the sequence of incidents. Luke has also used the sayings-source, as is shown by the above-mentioned parallels to the Sermon on the Mount (see Lk. 6:20ff. or Lk. 11:1ff.), but on the other hand he probably did not use our present gospel of Matthew. Above all, Luke offers us an abundance of material which is exclusive to himself; the best known bits of this are the introductory stories (e.g. the Christmas story, Lk. 2:1ff.) and a large number of parables (e.g. the good Samaritan, 10:25ff., or the prodigal son, 15:11ff., or Dives and Lazarus, 16:19ff., or the Pharisee and the publican, 18:9ff.). Almost one-half of the gospel consists of this special Lucan material. Even the structure and arrangement of the gospel as a whole shows marked peculiarities: whereas in both Mark and Matthew we found two main parts and as the turning point and link between them the confession of Peter at Caesarea Philippi, Luke clearly divides his narrative into three parts: between the ministry in Galilee and the preparations for the passion there lies a long report about the journey of Jesus to Jerusalem (9:51—18:14). Thus we shall have to say that Luke is the most peculiar and arbitrary of the synoptics.

2. *Luke the Physician*

Corresponding to all this is the ancient tradition which describes the gospel of Luke and its continuation in the Acts of the Apostles as the work of a Gentile Christian who was associated with Paul: namely the physician Luke. Here and there we find that Paul mentions him (Col. 4:14; Philem. 24; 2 Tim. 4:11). Also there is much that would indicate that the special ideas and outlook of Paul have in some ways influenced our evangelist. Both the deliberate historical method (of course in accordance with the ideas of the time) and in many ways the style suggest that the author is a man of culture: in fact it has been attempted to show that technical medical expressions are to be found in this gospel in rich measure. Thus the ancient tradition that Luke is the author gains some probability. We cannot say more; for none of the evangelists name themselves; the titles do not form an integral part of the text. In any event we may regard it as certain that a cultured Gentile Christian was the author. It must certainly have been a man who had at his disposal Palestinian traditions too; in particular the first two chapters show the existence of such traditions.

3. *The Saviour*

"To you this day is born a Saviour"; such is the message which rings out in the Christmas story, and the word is addressed to shepherds, a class of men who were despised both from a religious and social point of view. According to Luke, the Saviour is above all He who brings forgiveness to the sinner. Of course healing miracles are not wanting in this gospel; even in the special matter of Luke there are some specially impressive stories of healing, e.g. that of the ten lepers (17:11ff.): in fact we hear once more of a raising from the dead, in the case of the young man of Nain (7:11ff.). But narratives which deal with the relation of Jesus to the sinner are given far greater space. When Peter caught a miraculous draught of fishes (doubtless a symbol of the Christian world mission) he fell prostrate before the Lord saying: "Depart from me, for I am a sinful man" (5:8). We have already seen from the gospel of Mark that Jesus makes His own the cause of the sinner. But in the gospel of Luke this particular trait becomes predominant. Thus here, as nowhere else, we see Jesus in action as the Shepherd and Pastor of the rejected ones. Luke alone tells us the story of the woman who was a sinner (7:36ff.), the parable of the great supper (14:16ff.), the incident concerning the tax collector Zacchaeus (19:1ff.), the illustration furnished by the Pharisee and the publican (18:9ff.) and the parable of the prodigal son (15:11ff.). Everywhere in this gospel the great miracle is not the healing of the sick but the fathomless character of divine love in its pursuit of the lost. In line with this conception is the special emphasis on the Samaritans; one of this particularly despised race shows himself more merciful than the priest and Levite (10:25ff.), another is the only one who can find a word of thanks for healing he has been given (17:11ff.). This leads us to a further insight: the love of Jesus for sinners is all-embracing, "universal". It does not stop at the borders of the Old Testament covenant people; accordingly Luke omits the story of the Phoenician woman (Mk. 7:24ff.), whereas Matthew in his characteristic way impressively expands it (Matt. 15:21ff.). Luke does not of course intend to countenance the boastful pride of the Gentiles or of Gentile Christians; but his theme is that Jesus by the very fact of His interest in and solidarity with the lost has already crossed the border into the world of the heathen; the Saviour of sinners is the Saviour of all sinners throughout the whole world.

4. *The World*

It is characteristic of Luke that he traces the descent of Jesus (3:23ff.) back, not to Abraham (as does Matthew) but to Adam; Jesus belongs to humanity as such. The hymns of the introduction (of which the Magnificat is specially important, 1:46ff.) show that He is also the fulfiller of the old covenant; but again it is specially typical that in the Magnificat God is praised as the One who does what is inconceivable to man and who transforms and reverses present human relations. It is further characteristic that Luke is eager to stress the intercourse of Jesus with the despised Samaritans and that he alone mentions a second mission of the disciples (that of the Seventy) which proceeds from Samaria (10:1ff. after 9:51ff.): Jesus prepares a mission to the world from ground which to the Jews was certainly half-heathen! The universalistic tone of the gospel is heard especially plainly in the Christmas story so familiar to us. Luke fits the Nativity into the history of the Roman empire, names the emperor Augustus (as later Tiberius, 3:1) and Quirinius the governor of Syria, showing how a Roman enrolment decree was the occasion for the birth of the Son of David in the city of David. The song of praise of the angels ends with the proclamation of peace and salvation to all men with whom God is well-pleased, while the song of Simeon (2:32) likewise includes the heathen in its scope. The close of the gospel is completely universalistic: repentance and forgiveness of sin are to be preached, beginning at Jerusalem, to *all* peoples (24:47). This indication foreshadows the development in the Acts of the Apostles which is thus added as a continuation by the same author.

5. *The divine mercy*

In this gospel the very being of

Jesus is disclosed as inexhaustible mercy which turns in grace to all the lost. What He requires from man is nothing else but what He Himself inexhaustibly gives: love. The fact that the notorious Magdalene received a rich measure of forgiveness is clearly connected with the fact that she herself loves unreservedly and unstintingly (7:47). What in the parable of the Good Samaritan is the pattern which we are bidden imitate is the love which does not inquire on whom it bestows its favour (10:25ff.). What renders the rich man guilty towards the wretched Lazarus is just that he does not bother to concern himself with this helpless mortal (16:19ff.). It is typical that Luke offers us the saying given by Matthew (5:48) as applying to righteousness, in the form: "Be merciful even as your Father is merciful" (6:36). In Luke the superiority of Jesus to the law of the Sabbath is clearly shown to spring from the overriding demands of mercy (13:15ff.; 14:1ff.). Even in the suffering of the cross the tormented One prays for His tormentors (23:34) and turns in mercy to a repentant criminal, together with whom He will pass through the gate of death (23:39ff.). Thus in every respect according to this presentation the good news of Jesus can be summarized in the one word: Love.

6. *Riches and poverty*

More sharply than any other of the synoptics Luke brings out the attitude of Jesus towards possessions. Perhaps the most striking example of this is the parable of the rich farmer (12:15ff.): whoever wishes to render himself secure by means of his wealth is building in the void! Where the ultimate decision about man takes place riches are irrelevant; on the contrary, the careless enjoyment of wealth which pays no heed to the helpless, turns out to be disastrous to men (16:19ff.; Dives and Lazarus). In face of the imminence of the kingdom of God all wealth is but unrighteous mammon; this is the point of view which Jesus expounds in the parable of the unjust steward (16:1ff.). The heart of this parable is the thought that, in face of the judgment of God, wealth has lost its value and therefore should be used in order that in the divine judgment the rich man may have an advocate, namely the poor whom he has endowed with riches. The disciple of Jesus must renounce all that he has (14:33), must sell his possessions and give to the poor (12:33). Thus the demand of Jesus is in the highest degree radical and complete. Even the beatitudes in the form in which Luke presents them reveal the same trend of thought: "Blessed are you poor, but woe to you that are rich" (6:20ff.). The entire work of Jesus can be summed up in the fact that God puts down the mighty from their thrones and exalts those of low degree, fills the hungry with good things and sends the rich empty away (Magnificat: 1:46ff.): in other words, a complete reversal of current values. Nothing in the whole world can remain as it is. Jesus came to cast on the earth a flaming torch (12:49) but it is the torch of self-consuming love.

Chapter 15

THE ETERNAL WORD

THE GOSPEL OF CHRIST PRESENTED BY JOHN

1. *The general character of the fourth gospel*

The thought of the *word* is the keynote of the whole gospel. It begins with a profound mystical meditation on the eternal Word which nevertheless became flesh (1:14). The word of Jesus, His preaching, forms the heart and centre of the gospel and here it is expressed no longer in the form of terse pronouncements but in extended and ample periods. Again, these discourses of Jesus are predominantly concerned with the theme of His own Person; they are "revelational" in tone and content. In fact even the deeds of Jesus which are reported in this gospel are often specifically qualified as "signs" (2:11,23; 3:2; 4:54, etc.), and are self-revealing deeds: they have the character of a witness which Jesus bears to Himself in the form of special action. It is true that even in the first three gospels attention is wholly concentrated on the Person of the Lord; but there the mystery of that Person, as we have seen especially in regard to Mark, remains concealed, whereas in John it is from the very first regarded as fully disclosed (already in 1:29,41ff.). Historical occurrences such as the synoptics have in view, and which John certainly does not neglect, are decidedly envisaged by him as a process in which the Eternal is revealing Himself and it is on the Eternal that his gaze is concentrated. Sometimes in fact it seems as though a narrative almost imperceptibly fades away and in vain we seek a satisfying conclusion (cf. the story of Nicodemus, ch. 3, or of the Greeks, 12:20ff.). The historical event itself thus becomes merely an occasion for a self-revealing discourse on the part of Jesus, and the evangelist is obviously thinking not so much of the past as, so to speak, lifting his eyes upwards to the enthroned Lord whose ever living presence he attests. For it is integral to the whole scheme of the fourth gospel that it expressly bears "witness": nowhere else in the New Testament do the ideas of "witness" and "witnessing" occur so frequently as in the gospel of John. We might in fact summarily describe the whole gospel as the believer's witness to Jesus Christ regarded as the Revealer of the Father.

John still less than the other gospels

proposes to give us anything in the nature of a biography of Jesus. Nevertheless particular pieces of information are not wholly lacking. Here and there (e.g. 3:24) it looks as though John wishes to correct the synoptics. Much weight has been laid on the fact that according to John the crucifixion of Jesus did not take place on Passover day, as the synoptics imply, but on the previous day (cf. 19:14; 18:28). Further, it is plain that John presupposes a ministry of Jesus extending over several years (he refers to three distinct passovers, 2:13,23; 6:4; 12:1, and 5:1 is perhaps a fourth, whereas the synoptics report only the one passover on which Jesus suffered and died). Many critics are of the opinion that in this respect John is reporting events more accurately than the synoptics (who of course nowhere expressly state that the ministry of Jesus lasted only one year). But these historical details do not lessen the truth that John—as the church father Clement of Alexandria said—emphasizes not corporeal but spiritual things; he insists on the decisive and that which calls for decision (cf. 20:31). The fourth gospel is "central", it is focused on the heart of the Christian message.

This however must not be misunderstood in the sense that John had only in view the image of the exaltation and glory of the Lord. The fact is rather that the whole gospel is penetrated with the tension of a terrible conflict, the conflict between light and darkness, between Jesus and the prince of this world, between truth and the lie, life and death. This evangelist does not bear witness to the coming of the Revealer, the Son of God into the world in such a way as to suggest that that manifestation in its transcendent majesty eliminates all opposition and resistance, he depicts rather the terrible clash which His appearance occasions (so already in the prologue, 1:5; 1:11) and in which He glorifies Himself by His death (death as glorification, 12:23; 13:31, and as exaltation, 3:14; 8:28; 12:32,34). Only when we appreciate this tension and struggle can we truly understand this gospel.

2. *The Prologue* (1:1–18)

In all the gospels the unique quality which the disciples experienced about Jesus their Lord is brought into light from the very start. In the effort to express the uniqueness of Jesus, none of the evangelists confines his attention to merely earthly historical incidents: this uniqueness which they desire to attest consists for all of them in the communion of Jesus with God the Father.

But it is John who has expressed the mystery of Jesus, which strikes home to the believer, in a more comprehensive and profound way than any other of the evangelists. The prologue of the fourth gospel, which perhaps was elaborated from a much older hymn of the early Church, becomes in the hands of our writer a kind of "overture" striking the essential tones and harmonies of what is to follow.

We are referred back to the unimaginable beginning of things (so also 1 Jn. 1:1). In eternity God is no solitary self-contained God, but from the beginning was the Word which was "with God" and was God Himself (1:1). The creation took place through this Word (1:3); God was ever one with the Word (1:1) and yet in some way was distinct from the Word (1:2), was disposed to step forth out of His hidden self-existence, and the creation of all things is the first self-disclosure of God; creation is already revelation and the "life" (1:4) which was imparted to the creature is life springing from the Word and orientated to the Word.

With 1:5 there begins a new thought (up to v. 13). The "light" which the Word, as the Giver of all life, radiates, "shines in the darkness". We note that here begins what elsewhere we should describe as the Nativity story. The light shines in the darkness of the world, is attested by John the Baptist and in this world which nevertheless belongs to Him, this divine source of life and light appears as an alien element (1:9–11). Here for the first time we see that antithesis which we have mentioned. The astounding incomprehensible thought is expressed that the One who has His origin in the eternity of God and is the Giver of life and eternal light, appears in the thick darkness of the world as a stranger! But the still greater wonder is this, that there were men who received Him and to whom He gave power to become children of God, born of God (1:12,13).

The climax of the prologue now comes with 1:14; the Word became flesh and dwelt among us (in vv. 14,16,18 there comes to expression a confession of the first Church—the Johannine form of the primal Christian confession). The Word is not distant but very near, dwelling with human beings who are surrendered as a prey to death—"we have beheld His glory"! Once again in v. 15 the testimony of the Baptist rings out—but it is answered as it were by the choir of the fellowship of the Church which bears witness to the great things that Jesus has done for them (1:16). What Moses and the law could not achieve, grace and truth, the firm standing ground of life in God, has been accomplished through Jesus Christ, and He is the revealer of the Father whom no human eye has seen. Not until v. 17 is the name of Jesus Christ mentioned and therewith the meaning and the goal of the previous discourse, heavy with mystical significance, become clear.[1]

This is in essence the whole of the gospel that follows. The latter has sometimes in fact been divided up in accordance with the principle indicated in 1:11,12, and we may follow this method, for in the first section (1:19—4:54) the theme is how Jesus came to His own; in chs. 5–12, that His own, especially those

[1] The ideas which our gospel uses in the prologue, and often elsewhere also, flow most probably from gnosticism, a pre-Christian movement which later also influenced the Church. At the centre of the gnostic world of ideas was the theory that the soul, dying through its lapse into the world of matter and its link with the body, might be restored to its heavenly origin and home if by supernatural insight (i.e. gnosis) man could establish connexion with a semi-divine being emanating from God. It becomes at once apparent how repulsive 1:14 must have been to the gnostic world: the Word became flesh—hence not spirit, not the object of recognition and insight! According to Irenaeus this whole gospel is a polemic against gnosticism.

nearest to Him, the Jews, failed to receive Him; in the third (chs. 13–17) we have the words of Jesus addressed to those who confessed Him, and then finally (chs. 18–21) are described the events of the passion and resurrection and the way which Jesus takes to the Father. (We may state at once that ch. 21 is an appendix.)

3. "*He came to His own home*" (chs. 1:19—4:54)

As John the Baptist appeared in the prologue as the herald of the coming of Light, so also he opens the first narrative section of the gospel. In his testimony he describes Jesus as the Lamb of God (1:29,36). That, then, is the glory of Jesus.

In regard to "lamb of God" it is perhaps preferable to think of the passover lamb, perhaps also of the lambs which were daily sacrificed in Jerusalem, perhaps of Isa. 53:7. The essential point is that Jesus is the lamb of God slain for the sins of the *world*.

It is noteworthy that John the Baptist plays a specially emphasized role in the gospel of John; cf. also 1:35ff.; 3:22ff.; 5:31ff.; 10:41. There were probably in the environment of the evangelist gnostic circles who claimed to follow the Baptist.

From the circle of John the Baptist come also the first followers of Jesus (1:35ff.). The remark about the Lamb of God calls their attention to Him. We are told the name of one, Andrew the brother of Simon Peter (1:40). The name of the other we are not told—it is perhaps the same unknown disciple who appears in later contexts (13:23; 19:26; 20:2; 21:20), and whom critics have guessed to be the author of this gospel. Peter is then won over by the witness of his brother (1:40ff.); we have found the Messiah. He receives at once the descriptive name, Cephas, or rock (i.e. Peter). As a further disciple Jesus then finds one Philip who comes to the forefront only in this gospel: he again "finds" Nathanael, whom Jesus gives the honourable qualification of being a "true Israelite" in whom is no guile (1:43ff.).

John describes the calling of the disciples more colourfully than the synoptics. In the further course of the gospel some of the disciples are outlined with especial clarity. This applies above all to Philip (cf. 6:5,7; 12:21,22; 14:8,9) and Thomas (cf. 11:16; 14:5; 20:24ff.).

The ministry of Jesus itself begins with two symbolic actions: the turning of water into wine at Cana of Galilee and the cleansing of the temple (ch. 2). The first of these is not only expressly emphasized as the first "sign" which Jesus wrought (2:11), not only announces the "glory" of Jesus, and is not only a token of His divine epiphany (manifestation), but above all symbolizes His work as a work of renewal, as the inauguration of the age of salvation (wine rather than water!). The story of the cleansing of the temple (which in the synoptics belongs to the series of events circumscribing the passion) points in the same direction: 2:19 shows plainly that the evangelist is here thinking of the new Messianic age which Jesus (as the Risen Lord, 2:21,22) will bring to pass.

It is striking that in Mk. 14:58 reference is made to a similar statement which, however, is not to be found reported by the synoptics. In this instance John offers us the older tradition which is presupposed in Mark.

Two conversations constitute the centre of gravity of our section: firstly in ch. 3 the conversation with Nicodemus the Pharisee and member of the Sanhedrin, and in ch. 4 the conversation with the woman of Samaria. After the claim of Jesus has become clear in ch. 2, here in these conversations the full authority of Jesus to grant man new life and a complete reorientation of being is disclosed.

The fact that Nicodemus comes by night (3:2) shows how deep is his interest (it is not a matter of any supposed fear of the Jews). The manner in which he accosts Jesus (as Rabbi) raises the expectation that his purpose is to put a rather theoretical question. But Jesus answers him as though it were a question of something of immediate moment and urgency (3:3). When the kingdom of God is the issue, life as a whole comes into play.

It is remarkable that Nicodemus clearly does not understand what Jesus is talking about (3:4,9). The motive of lack of comprehension often appears in this gospel (cf. especially 4:11,15; 7:35; 8:22, 33,53,57; 12:34; 14:5). This lack of comprehension rests on the fact that men try to fit what Jesus says and does into the scheme of their own thinking. The new birth of man takes place "from above" (3:3) and according to the following verses through the Spirit (granted in baptism, 3:5).

From 3:11 onwards we are concerned with the exclusive speech of Jesus. Nicodemus himself disappears from view. Jesus speaks of heavenly things; but the most important point is that although in this connexion the exaltation of the Son of Man is the theme (3:14) yet this exaltation is focused on the crucifixion (cf. 8:28). The remarkable thing about "these *heavenly* things" is this, that we have here no outline of a transcendent ideal but a speech about the supreme saving gift, which is brought out most plainly in 3:16. Hence the work of the Son is seen not in judgment but in salvation (3:17); the judgment consists essentially in this, that men reject and spurn this salvation (3:18ff.) whereas the believer escapes condemnation and is assured of eternal life (3:18 and 3:16,36).

That Jesus is found speaking to a woman (ch. 4) amazes the disciples (4:27) for the Jews considered women of no importance religiously. And furthermore this woman is a Samaritan! She herself finds this sufficiently extraordinary (4:9). She understands Jesus just as little as the Jew who was learned in the law, in ch. 3 (4:11). But she begins to have some dim surmise (4:12) although again her approach rests on a strange misunderstanding; the image of the water of life she takes in the most material sense (4:15). Only when Jesus tells her the truth about her own life does she begin to grasp things (4:16–19) and then she desires to clear up with the "prophet" that old question in dispute between the Jews and Samaritans: where should God be worshipped? But Jesus refers her to the new age in which both Jerusalem and Gerizim lose their significance (4:21–24) and the woman at last understands that He is speaking of the Messianic age (4:25). Then Jesus Himself unlocks the mystery with His "I am he" (4:26). But the woman herself now becomes the proclaimer of Jesus as a result of all that she has heard (4:28–30,39–42). It is to be noted that according to our text it is just here that Jesus speaks about the harvest and the disciples' duty of labouring (4: 35–38). A harvest beginning with the despised Samaritans!

4. "*His own people received Him not*" (chs. 5–12)

More sharply than is the case with the synoptics, the ministry of Jesus in John's gospel is characterized by the clash with the Jews (here the term Jews does not connote the people as such, but their typical representatives who oppose Jesus).

In ch. 5 the battle flares up—we are reminded of the synoptics!—around the question of the Sabbath. Jesus heals at the pool of Bethesda a paralysed man and bids him take up his pallet and walk home. It is just this which provokes the quarrel (5:10). The healed man refers them to the authority of the one who healed him, whose name however he does not know (5:13). Later Jesus meets him in the temple: now the Jews realize who the Sabbath violater is and Jesus pushes the conflict to an extreme pitch by equating His own work with that of the Father (5:17). The Jews understand very well how monstrous is the implied claim, especially as it is a violation of the Sabbath which Jesus characterizes as a ministry reflecting the action of *God Himself*. Now they seek all the more resolutely to kill Him. His beneficent deeds reveal at the same time His emancipation from the law.

The work of Jesus is the work of God, the Father's work! The Jews feel this claim to be wantonly wicked. In 5:19–47 the relation of Jesus to the Father is set forth in some detail. On the one hand the perfect communion of Jesus with the Father is declared with vigorous emphasis: the Father loves Him, and the office of judgment which the Father exercises is also that of the Son (5:21,22, 25ff.); the honour and the glory of the Father also redound to the Son and whosoever refuses to honour Him refuses *ipso facto* to honour the Father (5:23). But on the other hand it is plain that the communion of the Son with the Father consists in obedience: of Himself the Son can do nothing (5:19,30). He does not do His own will (5:30). He does not bear witness to Himself, i.e. on His own authority (5:31) but is wholly dependent on the Father who of course bears witness to the Son, a witness far more powerful than that of the Baptist (5:36). In fact the witness of the Father has long existed: it stands in scripture, which the Jews so eagerly search (5:39: "You search the scriptures") in which they might have found the testimony to Him (5:39,47) but to the power of which their hearts are in reality closed, because they covet honour from each other, i.e. are concerned about their esteem among men, desiring for themselves religious authority (5:44). This means that their insistence on the scriptures is in truth hypocrisy, blindness to the message of the scriptures, and hence blindness to God and therefore to His Son!

The theme of chapter 6 is a further and fiercer clash with the Jews. Here two stories which we find in the synoptics are retold: the feeding of the 5,000 and the mysterious encounter of the disciples with their Lord on the Sea of Galilee. In comparison with the synoptic account one new point is above all noteworthy: after the feeding miracle Jesus can only escape being proclaimed as Messiah by fleeing (6:15); the people have come to believe that He is the "prophet" (6:14). The latent motive of the feeding then controls the whole subsequent fierce debate of Jesus with the Jews, which we find in 6:24ff.

Here the decisive point is that Jesus refers away from the "food which perishes" to the "bread of life": the Jews have perceived only the external and this provides the motive for their action (6:26); but they desire something further which they imagine equally materialistically—namely the bread from heaven which in their opinion the Messiah must grant, just as once Moses gave them manna in the wilderness and which they think to be one of the demonstrative signs of Messiahship (6:30–32). But Jesus, whose own food consists in doing the will of God (4:34) desires to give them the true bread from heaven, which the Father will give—in fact Jesus Himself is this bread (6:35,48). What He offers is not bodily nourishment but eternal life (6:40,47,33,35), life in God which is stronger than death (6:39). He promises no intoxicating miracle but the supreme wonder, which is conferred on the believer who comes to Him (6:35,37,44,45). Thus He Himself is the One who confers fullness of life in God.

In 6:51ff. this theme is then brought to a head in a certain specific direction: the thought is now presented that He wishes to give Himself as food to His own, that He grants to His disciples His own "flesh" and "blood", i.e. He grants them a share in the sacrifice of His life "for the life of the world" (6:51). This new turn of the discourse is certainly an allusion to the Last Supper. John gives us no account of the latter. Only in this passage is the theme brought forward.

The enormity and "hardness" of the words of Jesus are intolerable to many of His "disciples"; they turn away from Him. (Likewise 8:31ff.) So much the more vividly stands out the confession of those disciples who remain with Jesus—at this point we are reminded of the confession at Caesarea Philippi given in the synoptics (cf. Mk. 8:27ff.). But already the shadow of the traitor is outlined (6:64,70,71).

Yet the clash becomes still sharper. If already in 5:18 the Jews sought all the more to kill Him (hence they had had the intention earlier), in chapters 7 and 8 the net is drawn closer: they try to seize Him (7:19, 25,30,44ff.; 8:20,40), declare Him to be a Samaritan, or one possessed of a devil (7:20; 8:48), and even take up stones to stone Him for blasphemy (8:59). The shadows of the coming passion lie heavy on these chapters.

Events are now ever more clearly centred in Jerusalem; chapters 7–10 (as far as 10:40ff.) imply the capital city and ch. 11 (Bethany as also at the beginning of ch. 12) takes us not far from Jerusalem. Yet 10:22,40; 11:7 show that this concentration of events on Jerusalem indicates neither a strict temporal sequence of the incidents nor in fact is it quite strictly maintained. It is more probable that with this intense accumulation of traditions pointing to Jerusalem the evangelist wishes to emphasize the vital decision with which the contemporaries of Jesus are confronted and which they make in a sense leading ultimately to the passion. It is significant that the fourth gospel, which so emphatically declares the exalted status of Jesus, also emphasizes—and still more strongly than the synoptics—the fundamental significance of the passion. Chapters 7–19 (i.e. the greater proportion of the material of this gospel) belong to the wider or narrower circle of the passion narrative. Moreover we have noticed already in the prologue (1:11) and in the further course of the gospel almost from chapter to chapter (1:29,36; 2:21,22; 3:14–16; 5:18; 6:51ff.) clear foreshadowings of the passion of Jesus.

In 7:1–10 the imminence of the decision is already clear: the brothers of Jesus —who do not believe on Him—try to persuade Him to show Himself openly to the world, *now*. Jesus evades their pressure; His "hour" is not yet come. When the brothers have gone away, He too goes up to the feast privately. In Jerusalem it is the feast of tabernacles which draws large crowds of pilgrims. The people are divided in their opinion about Jesus (7:12). The question as to who Jesus is, is a theme which runs through the whole of chapter 7 (7:26,27, 31,32,40–42,46ff.).

Here the self-testimony of Jesus is strongly reminiscent of ch. 5: His teaching is not His own affair (7:16,18); He has not come of His own accord (7:28); He has been sent by the Father (7:29). His high dignity consists in His obedience! But it is an exalted dignity. This is shown in a dramatic climax in 7:37ff. The feast is at its height. As every day during the feast, the priest draws water from the spring of Siloam which is then carried in joyful procession to the temple and poured out on the altar, to the accompaniment of the people's chanting: "With joy you will draw water from the wells of salvation" (Isa. 12:3). And just at that moment Jesus comes forward and speaks to the rejoicing people of the inner thirst of the spirit (which it certainly is not aware of) and which *He* will satisfy: "If any one thirst let him come to me and drink. He who believes in me, as the scripture has said, 'Out of his heart shall flow rivers of living water'." This was both claim and promise in one.

It is not otherwise with the tremendous saying: "I am the light of the world" (8:12) which again reminds us of 6:55. But at this moment it is much more evident that the light shines in *darkness*; the allusions of Jesus to His going away become ever plainer (thus already 7:33ff.; now especially 8:21ff.)—a withdrawal which will deprive the Jews of the light and will leave them to die in their sins (8:21,24). In fact the Jews now show themselves to be men who are determined not to see the light. Even those who believe on Him (as described in 2:23–25 or 6:60ff.) are not prepared to accept His *gift*. He calls them to discipleship and gives them the knowledge of the truth and thus freedom (8:31,32). But they brag about the freedom which they enjoy as sons of Abraham and do not notice the fact that sin holds them prisoner (8:33–36). And are they really the sons of Abraham? Do they then do what Abraham did? Are they the children of God? Does not their refusal of Jesus and thus of the truth show they are children of the lie? The words with which Jesus reproaches them are here unspeakably harsh (8:37–45). And again unfathomably deep is on the other hand the self-testimony of Jesus here, perhaps the most audacious saying in the whole of the gospel. Yes, to be sure, you appeal to Abraham and you suppose that after all I cannot be greater than he. But Abraham saw in vision my "day", for: "Before Abraham was, I am" (8:58). He is at one with the Father and shares in the eternity of God! No wonder that the Jews wished to stone Him. For in face of such a man there are only two possibilities: either he finds faith or he finds the death of the wanton blasphemer.

The Jews have shown themselves to be such as prefer darkness to light (cf. 3:19). In the deep symbolism of the man born blind, this truth is illuminated (ch. 9).

Once again, as in ch. 5, it is a question of a Sabbath healing. The Pharisees, those professional guardians of the Sabbath rule, consider that this very desecration of the Sabbath proves that Jesus is not from God (9:16). But the formerly blind man contradicts them. They try to dispute, unsuccessfully, that he has been healed at all (9:18ff.). They then seek to persuade the healed man that Jesus must be a "sinner" (9:24). But the man born blind refuses to be so persuaded—until at last they cast him out (9:34). At this point he comes to an open confession of his faith (9:35ff.) and the whole incident is summed up in the words of Jesus: "For judgment I came into this world, that those who do not see may see, and that those who see may become blind" (9:39). Such is the situation of the Jews. The Pharisees, and the most pious, hear the words specifically (9:40,41).

Why do the Jews harden their hearts? Why is it that precisely those are blind who yet see (9:39)? The mystery which appears very pressingly here is discussed by Paul in the three hardest chapters of his Epistle to the Romans (9–11) and is answered by reference to the predestination of God. John offers us no other answer. Why do the Jews not believe? They do not belong to the "sheep" of Jesus (10:26). His sheep hear His voice and remain in His, i.e. the Father's, hand (10:27ff.). But the Jews, the standard representatives of Israel, can do nothing with the Good Shepherd except try to stone Him (10:31) as they had already tried to do (8:59). He had "made Himself God" (10:33). This of course is the only reaction possible when faith is refused. It is remarkable that in this tenth chapter in which Jesus confesses Himself the Good Shepherd, the decision of man is finally taken against Him, with the consequence that the way of the Good Shepherd can be no other but that of laying down His life for the sheep (10:11). He is the true, right Shepherd, and no hireling like the others. In fact He stands over against all who are called shepherds in the world as the one true Shepherd.

In this 10th chapter two thoughts are closely bound together: firstly the thought that Jesus alone has a real right to the "sheep" (whereas all others, especially the present leaders of the Jewish people, are false shepherds) and secondly the thought that the right of Jesus to the sheep, to all men who belong to Him, is the right of One who gives Himself for the sheep: His claim is the claim of love (10:11,12,17,18) which is consummated in the offering of His life.

The die is cast. The people of Jesus have disclaimed their connexion with Him. But the plot against His life has not yet found the moment of fulfilment. Everything however is in shape soon to bring it to execution. Darkness has not understood light. But neither can it extinguish light. The very One who is going towards the death that has now become unavoidable, manifests Himself (ch. 11) as the sovereign Lord of death, as "the resurrection and the life" (11:25).

Death and life are here deeply interwoven: the disciples of Jesus warn their Lord not to go to the help of this seriously ill friend—only here do we learn that Lazarus is the brother of Mary and Martha (Lk. 10:38ff.; yet cf. Lk. 16:19ff.)—and when finally He decides to depart from the land east of Jordan, Thomas says with deep insight: "Let us also go, that we may die with Him" (11:16). The One who here wins this overwhelming victory over death is He who goes forth to meet—death!

But conversely: He who now goes to meet death, is the One who confers (through prayer, 11:41,42) life on the dead. Thus this story, which in its whole structure and mode of presentation is the most powerful miracle story in the New Testament, becomes a symbol of the truth which is now to be actualized: The dying Lord grants life (11:26) and indeed eternal life beyond the reach of the power of death. How terrible—but at the same time in the mind of the evangelist how meaningful and appropriate—that precisely in connexion with this miracle (11:46) the religious officials finally resolve to put Jesus to *death* (11:47–57)!

The narration of the council's deliberation in which the death of Jesus is determined is saturated with dramatic irony like the whole of chapter 11. No doubt the high priest means what he says from political motives: far better that one man should die than that the whole nation should be destroyed in a Messianic uprising (11:50). But the evangelist is concerned to make an ironic point: this man, high priest as he is, is speaking the truth without realizing it (11:51ff.).

At this decisive juncture (ch. 12) the drama proceeds as the synoptics relate—the death of Jesus is not really the result of the resolve of the Jews, but flows essentially from His own free will. After the anointing of Jesus in Bethany and His solemn entry into the holy city, certain "Greeks" come and desire to see Him. They are, as it were, the representatives of that wider world in which the "other sheep" are to be sought, the scattered children of God (11:52) whom He will bring into the one fold. It is just the appearance of these men from that wider world (even though they are in all probability Greek-speaking Jews or proselytes, i.e. Greeks who have embraced the religion of the Jews) which elicits from Jesus the confession that the hour of His glorification has come (12:23). But His glory has come as death! For, says Jesus, there can be no bearing of fruit unless the grain of wheat dies (12:24). It is His decision to be this grain of wheat. But by this very decision He yields Himself to a bitter hour of darkness (12:27) which is not only the hour of His solemn and saving purpose, but also the hour of the judgment on this world—just in so far as *He* treads the way of obedience, the power of the lie, of negation, "the prince of this world", is cast out (12:31). The dying of Jesus spells the victory of light at the very heart of the apparent victory of darkness; it is the victory of love achieved within the victory of hate.

5. "*But to all who received Him . . .*" (chs. 13–17)

Jesus bids farewell to His own. Such is the theme of the extended section of the gospel which now lies before us. But this particular farewell foreshadows the future rather than implies the past: what is in question is the future of the disciples and of the Church. For the death of Jesus according to John is not the end but the beginning, not a catastrophe but an act of salvation.

As has been said, the theme of ch. 13 is the foundation of the Church. The foot washing is a symbol of the fact that the work of Jesus is a ministry rendered to His own (and here Simon Peter refuses at first to accept the service, 13:6), but on the other hand it expresses the rule of life which is to prevail in this new community of God: the rule of love, the "new commandment of Jesus" as is said later (13:34). The two things belong together (as also we find in Mk. 10:35–45). Again it is characteristic of the dramatic irony inherent in these events that in the very scene where the new community as the community of love is founded, there takes place also the recognition that treachery lurks in the midst (13:21ff.).

Chapter 14 continues the theme of the preceding chapter inasmuch as here too love appears as the commandment of Jesus (14:23ff.). But the point which here stands in the foreground is that the fellowship of Jesus with His own is not to be interrupted by His own departure to be with the Father: He goes before them (14:1–4), and is indeed the way, the truth and the life for them (14:6) as also He is the light of the world (8:12) and the bread of life (6:35). In order that the disciples may not be abandoned and comfortless after His going away, He will pray the Father to send "another Comforter" (14:16). He will Himself send such a Counsellor (15:26). This Counsellor is the "Spirit of truth" (14:17). The translation "comforter" is according to the basic text the "Paraclete": Paraclete means advocate, help, intercessor. This idea is peculiar to John.

From 14:31 it is clear that the farewell discourses once ended here. It seems probable that chapters 15–17 were previously situated elsewhere, in any event before 14:31.

At the centre of ch. 15 stands the metaphorical speech about the vine. As in the speech about the Good Shepherd, the sense is not: I am what a good shepherd or the true vine is, but on the contrary: I alone am the true, the real vine, alone in abiding fellowship with Me (by remaining with Me) can you bear fruit, "apart from me you can do nothing" (15:5). It is part of the same sequence of thought that Jesus calls His disciples His friends (15:14ff.) whom He has freely chosen (15:16). The truth emphasized is that just in face of the hatred of the world (15:18ff.; 16:1ff.) Jesus grants His disciples fullness of communion with Himself.

Because the disciples are so utterly linked with their Lord, ch. 16 can speak of the hope which is theirs: "after a little while" He will once more be seen by them (16:16ff.). Probably what is implied here is not His second coming, but the vision of the Lord which since the resurrection has been given to faith.

The full disclosure of the communion between Jesus and His own is the theme of the high priestly prayer (ch. 17) which is penetrated with the thought that the oneness of Jesus with the Father is the basis of His oneness with those whom the Father has given Him and who from henceforth, just as certainly as that they are in the world (17:11), are nevertheless to be where He Himself is (17:24). Their life is linked with His life and held secure in His life.

If we were to ask what now remains to the disciples, we might answer on the basis of these farewell discourses that *Jesus* remains to them, as the One who is ever present with His Church; and the whole of this gospel of John, which more markedly than the synoptics has been fashioned by the mystic life of the Church, is one sustained impressive witness to the fact.

6. *Passion and resurrection* (chs. 18–21)

In its representation of the passion, the gospel of John shows most point of contact with the synoptics. The most significant difference consists in the far greater emphasis on the share of Pilate in this event. Roman troops are already concerned in the arrest of Jesus (18:3,12).

The Jewish trial before Caiaphas is dealt with only briefly (18:24). In lieu of it we find a short account of a hearing by the former high priest Annas (18:12ff., 19ff.). But it is obvious that for this evangelist the main thing is the various phases of the trial before Pilate; a vivid light is cast on the failure of this representative of Rome. How soul-piercing is the opposition and contrast between the Roman glorying in his consciousness of power and the prisoner denuded of all power, who yet spontaneously confesses that He is a *King*, "For this I was born and for this I have come into the world that I should bear witness to the truth" (18:37). How often in this fourth gospel has the world come into view—and now Jesus stands before the exponent of the power of the world! and this latter abruptly dismisses the question of all questions as something of no political significance: "What is truth?" (18:38). Nevertheless Pilate attempts to get rid of the whole wretched business while triumphantly vindicating the authority of Rome. He tries to do so by means of Barabbas (18:38–40). He orders Jesus to be scourged and exposes Him to the public gaze perhaps in order to give to the Jews palpable evidence that here is no common State criminal and again he utters a word of truth fraught with ironic implications: "Here is *the* man!" (19:5). But the Jews remain relentless. They urge the primacy of their law (19:7), confronting the Son of God with the law of God! After Pilate has failed to refer the trial of Jesus to the Jews (19:6ff.) he tries a new hearing. Jesus maintains silence. The governor insists on the completeness of his authority. In reply Jesus addresses to this sorry exponent of the power of the State a truly majestic word: "You would have no power over me unless it had been given you from above" (19:11). Finally Pilate gives up his attempts; the threat of denunciation to the emperor has its effect and things are allowed to take their cruel course. But the Jews caught up in the vortex of this drama, in their madness and blindness surrender their entire Messianic hope: "We have no king but Caesar" (19:15).

As we have already mentioned, John dates the crucifixion (19:14) as taking place on the day of the passover—in the very hour when the verdict is passed on Jesus, the preparation for the passover begins in Jerusalem. At that moment the lambs are slaughtered which are to be eaten in the evening. For John, Jesus Himself is the passover lamb. This idea is reflected in 19:36: the passover prescriptions provide that not a bone of the lamb shall be broken. The synoptics date the crucifixion a day later. There is much to be said for the correctness of John's dating.

The three words from the cross which John records are found only in his gospel. It is especially significant that the mother of Jesus too stands beneath the cross. She is committed to the care of the unknown beloved disciple (cf. 13:23–35; 20:2ff.; 21:20). Perhaps the incident should be understood thus: the mother of Jesus symbolizes Jewish Christianity, the beloved disciple Gentile Christianity—the word of the crucified joins them together!

John reports only Jerusalem appearances of the Risen Lord in ch. 20 (in 16:7 Mark presupposes Galilee, and Matthew at the close of his gospel likewise reports an appearance in Galilee, while Luke confines the appearances to Jerusalem). Without any parallel in the synoptics is, in particular, the story of Thomas who refuses to believe in the resurrection without tangible evidence, which in fact Jesus offers him, thus convincing him—though at the same time he is warned: "Blessed are those who have not seen and yet believe" (20:24ff.).

Chapter 21 is an appendix. The gospel obviously closes with 20:30,31. In ch. 21 we have in distinction to ch. 20 the report of an appearance of the Risen Lord in Galilee, which in certain essential features (the fishing of Peter) is reminiscent of Luke 5:1ff. In the second part also Peter stands in the foreground: to the three denials there here corresponds the thrice-repeated question of the Risen One, who now institutes the man who denied Him as the shepherd of the Christian flock and foreshadows his coming martyrdom.

7. *The question of authorship*

To whom do we owe this most profoundly reflective of all our gospels? The gospel itself, like the others, does not mention the name of its author. Since the second century, Church tradition has affirmed the disciple John to be the author. The gospel itself at all events contains a possible allusion to the author: it has often been wondered whether that unknown disciple whom we find mentioned in 13:23ff.; 19:26ff.; 20:2ff. (21:20) and perhaps also in 1:37,40 is not the figure behind which the author conceals himself. And is it not also striking that precisely the disciple John is never mentioned by name in this gospel? Should we not also give due weight to the emphasis on eye-witnessing in 1 Jn. 1:1? It cannot be denied that the ancient tradition has obviously certain points in its favour.

However, the fourth gospel is without a doubt later than the synoptics. It will have been written about the year A.D. 100; not later, since we have a papyrus MS. from Egypt dating from the early second century which contains a part of this gospel. Church tradition contains the information that John worked in Ephesus up to an advanced age and wrote his gospel there. Recently however this datum has been disputed and the authorship of John has also been questioned by many critics. The reasons for this doubt are partly that the residence of John in Ephesus has been questioned, partly the uncertainty of other indications which tradition gives about the life of this apostle, and partly also the character of the gospel itself.

It is undeniable that the witness which our evangelist bears to Jesus is at all points refracted through the medium of his own characteristic experiences and insights which he has acquired by his communion with the fellowship of the Church. But it is not essentially otherwise with the synoptics; in their witness too we hear the voice of the community and not the critical conclusions of a historian. Yet the traces of a process of meditation flowing from vision of the being of Jesus Christ are especially plain in the fourth gospel, and it is just to this circumstance that we owe its depth and power, the authority of which strikes all who read it with an open mind.

The differences which exist between this gospel and the synoptics both in mode of presentation and important features of the historical picture have been discussed above and cannot escape any attentive reader. On the other hand the historical indications of the fourth gospel (e.g. with regard to the date of Jesus' death) are to some extent taken much more seriously to-day than they were a century ago.

The question of authorship, however, is not of decisive importance for the value and authority of the witness given here. Hence, if we do not consider the ancient tradition of Johannine authorship sufficiently assured, we may still agree with Luther that this is the "chief of the gospels" and in earnest attention and faith lay our hearts open to the truth of its message.

John reports for us a word of Jesus (14:26) according to which the Holy

Spirit will teach the disciples all things and bring to their remembrance all that He said. The Christian community was certain that through the Spirit the reality of Jesus remained for it a living and present fact. For the true believer Jesus does not simply belong to the past, for there is always the possibility of living and present communion with Him. Hence there is no need to be surprised that the Church's testimony to the Christ assumes the traits of the rich spiritual experience which it has won in fellowship with its ever-living Lord. But if this is so, then we can understand the discrepancies in the evangelistic testimony —it is as though the stream of light radiating from the one reality of Jesus fell in different directions and became broken up in varying media.

Chapter 16

THE AGE OF THE APOSTLES

(Acts 1; 2; 6–7; 9; 11; 13–20; Galatians 1; 2; 1 Corinthians 1)

1. *Jerusalem and Jewish Christianity*

(*a*) *The beginnings.* The Risen Christ appeared only to His disciples. Just as before the crucifixion He had refused the "sign" which should prove His divinity without the need of faith, so afterwards He did not appear to those who demanded only the demonstrative power of a sign. The disciples experienced the resurrection event as something utterly unique, incomparable, and unfathomable, and we shall do well on our part also to renounce any attempt at explanation. In any case, these disheartened men now experienced the gift of a faith and zeal which proved its power even unto death. They were now imbued with the assurance that Jesus was the Christ, the Son of God. And after all their failure, their flight and defection, they now had the joyful awareness that their Lord showed Himself to them as the ever-living One and the Conqueror of death: the resurrection event was the consummation of their forgiveness. There was a considerable number of encounters between the disciples and the Risen Lord: in 1 Cor. 15:1ff. (the oldest report) Paul enumerates more of these appearances than the evangelists. But the disciples (or apostles) first found the courage to make an open proclamation of their Lord when they were permitted to experience in the outpouring of the Holy Ghost a new and mighty act of God on their behalf.

We allude at this point to the feast of Pentecost, fifty days after the Passover (among the Jews called the feast of weeks and originally a festival of rejoicing over the harvest). In order to make clear to some extent the apostolic development, we must take as our point of departure the fact that—regarded from a purely human point of view—the spread of the profession of faith in Christ in Jerusalem, in the whole of Judea, and beyond into the whole of the known world at that time, represents an incredible achievement on the part of the apostles and preachers of the Christian faith. Yet from the outset Christians were convinced that what we call "faith", "witness", Christian proclamation or Christian life and thought, was something that was not engendered by man and did not spring from the power of the human soul, from greatness of character or from depth of thought, but was nothing but a pure *gift*. Hence the apostles were not religious geniuses or heroes of the faith, but were simply the first recipients of the gift of the Holy Spirit. To become and to be a Christian, to believe, to bear witness, is something that is not humanly possible although it is human. When the Bible speaks of the Holy Spirit, it means that capacity to believe and be a Christian which flows from God and is bestowed on us by Christ Himself. Similarly every type of ministry within the Christian community (leadership, preaching, healing of the sick, etc.) is equally the result of the gift of the Spirit. Indeed, the fact that there is a Church at all, that we can speak of the Christian Church, is something that rests solely on the work of the Spirit.

(*b*) *The Church in Jerusalem.* From the earliest apostolic preaching there arose a Christian community of probably fairly considerable proportions. The members of this community and of the many others which took their rise from the centre at Jerusalem, adhered to the traditional Jewish law, and thus practised circumcision and attended the temple cult. Their meetings together took place in private houses. What went on in them is summarized in Acts 2:42: the teaching of the apostles (the root of all Christian proclamation), the fellowship (life in common extending even to a certain community of goods), the breaking of bread (i.e. the holy meal) and prayer. In other words, this was an all-embracing life in fellowship and in the service of God. The so-called early Church sharing of goods seems to have been limited to the pooling of the yield from work and property; only in exceptional cases does there seem to have been a real renunciation of possessions. The primary concern was that no one should suffer want. This living together of Christians certainly made a deep impression on the other inhabitants of the city. Christian messengers soon went out from Jerusalem to the neighbouring country, but Jerusalem itself remained the mother church—a position which it retained in the eyes of Christianity for decades to come; Paul himself is a witness to this.

(*c*) *Persecution.* It was only natural that a Church which proclaimed as Messiah and Risen Lord One who had been executed as a blasphemer of the divine should meet with opposition and persecution. The Acts is able to tell of many a clash between the apostles and the religious leaders of the Jewish capital city. The most violent persecution flared up as a result of the activities of a certain Hellenist (i.e. Greek-speaking Jew from the diaspora) by name Stephen. The latter vigorously emphasized the opposition of the gospel to the law and the temple cult, and suffered stoning. In the wake of these events there followed a persecution of the believers in Jerusalem and the whole neighbourhood extending right to Damascus. But those Christians who as a result of this oppression were driven out of Jerusalem became preachers of the gospel even in their places of refuge, and it is just they who were probably the first to turn to born Gentiles. The first Church composed of both native Jews and native Gentiles arose in the Syrian capital city of Antioch. And here, according to the account given in the Acts, believers were for the first time called Christians.

2. *Paul and the mission to the Gentile world*

(*a*) *Conversion.* Saul (or Paul) was one of the chief participants in the persecution of Christians which followed the death of Stephen. He came from the Asia Minor town of Tarsus (in Cilicia) and no doubt was of well-to-do people: by birth he was a Roman citizen, a privilege which only members of the upper classes enjoyed. He must have been bilingual throughout his life. His education as a theologian he acquired in Jerusalem; he was a pupil of the famous Gamaliel. Thus Paul belonged to the Pharisee group, and we can well understand that the attitude of Stephen and those who thought like him provoked him in the extreme. He was a champion of the traditional law. But in the midst of his zealous rage against the Christians there came to him, in the neighbourhood of Damascus, that encounter which orientated his life in a completely new direction. The persecutor became a missionary.

Paul himself has left us some personal notes concerning his "Damascus hour". In Gal. 1:13ff. he reports how God "revealed His Son" to him the persecutor, and in 1 Cor. 15:8 he counts this phenomenon as the last of the appearances of the Risen Lord. The three accounts (not quite consistent) which the Acts gives us agree in essentials with these personal records. By a "vision of the Lord" (1 Cor. 9:1) Paul became convinced that the Jesus whose disciples he was persecuting was the Conqueror of death and the Messiah of God. Was this Damascus experience in preparation in his inner life long before? Had a previous impression of Jesus bitten deeply into him in such a way as to leave him no peace? Had he not long since attained the insight that fellowship and harmony with God was not to be obtained by way of the pious works of the law? that the righteousness of which he so often speaks later could never be earned through such meritorious piety? None of this can we know, and it is the secret of God. It is certain however that without much hesitation or deliberation (Gal. 1:16) Paul reversed the direction of his whole life. The conversion of Paul may not be universalized in the sense that every Christian may be supposed to have experienced something similar. In fact Paul himself sees in his experience something quite singular: an appearance of the Risen Lord. Certain as it is that every Christian is a "converted" man, i.e. a man who has changed the direction of his life through the power of God, just as little can any uniform pattern be imposed on these phenomena.

(*b*) *The missionary activity of Paul.* We have but little information about the early years of the missionary activity of the great apostle of the Gentiles. It was exercised particularly in Syria, in his native Cilicia, and at first in Arabian territory bordering on Syria. The most significant aspect of it must have been the work of Paul in Antioch, that mixed community of which we have spoken. From thence as his point of departure Paul seems to have undertaken (Acts 13) a first fairly considerable missionary journey.

In Acts 13:9 we find mentioned for the first time the name Paul. As a Roman citizen the apostle would certainly have in addition to his Jewish name, Saul, a Latin name too. In his letters he always refers to himself as Paul. As seems evident, this name is *not* the Christian or apostolic name; the suggestion that "Saul became Paul" is thus inappropriate.

About the time of the early full-scale missionary journeys there occurs the important event called the apostolic council, about which Paul himself (Gal. 2) as well as Acts (ch. 15) gives us an account. It is somewhat difficult to elucidate the details. So much is certain, namely, that for the purposes of his work among the heathen Paul required the approbation of the Jerusalem apostles (he names James the brother of Jesus, Peter and John). Yet even later there were still differences of opinion: Paul did not require the Gentile Christians to observe the law in its full scope and found it hard to obtain the concurrence of the Jewish Christian apostles for his course of action.

The missionary journeys of Paul comprised at first the south of Asia Minor, later, parts of the north and west also, and then (on the occasion of the second journey) were extended to Europe. The year 50 of our era is one of the most important years in the whole of world history. Paul in Greece! In consequence there arose Christian communities (e.g. at Philippi and Thessalonica, both in Macedonia) and then—more important than the others—one at Corinth. Paul renewed contact with these Churches on a further journey of which the richest harvest however was the founding of the Church at Ephesus.

Thus Asia Minor and Greece are the areas which we know to have formed the centre of gravity of the work of Paul. But his goal was Rome, the chief city of the world. And he did reach this goal—but as a State prisoner! In Rome there was already in existence before his arrival there a Christian Church, to which he had previously addressed a letter. He was able to work in its midst even as a prisoner. Then the threads of our historical accounts snap. Yet many indications seem to suggest that Paul was eventually freed from his imprisonment at Rome and for a few further years was able to visit his Churches and make new arrangements for them; perhaps also, if a good tradition is to be believed, he extended his travels as far as Spain. But later he was again imprisoned and in the reign of Nero died the death of a martyr, probably a few years after the Neronic persecution of Christians.

Both Acts and the letters of Paul give us reliable information about the character of his missionary work. His stay in the various places which he evangelized varied considerably in length; the Macedonian Churches were built up after only a brief period of activity by the apostle, whereas his stay in Corinth lasted at least a year and in Ephesus several years. Paul regularly addressed his preaching to the Jews first of all, when he found them on the spot (which in the larger towns was always the case). Afterwards however he took every opportunity to turn to the Gentiles, preaching to them partly in public places (as on the Areopagus in Athens), partly also by talks in hired rooms (as in Corinth) or in private houses. The size of the Churches he founded must have varied a great deal; they mostly assembled in private homes. In his preaching Paul made good use of the experience he had acquired in Jewish methods of propaganda which had long been elaborated (for example in combating polytheism) as also no doubt of the methods of instruction used by Greek philosophers (which he knew of from his native town). The essential core of his message was "Christ crucified", "a stumbling block to the Jews and folly to the Greeks" (1 Cor. 1:21ff.; 2:2). Much as he became "all things to all men" in the form of his message, so certainly had he always but one message to give! In this, apart from apostolic tradition, he based himself on the Old Testament. His proofs were predominantly scriptural. He met with hostility and persecution in almost every town, mostly from the Jews, but also from the Gentiles, as in Ephesus.

(*c*) *The Gentile Christian communities.* In the earliest period Christian communities are found almost exclusively in the towns. From the towns the gospel message then radiated to the country. In many of these Churches poor people must have formed by far the larger numbers; but sometimes there were also people of higher social status who placed their house and assistance at the disposal of the Church. From the outset, mutual help was a keynote of the Church's life. Thus at Philippi the needs of the apostle were met, and generally help was given to other Churches, especially the severely oppressed Church in Jerusalem. In some town Churches there were also "educated" people; in this connexion we must mention Corinth especially. But what in his letters Paul presupposes among his converts is not in the first place general instruction but constant study of the Bible, efforts to interpret it and to apply it in the sense of the gospel.

The meetings of the Church had a twofold bearing: the preaching of the word (or prophecy) and the supper of the Lord. The task of preaching was not at first incumbent on a special class of ministers, but it was rather the case that all could share in it who possessed the necessary spiritual gifts. In this matter things often became very heated and glossolaly was not lacking (i.e. ecstatic speaking with tongues in unintelligible terms—1 Cor. 14). Christians who by their gifts were marked out to fulfil a special office in the Church (preaching, declaration of the word or ecstatic speech and conduct) were described as charismatics (i.e. endowed with the gift of the Spirit in a special sense).

The guidance of the Church meetings and the administration of the Churches generally belonged among such spiritual gifts; such leaders were called "shepherds" or "bishops", or "overseers". It is not possible to say how ancient are firmly moulded forms of ministry, but it is to be supposed that such developed only gradually and slowly. In any case the criterion was always the extent of spiritual endowment and inner authority.

(*d*) *The letters of Paul.* While Paul certainly did not govern autocratically the Churches founded by him, he cared for them as an apostle invested with special authority in their regard. This authority he not merely exercised by his personal presence, but he asserted it effectively from a distance. His letters, which are almost all addressed to entire Churches and were openly read to the congregations, may in a certain sense be characterized as *official* writings. Now he discusses questions arising out of the circumstances of the community in question, now he opposes heretical teachers, or refutes such as wish to turn the gospel into the law, or to make it a sort of philosophical system, or he corrects those who will not subject themselves to the discipline of the Spirit. At other times he gives instructions for the arrangement of their worship and life in common, or again he pleads for contributions to help the severely distressed mother Church in Jerusalem. But with Paul person and office have grown together and become fused in one. Hence his letters are also, and that in the most impressive way, self-revelation from the heart of his personal experience: they disclose to us the bitter sufferings which he undergoes, the bodily and spiritual distresses to which he is exposed, and his wrestling in the faith and for faith. We are here faced not by an accomplished man who is at his ease, but by one who wills to be nothing and to possess nothing in himself, and whose whole existence has only one content and theme: Jesus Christ. These letters are edifying in the sense that they are intended for the spiritual admonition and fortification of the various Churches, and they have such a wealth and abundance of insights, such power and clarity of thought and exposition, that it is hardly possible to escape their overmastering inspiration.

The oldest letter of Paul, the first to the Thessalonians, was written during the second missionary journey, probably in the year 51. The same no doubt applies to 2 Thessalonians. In the following years there came the letter to the Galatians, the two letters to Corinth, and that to Rome. During the time of the imprisonment of the apostle were written: the letter to the Philippians, that to the Colossians, and that to Philemon. It is possible that the letter to Ephesus also belongs to this period; yet the Pauline authorship is here disputed. It is probable that, in regard to those letters which are doubtfully authentic, notes or phrases and formulae of the apostle lie at their basis.

3. *The other apostles*

Paul was by no means the only missionary preacher to the Gentiles. Thus, for instance, the Church in Rome arose before the arrival of the apostle and was composed of both Jews and Gentiles. There were in fact whole areas which did not receive the gospel either from Paul himself or from any of his numerous pupils. In particular there is much to indicate that later on the Jerusalem apostles left the holy city and devoted themselves to missionary work among the Gentiles. In all probability Peter went to Rome and there died as a martyr to his Lord during the Neronic persecution. John, as we have already mentioned, was active up to a very advanced age in Ephesus (so an old tradition states). The general pattern of life of primitive Christianity was far richer and more varied than is generally supposed. We cannot be surprised therefore that the New Testament gives us letters which are ascribed to Peter, John, Jude or James. How far such ascriptions are accurate cannot be established with certainty and in detail: but most important and weighty letters from these other centres of missionary work are the first letter of Peter, the first of John, and the—anonymous—letter to the Hebrews. As a whole such letters take us into the time of the last phase of Paul's life or the early decades after his death as a martyr, and show us how in many other forms and in other places the same gospel was preached and believed.

Chapter 17

BASIC IDEAS OF THE PREACHING OF PAUL

AS SET FORTH IN THE LETTER TO THE PHILIPPIANS

1. *Introduction*

Paul was a theologian; his great significance for Christianity rests on the fact that he understood the import of the gospel of Jesus Christ as a thinker and expounded it as a thinker. But Paul the theologian is also and always a Christian and a missionary. This threefold qualification is expressed in all his letters; hence they are never merely intellectual expositions. In the letter to the Philippians all three aspects of his life and work are fused together in a specially profound and interior way. A relationship of warm-hearted trust and affection bound the apostle to the Church in Philippi (in Macedonia), and our letter is a most moving testimony to this relationship. The apostle is a prisoner at the time of writing. We know certain details about one imprisonment of Paul, namely the one which was consequent upon his arrest in Jerusalem; at that time Paul was held for two years in Caesarea by the Romans and then was transferred to Rome. Hence the letter to the Philippians might have been written from either Caesarea or Rome, in which case it would date from the period between A.D. 59 and 63, roughly a decade after the foundation of the Church in Philippi. Many critics however are of the opinion that some years before this Paul had suffered a fairly lengthy imprisonment in Ephesus, and that our letter comes from that phase of his life. In any case the detention of the apostle did not hinder his active correspondence with his Churches, and, as we shall see, Paul is looking forward to a speedy and favourable end of his arrest.

Hence our letter takes us into the world of a prisoner and at the same time it shows the freedom in which such a man can live. It comes from the pen of a martyr and is addressed to a martyr community. It is times of distress and oppression that most plainly reveal what are the fundamental motives of the Christian life.

2. *The introduction to the letter* (ch. 1:1–11)

According to the custom of the time, Paul begins his letter with what we put at the end: that is, with the name of the sender. Then come the names of the addressees and usually a word of greeting is added (here v. 2).

But Paul uses the opportunity of mentioning his name in order to emphasize at once who he is: he is—like his friend Timothy—a "servant of Jesus Christ". This means that he has surrendered his own will to Jesus, the Christ. In v. 21 he says this still more plainly. "For to me to live is Christ." We find the same thing in Rom. 14:8: "If we live we live to the Lord, and if we die we die to the Lord." Or in Gal. 2:20: "it is no longer I who live but Christ who lives in me." But one who lives in such deep communion with Christ has no message of his own to proclaim; by describing himself as a servant of his Master, Paul claims authority for his utterances. Wherever in Christianity there is authority it can be only the authority of Jesus Christ Himself, and men have exactly so much authority as they are servants of Jesus Christ.

Just as the writer of the letter has his own special qualification, so it is with the community to which it is addressed. They are described as the "saints in Jesus Christ". The word "saints", i.e. the "holy", means in the Bible not so much the faultless or perfect as those who belong to God. Hence the meaning here is: you Philippians, you belong to Jesus Christ, and thus you are the devoted servants of God, you are not your own masters! Now this reminder is of great significance for a persecuted Church—as indeed for every Christian who is living in distress—and it spells great encouragement: whatever you encounter, whatever your sufferings, you belong to God and God will vindicate His own!

Contrary to his usual custom, Paul then mentions the bishops and deacons, i.e. the overseers and church officers to whom in a special way was entrusted the care for the true well-being of the Church. Later there was only one bishop for one Church; but here there are several. There is no suggestion here of a rule of the Church by a bishop. The fact that Paul here mentions these men probably implies that the Church had cared for him in his need (cf. 4:10–20). Paul is no ecstatic heedlessly disregarding the efforts of men.

Almost all the letters of Paul contain at the beginning a word of thanks to God. It is clear from the expressions of thanks and prayer at the opening of this letter that the relation between this Church and the apostle is very close.

Everywhere Paul shows himself to be a grateful man. He realizes that all Christians live by receiving. Thus the note of gratitude is closely bound up with the core of his message: our relationship to God rests not upon our own achievement nor upon our own obedience to the law but purely upon the free gift of God, and His grace.

Great events have been taking place among the Philippians. Men who were heathen by their origins have acquired (v. 5) a partnership in the gospel and thus their whole life has been fashioned anew. Whoever comes into relation to Christ obtains not only new thoughts, but a whole new manner of life! From the standpoint of man, this great change was not conceivable without the work of the apostle and the decision of the Philippians. But Paul realizes the inner truth: there is another who began a good work (v. 6). Had it been a merely human work, it would be without any solid foundations and unable to withstand persecution. But because it is the work of God, the Philippians can entertain confidence and faith even amid their trial.

How little importance Paul ascribes to himself can be seen in v. 7. He knows that the Philippians have been partakers with him of grace. Whatever has happened was due to the grace (i.e. the kindness) of God.

But because God was the initiator and will be the consummator of this work of salvation, therefore there can be joined to this word of thanks the note of confident prayer (vv. 9–11). It is noteworthy that in all that Paul prays for on behalf of the Church, love stands first: they are to abound more and more in knowledge and discernment. Hence knowledge comes not from anxious brooding but from the practical performance of the works of love. But love is a gift.

3. *Paul's account of himself* (ch. 1:12–26)

Paul feels a twofold debt to give some account of himself to a Church which has so energetically concerned itself with his wants. But it is important that everything that happens to him should be envisaged from the point of view of the advance of the gospel; to that end his personal life is wholly subordinated; he is completely absorbed in his missionary task.

(*a*) vv. 12–18. Here the apostle speaks above all of his environment. Even his chains are a means of missionary activity (13) and serve to increase the confidence of other Christians (14). Of course he is not spared the grief of seeing that certain all too human things are taking place around him; there are men who in preaching the gospel are solely concerned about the advancement of their own influence and the elimination of the imprisoned apostle (vv. 15–16). But Paul is concerned solely about the gospel itself and thus he does not allow himself to be agitated by such ignoble conduct on the part of others (18).

Dishonest self-interested actions on the part of men are repeatedly reported in the New Testament. Thus Acts tells of two members of the primitive Church who behaved in such a way as to pretend that they were giving all their goods to the Church and yet nevertheless retained a portion for themselves (Ananias and Sapphira; Acts 5). Especially in Corinth Paul experienced violent personal opposition. Also there were quarrels between the apostles themselves (the most obvious example being that between Peter and Paul at Antioch, Gal. 2). The Bible is nowhere inclined to idealize man!

(*b*) In vv. 19–26 the discourse turns on Paul himself. These words also are completely moulded by his passionate concern for his life's work. He is a prisoner, but his chains are for Christ and this has become known throughout the whole praetorian guard and to all the rest (i.e. his very imprisonment is serving the cause of Christ, v. 13). His trial is not yet decided; he may have to suffer death or he may be allowed to go free—but in either case it matters not as long as Christ is honoured in his body (v. 20). This man has in truth surrendered his whole life: "for to me to live is Christ and to die is gain!" (v. 21). Yet he knows that he has much work to do yet. Thus he is uncertain what he ought rather to prefer: for himself he would rather depart and be with Christ; but for the sake of his Church he would rather go further on the hard way of this life (vv. 22–24). He expects the latter course to come about and so foresees a favourable issue to his trial. Thus he can give the Philippians the hope that he will once again come to them.

Have we here an intimation of an other-worldly Christianity? If we read these verses attentively we shall have to answer both yes and no. The theme is certainly not "the beyond"; yet Paul explains that the real goal of his aspirations is to be with Christ (v. 23). Since in this world Christ is the true content and meaning of his life, there can be no fulfilment of such a life except in union with Christ in the eternal world of God. But just because for Paul life has its stay and its end in eternity, he can take joyfully all that happens to him here, suffering and death included, and live in contentment. But he who lives only for this earthly life fails when crisis occurs. If on the other hand our life has an eternal foundation, then we know how to finish with this life. And in that case our existence here, instead of being a round of enjoyment, becomes a task to be fulfilled.

4. *The trial of the Church* (chs. 1:27—2:16)

The Church too suffers persecution; you are, says Paul, "engaged in the same conflict which you saw and now hear to be mine" (1:30). It has been granted to the Philippians, "not only" to believe in Christ, but also to suffer for His sake (1:29). And yet the characteristic admonition of the apostle here is not: be steadfast! That is something which will come as a matter of course (v. 28). His real admonition is: stand together!

(*a*) 1:27—2:4. *Unity and unification of the Church.* By his emphatic "only" in v. 27 the apostle emphasizes: you have shown your concern for me, and you yourselves are in distress—that does not matter so long as your manner of life is worthy of the gospel, which means: be of one mind in your struggle! Whoever, whether in the face of such threats or in peaceful times, is actuated by selfishness or conceit (2:3) is not measuring up to the high dignity of the gospel.

We see how Paul is here making the gospel the criterion of the conduct of believers. For here we are told that God, by showing His concern for us in Christ, does not allow us to shape our lives by our own outlook, our own thoughts or our own efforts, but by His gift and grace. But whoever is anxious to carry out his own ideas or to succeed by his own efforts, is not living by the gift of God and is eager to be right by his own intrinsic worth! In the letter to the Romans and elsewhere Paul speaks about the justification which God grants to us: we are just in the eyes of God (i.e. in the way which God wishes us to be) not by our own merits but entirely by the action of God towards us, in Christ, whom God made "our wisdom and righteousness and sanctification and redemption" (1 Cor. 1:30). Hence we have our righteousness not in ourselves. Whoever walks worthy of the gospel cannot possibly therefore wish to be right through his own efforts. Thus both "love" (which does not insist on its own way, 1 Cor. 13:5) and humility (Phil. 2:3) spring directly from faith.

(*b*) 2:5–11. Here Paul takes us to a deeper level of thought. The spirit of the Church can only be that which is seen to animate Jesus Christ. He emptied Himself, sacrificed Himself utterly, taking on Himself the form of a servant, and being found in fashion as a man, becoming obedient unto death—for which reason God has highly exalted Him! You say, Jesus Christ the Lord (2:11). Yes, He is Lord, and has been made by God Lord of the whole universe. But He only became so after taking the way of fullest humiliation.

The very powerful passage 2:6–11 is a psalm to the glory of Christ. It is hardly supposable that Paul himself wrote these splendid sentences, it seems rather that he is quoting them: we have here no doubt a hymn well known in the services of the ancient Church, and probably one that crystallized at a very early stage. Col. 3:16 shows that there were such hymns and psalms in the oldest period of Christianity.

This psalm reads as though it were a comprehensive confession of the Church's faith: here the Church in the most solemn form expresses the faith that sustains it. It states who this Jesus Christ is in whom it believes. Self-emptying and exaltation, these are the two contrasted truths which it crystallizes out concerning Him. He came not from below but from above. He was in the form of God, in fact He was equal to God. But He did not consider this His dignity as a thing to be grasped at: He was God and not the Satan who steals the status of God; thus He did not clutch His equality with God as though it were booty, but because He *was* in truth God, He did the most unheard-of thing—He emptied Himself. One cannot help thinking of the fall at this point: sin originally sprang from the fact that man allowed himself to be tempted to wish to become the equal of God (Gen. 3:5). The triumph over sin springs from the fact that One who is equal with God voluntarily deprives Himself of that dignity. The method of sin is man's self-willed grasping of what is superior to him. The method by which sin was overcome was the self-humiliation of One who was by right above. His condescension to this world was not a merely figurative and apparent becoming man: He who had the form of God took the form of a servant (we are reminded of the servant of God of Deutero-Isaiah) and His condescension, through obedience, led Him to death, to the shameful death of the cross. But *therefore* has God exalted Him! This means that this very way of condescension, this way of self-emptying was the way which God willed. *Thus* is the eternal will of God. And the proof of the fact that Jesus went the way the Father willed, lies in His exaltation, in the "name" which is above every other name, and before which (as before God) every knee must bow, that name which already constitutes the essential creed of the Church—the name "Lord" (*kyrios*).

"Jesus is the Lord, the Christ"—in Greek "*kyrios Jesous Christos*"—such is the very oldest Christian creed known to us. Paul quotes it already in 1 Cor. 12:3. What is the meaning of "Lord"? In the language of the time it unquestionably denotes divine dignity. It reminds us of the fact that at that time the name Yahweh was avoided by the use of the title "Lord". It also implies that such a one has the right to command. At bottom every later confession of the Church says only what is already implied here: no other discloses to us the being of God, no other has power over us, no other has the right to command us. There were at that time many "lords" of all sorts—gods who were so called and men who wished to be considered gods—but we, says Paul (1 Cor. 8:6) have "one Lord, Jesus Christ, through whom are all things and through whom we exist". Thus it has always been in the Christian faith.

Why does Paul introduce this psalm to the glory of Christ just at this point? He wishes to impress upon the Philippians what we have already seen in Mark 10: 43–45: "Whoever would be great among you must be your servant, and whoever would be first among you must be slave of all. For the Son of Man also came not to be served but to serve and to give his life as a ransom for many."

(*c*) 2:12–16. *Discipleship to Jesus*. As is clear from the very first word of this passage, Paul now wishes to draw the conclusions from what precedes, and his period begins with a certain solemnity (12,a). And then comes the warning: "Work out your own salvation with fear and trembling" (12,b). Fear and trembling—that is the attitude which becomes the "servant": these words could in fact be paraphrased as "awe" and "meekness". Hence Paul wishes to say: if you want to belong to the saved—and you do indeed belong among that number—on the coming "day of Jesus Christ" (1:10), then the way for you is the way which Jesus your Lord has trod: the way of self-emptying! That way is the way of Christ; for you are not such as had merit in the eyes of God, but "it is God who is at work in you, both to will and to work for His good pleasure" (v. 13).

Thus "fear and trembling" do not mean: you are to be anxious about your salvation, but: you will obtain it inasmuch as you go the way of the servant, the way of condescension, as we have said. It should have now become clear that there is no antithesis between v. 13 and v. 12, but unity: because God is at work in you (who works by the way of condescension) therefore you must work similarly in all humility. You can choose no better way than the way which God in Jesus Christ has trod. That way leads to glory.

Thus Christians live differently from other men, from the "crooked and perverse generation" of v. 15. Man in general seeks power. The Christian seeks his Lord. Hence he does not grumble and brood over his difficulties (v. 14) but obeys and with his silent obedience he shines as "a light in the world" (v. 15).

5. *A personal interlude* (ch. 2:17–30)

How truly we have here a genuine letter (and not a dissertation clad in the form of a letter) is shown by nothing better than this episode. Paul has not only to teach but also to act. And he has also to act in regard to the Philippians. It is in particular a question of the coming to them of two men, which he announces: Timothy, his proved fellow-worker and champion in the faith, and Epaphroditus whom the Philippians recently sent to him will shortly be coming to convey the letter. Timothy receives high praise—how clearly his portrait stands out in contrast to the many who have disappointed the apostle because they looked after their own interests (v. 21). The Church is earnestly enjoined to receive and honour the Philippian Epaphroditus. The latter was sent by the Church to care for the apostle in his imprisonment, but then he became seriously ill, and in fact through the service which he rendered Paul he risked his life. Thus the prisoner pleads for and supports a fellow-worker.

Once again with 3:1 the apostle interrupts his writing: he speaks of joy with particular emphasis in this letter—it is as if he felt almost obliged to excuse himself for repeating the same things—he the prisoner to the persecuted Church!

6. *Warning against the distortion of the gospel*

Abruptly as though with the crack of a whip, the warning of v. 2 cuts into the flow of the letter: "Look out!" We have already realized that the Church at Philippi is persecuted from without. Here we see that danger threatens it from within. And such inner danger is always by far the greater for Christians. What is to happen if they lose the very thing by which they live—the gospel? And it is against the gospel itself that the false teaching is aimed which the apostle here opposes. Harsh words of condemnation spring to the pen of this impassioned fighter for the faith: "Dogs" (i.e. impure), evil, deceitful heroes of good works (as a modern exegete so excellently paraphrases) mutilating the flesh (in contrast to true circumcision).

To whom is Paul alluding? The following words show plainly: it is a question of people who boast of their Jewish descent, their achievements in the fulfilling of the law, their circumcised status, their possession of the ordinances of the fathers. Paul reminds them of all that he might say in that line were he to insist on his hereditary privileges. It is obvious that these men have appeared within the Church: they are Judaizers, who are requiring from Gentile Christians the keeping of the law, the observance of food laws, perhaps even the practice of circumcision! Thus the danger at Philippi is the same as that in the Galatian Churches (in just the same situation was the passionate letter to the Galatians written) also in Rome and Corinth. Everywhere there is the same struggle for the freedom of the gospel. Is the gospel to be regarded as merely a completion of the law? Is a man first of all to take up the keeping of the law, and then, when he fails, to receive the gospel of divine forgiveness? Does the gospel as it were merely extend the line which man begins to draw by the power of his own piety? Paul says an emphatic no. The gospel stands not at the end, but at the beginning. And it needs no preparation and no completion, but includes everything in itself. Here too, then, Paul feels compelled to draw out the heart of his message. Christ alone, faith alone!

(*a*) 3:2–6. *True and false pride*. These "Judaizers" who are so proud of their traditions, Paul finds he cannot recognize as the cultically pure, fulfilling the will of God by their conduct, and holding the true circumcision, as they claim. Verse 2 suggests that they are the exact opposite. "We" are the true circumcision! Hence the Christians who know no other power in the service of God except the spirit of God, and no other glorying than glorying in Jesus Christ (v. 3) and who are not therefore confident in the flesh (i.e. in the unaided efforts of man)—such are the true circumcision, the true people of God. This is the proud and yet so humble claim which Paul makes to refute self-glorying. He then continues saying that he too could boast of the same false security to which the Judaizers have succumbed. There follows an enumeration of all that might be considered the claims of the flesh: descent, circumcision, status as a Pharisee, persecution of the Church! Hence this is what the claims of the boastful man amount to, of the boastful Paul of former days before the day of Damascus. The fact is that wherever man relies on what he is and can do in himself, he becomes an enemy of the Church of Jesus.

(*b*) 3:7–11. *Justification by faith*. The argument takes a completely new turn at v. 7. Paul had plenty to boast of from the point of view of one who was proud of the law: he could adduce many things in his own favour. But all this he has counted loss for the sake of Christ: not only does it mean nothing, but it has only hindered him on the way to the attainment of true salvation, has merely misled him: how much, is shown above all by his share in the persecution of Christians. The man who is proud of the law is building for himself a rampart behind which he fondly imagines that he is secure against God. But to build a rampart against God, to take up a position over against God, means that one does not love God, and hence does not keep the law. Such a one becomes ever more entangled in his self-centredness (cf. Rom. 7) and in his despair. Hence it is really "loss" for man to wish to stand on his own merits in the face of God. Really to come into fellowship with God, and to attain newness of life, is possible only through Jesus Christ (such was the experience of Paul). To "know" Him (v. 8) and so to be in harmony with the truth that the way of God is the way of condescension and that the divine mercy effects what all our efforts cannot—that is for Paul the sum total of the gospel, and in contrast all the works of the law are simply nothing, in fact "refuse".

In v. 9 Paul expresses very pointedly the motives which inspire him. It is a question of "righteousness" (i.e. the right relation to God). The righteousness which Paul thought he had earlier was the righteousness of the law, i.e. his own. He believed that he was able to show piety and religious works, and so to be in the right before God. But the man who calculates thus is seeking himself and not God. What Paul has found in Christ is the righteousness which stems from God, and this he assimilates "by faith in Christ": it is no righteousness of his own, but—as Luther says—the righteousness of another, which is conferred on man as a gift. In Rom. 3:24 the apostle calls it "being justified by grace as a gift". The righteousness which "is valid in the eyes of God" (Luther's translation of Rom. 1:17) is that which God imputes. Hence the right relation to God is something which God Himself effects and it consists in His gift of Christ to us. Hence for Paul the most important thing is "to be found in Christ"; if Christ is his true life, then he has the life which flows from God!

These thoughts must be clearly grasped. Here is the heart of the message of Paul and also the heart of the message of the Reformation. If we grasp the content of Phil. 3 we have also the key to the "difficult" letters of Paul, those to the Galatians and Romans. Here it becomes quite plain how the gospel confers freedom. Where it is believed, there reigns no longer the tense effort to achieve ever more and more in order to earn the good pleasure of God. Here the whole of life becomes nothing other than an act of thanksgiving: in Christ God has in fact taken us into fellowship with Himself.

Yet the believer in Christ is not merely one who knows the power of His resurrection (v. 10), he is also one who becomes like Him in His death; the ideas of ch. 2 are still applicable here: there is no path to glory, to fullness of life, and to the resurrection of the dead except the path that runs through participation in the sufferings of Christ. The cross is the very fashion of the life of the Christian.

(*c*) 3:12–16. *The race to the goal.* Is it not tempting, in view of what we have just been saying about the divine righteousness, to take things easy? If all depends on the deed and initiative of God, which has taken place once for all in Christ—should one not idly rest and leave all to God? Paul obviously thinks just the opposite. He feels that he is comparable to a competitor in the arena—this image which lies at the back of our passage, occurs constantly with him (esp. 1 Cor. 9:24–27). Whoever is really seized on by Christ, is a man in movement, for Christ is no abstract idea but the living Lord.

Paul has not yet attained the goal. He does not by any means say: day by day I am becoming more and more pious, better, wiser. That would be the mentality of the man whose effort is directed to the keeping of the law. The goal, the consummation is not a state to be reached by himself, but is the reality of the Christ; just as Christ stands at the beginning of the way, so He stands at the end (v. 14).

Christ stands at the beginning: Paul is determined to obtain the crown, because he has been marked and mastered by Jesus Christ. We may say that the idea of predestination is expressed here. Likewise it is latent in 2:12,13. Paul and every believing Christian realizes that faith rests not upon our deed but upon the deed of God. God has chosen, Christ is given to us. To believe does not mean: *I* give myself a jerk in order to believe what I am supposed to believe. To believe really means that I am seized on and called by Jesus Christ, apart from any doing of my own. But it is just he who believes that and knows himself to have been called by Christ, who feels himself to be not a dead log, but one to whom Jesus Christ offers life—a life which consists in movement, obedience, decision! The true doctrine of predestination has never made men idle and sluggish, but always active and energetic in the extreme. We see this most plainly here in the example of Paul. The "upward call of God in Christ Jesus" has set a goal before him which he fiercely pursues forgetting all that lies behind.

But why in v. 15 does Paul speak of those who are "mature" in the Church, reckoning himself among that number? We must think of the word as if it were in inverted commas. At Philippi there was a special class of Christians called the mature or perfect and composed of such as had proved their loyalty in the face of persecution, hence the martyrs, the witnesses to the faith. Paul wants to warn them that though they may be mature, they should not allow the qualification to make them conceited. The truth is that we are all on the march and paradoxically enough the perfection of the Christian lies in his imperfection. He is as he should be when he is engaged in striving towards the goal. Thus he exhorts the mature not to rank themselves above the others.

(*d*) 3:17–21. *Renewed warning and joyful prospect*. The Philippians are to take Paul and his fellow workers as a model. In what? Paul does not set himself up as a moral example, but as one who having nothing yet has all things (so he puts it in the splendid text of 2 Cor. 6:10). He is not yet at the goal—as is shown too in the conclusion of the chapter. But he wishes to be an example just in virtue of the fact that he is engaged in running his course to the goal, and in so doing forgets all that lies behind. Others however live as enemies of the cross of Christ (vv. 18, 19). Their minds are set on earthly things; they glory in their shame. It is clear that those who prided themselves on their being circumcised are meant. It is just these proud champions of the law who are materialistic, and enslaved by sensuality—"their god is the belly" says Paul sharply.

Our commonwealth is in heaven (v. 20). This on the contrary is the assurance of the Christian. On this earth his situation is that of a pilgrim. But he can look forward to coming home. He awaits the great day when Jesus, the Lord and Saviour, will come in majesty and change all things. Such is the Christian hope!

7. *Life in joy* (ch. 4)

Again and again the note of joy is struck in this letter (1:4,18; 2:2,17, 18,28,29; 3:1; 4:1,4,10). And yet this note is so clearly combined with that other, the "not yet", with the way of the cross and of meekness. Both belong together. Only he can truly experience joy (when it is essential) who does not pride himself on his religious security, and is not in bondage to the earthly and visible things of this life. Hence (4:4): "Rejoice in the Lord!" A curious abandon controls the close of the letter; Paul encourages the Philippians to be free from anxiety in spite of their troubles (4:6) and he says of himself that he is able to take both plenty and hunger, abundance and want (4:12). It is essential to realize that all this stands in the closest connexion with the rest of the letter.

After a note of personal admonition to two women who cannot agree (vv. 2–3) Paul exhorts the whole community: "Rejoice in the Lord always" (4:4). We might ask what is the point of such exhortations since joy cannot be controlled and forced joy is no joy at all. What Paul means is that the Christian has reason to rejoice. He reminds his flock that they have their Lord to whom they belong even in their distress, and that thought is a motive of rejoicing. You know, he says, that the Lord is at hand: His return confronts your souls. You have a God who hears your prayers, hence you need not be anxious. The peace of God protects you (4:7) and therefore you must not be discouraged. The exhortation is thus an allusion to the *realities* on which faith lives.

The personal remarks at the close remind us of what we heard in ch. 2 about Epaphroditus. The Philippians were privileged to be the one community to look after the needs of Paul regularly (4:15). Paul has no pressing needs, but the proofs of affection he has received show that the right spirit is prevalent in this Church. It is noteworthy that among the Christians who send their greetings by Paul are some from "Caesar's household" (4:22), i.e. imperial slaves such as were to be found here and there.

One further point. Paul says (4:5): "The Lord is at hand". In the expectation of His advent Christians must show meekness to all men and not be ambitious and grasping. What are we to think of the expectation of the future which Paul shares with the whole of primitive Christianity (cf. the gospels)? There is no doubt that these men did not reckon with a centuries-long future history of Christianity. They expected their Lord to return "soon". If we interpret this "soon" in terms of years, then we must conclude that they erred; most of them really believed that the present order of things would soon be terminated. What are we to think of the eschatology of the earliest Christians? First, if we read the Bible attentively we shall see that it gives no ground for the optimistic faith in continuous human progress. The Bible does not suggest that the world will become ever more beautiful or more pious. This implies the second point, namely that the Bible teaches us to view reality soberly. The world remains the world, the earthly remains the earthly, and "flesh and blood cannot inherit the kingdom of God" (1 Cor. 15:50). What the Christian expects is not the gradual betterment of conditions in this world. Should he therefore calmly let things slide? Certainly not: if he exerts himself for the right, for humanity, for the weak and oppressed, he does so because God in Christ vindicates the right and the cause of man. That the world "passes away and the lust of it" (1 Jn. 2:17) means the world in so far as it "lies in the power of the evil one" (1 Jn. 5:19), and inasmuch as evil controls the world, the world destroys itself and falls under the judgment of God. But what belongs to God remains. Thus the Christian is always poised between this world and that which is to come. We must interpret the eschatology of the Bible as an emphasis on pilgrimage, on running the race, of which Paul speaks (ch. 3). Such a race has a goal, when and how it pleases God.

Thus we have examined only a limited portion of the fullness of apostolic testimony. But if we know the letter to the Philippians, we can easily master the other letters of Paul and then go on to explore the remaining letters of the New Testament up to the Revelation of John, which in conclusion stands as a witness to Christian hope.

Chapter 18

THE DOCTRINE OF PAUL

(THE LETTER TO THE ROMANS)

The rise of a Christian Church in Rome was an event of world-wide importance. The message of Christ in the city of the Caesars! Those two powers which in their clash were to determine the course of centuries were thus rooted on the same soil.

We do not know when this decisive event took place. Paul's letter to the Romans implies it. Paul explains that he had often had the intention of visiting this Church. Thus it must have been for some time already in existence. In view of the relative ease of communication prevailing at that time, we may assume that at quite an early stage Christians from the East reached the capital city of the empire. We may take the year 50 as roughly the date of origin of the Roman Church.

The repercussions of the letter which Paul wrote to the Church in Rome have also been of first-class historical and world importance. Aside from the gospels, no part of the New Testament has so strongly influenced the thought and action of Christianity. For example, who would propose to understand the Reformation without taking into account this letter of Paul?

It bears unquestionably a programmatic character. Paul did not found the Church in Rome. But at a crucial point of his career he wishes to feel sure of its understanding of and support for the work which he is doing. Hence in a rigid summary he expounds for it the gospel which he preaches. The letter is a doctrinal document. Here the personal note falls away into the background. Everything turns on the cause which Paul is serving.

The situation in which Paul writes can to some extent be defined. Paul feels that his missionary work in the East is finished (15:23). He proposes now to visit Jerusalem first (15:25–27) in order to bring to the impoverished Church there the gifts of the Gentile Christian Churches. But his ultimate goal is Spain (15:24,28), and on the way there he wishes to visit Rome. The letter is intended as a preparation for his visit.

The time of composition of the letter is accordingly just before the start of his journey to Jerusalem, *circa* A.D. 58. It is very probable that the place of its completion was Corinth.

1. *The theme of the letter*

The letter to the Romans is concerned with the question of the "righteousness of God". Paul says in 1:16,17: "I am not ashamed of the gospel [the good news of Jesus Christ]: it is the power of God for salvation to every one who has faith, to the Jew first and also to the Greek. For in it the righteousness of God is revealed through faith for faith; as it is written, 'He who through faith is righteous shall live'."

What is the implication of the righteousness of God? The clearest explanation might be found in 3:26: God alone is righteous and justifies the one who has faith in Jesus, and lives by that faith.

God is righteous. Such is also the message of the Old Testament. God grants to man a share in His life, when man does the divine will. That will is expressed in the law. Judaism, however, understood this to mean that the will of God was fulfilled when man painfully obeyed the various individual prescriptions. In the light of this conception, the fulfilling of the law became an attempt on man's part to procure for himself a "righteousness" over against God, i.e. to protect himself against the wrath of God and at bottom to win salvation by his own achievement. But this point of view failed to take into account that God requires not man's punctilious performance of the law, but man himself. As He gives to man life, so He wills that the very being of man should be open to Him and that man in his innermost spirit should depend on God. But then there can be no relation between God and man which so to speak depends on bargaining.

Paul too is firm on the point that God is righteous. He does not propose to be lax. Hence he does not despise the law: he calls it "holy" (7:12). He does not say: now I will give you quite a new idea of the matter.

The new element of which Paul speaks is not a thought, but a person, the Person of Jesus Christ. Paul says that the righteousness of God is revealed in the gospel of Jesus Christ (1:17). The new thing which has happened in Jesus is that God has established a new relation between Himself and man. He has made Jesus Christ our righteousness (1 Cor. 1:30). Whoever believes on Jesus *receives* the righteousness of God, i.e. is in harmony with God.

Hence the righteousness of God is a gift to man. God is righteous in that He justifies the believer. Or, to put it in other terms, God Himself brings man into a right relation with Him, by sending His Son Jesus Christ into the heart of the situation. The believer on Jesus Christ who becomes His own stands in a right relation to God and is "righteous".

Such is the theme of this letter. It is nothing less than the new order which God has set up for both Jews and Greeks in the person and work of the crucified and risen Lord. In other words the letter to the Romans is concerned with the new life which God wills to give to man.

2. *The unrighteousness of man* (ch. 1:18—3:20)

It is the will of God to establish between Himself and man a new order and harmony, and to this end He has disclosed His righteousness. Man, however, Paul now desires to show, lives by his natural instincts in a state of disharmony with God, in godlessness and wickedness (1:18). This revelation of the righteousness of God is accompanied by the revelation of the wrath of God. If in His righteousness God says "yes" to man, His wrath spells His judgment on the "no" which man speaks to God.

The "no" of man takes different forms with Jew and Gentile.

The Gentile world (which is in question in 1:18–32) says "no", in that while knowing something of the existence of God, it refuses Him the honour and thanks which is His due (1:21). God has provided for them in such a way that they need not grope in thick darkness (1:19,20). If they say "no" nevertheless, then they have no excuse. Their sin therefore consists not in ignorance and incapacity, but in refusal of the gift of God. Real sin consists in a guilty reversal of the right relationship with God. From this follows the perversion of both thought and action (1:24–32). What is usually called sin, is for Paul the consequence of sin—"God gave them up to . . ." (1:24,26,28).

But the Jews also say "no" (2:1ff.). Not in so many words. They of course recognize the validity of the law. But they commit sin. They have received the gift of the law—they know what the will of God is. But it is a question of *deeds*. The mere knowledge of the law is not the decisive factor (2:12,13). On the day of the divine judgment (2:16) it will be shown that even the Gentiles were not entirely without law (2:14–16). If, however, the Jews commit sin, it is of no use for them to claim the protection of the law (2:17ff.) and even circumcision as the sign of God's covenant with Israel will be of no avail (2:25ff.).

Paul does not dispute the fact that the Jews have an advantage (3:1,2). But this consists in nothing other than the fidelity of God (3:3). God keeps His covenant mercies. He does not break His promises. But man has not the right in consequence to say, with frivolous wit, that one sin more or less makes no difference. For the God who keeps His promises is the Judge (3:5ff.). Since then Jews as well as Greeks are sinners (3:9) the Jews cannot on their own initiative claim the protection of the privileges which *God* has granted them—the law of which they so fondly boast, really effects the knowledge and awareness of sin (3:20).

"All have sinned"—that is Paul's judgment on mankind (3:23). And they are sinners standing under the revelation of the wrath of God (1:18). The gospel does not spare man, for only so can he be helped.

3. *The righteousness which is freely bestowed* (chs. 3:21—4:25)

"But now", thus Paul begins a new section (3:21). Something utterly new has entered into the situation. The indisputable wickedness of man is not the only element in the situation; the righteousness of God is now made available to this wicked, impious man. God speaks His "yes" to men, involved as they are in refusing God. This "yes" is spoken apart from the law (3:21) and confirmed "without the works of the law" (3:28). It has nothing to do with human performance intended to compel from

God recognition, it is something bestowed without merit on the part of man and as a pure gift (3:24) by the free grace of God. This is the marvel which stands at the centre of the Pauline message. Paul considers that the Old Testament in the law and the prophets bears witness to it (3:21) and that the true meaning of the latter now for the first time stands revealed (3:31 and ch. 4). But this marvel has now been actualized in the "redemption which is in Jesus Christ" (3:24).

Paul describes Christ (3:25) as the "means of expiation" ("mercy seat"). This means that by His death, His blood, Christ has effected atonement for us, i.e. has restored the broken relation with God.

What can man do in order that this marvel shall bear fruit for him? "The works of the law" merely serve to confirm man's rejection. In fact man has no achievement to his credit to which he might point. Furthermore, God destroys every conceivable boast of man, every pious claim (3:27). The only thing which man can do is this, namely, to be content with the righteousness of God, to *believe*.

Hence belief is not a performance, not a "work". The believer does not adopt this attitude in order to deserve the good pleasure of God. Belief means to receive a gift, it implies surrender, the resignation of all human claims before God, yet also for that very reason obedience (1:5).

Does this new dispensation which God has inaugurated signify the end of the Old Testament? This question is so important for Paul that it predominates in several whole chapters of the letter to the Romans (chs. 4 and 9–11), and even elsewhere is constantly in the background. We must not forget that the Old Testament ("the law and the prophets" of 3:21) was the Bible of early Christianity. But if "now" God has disclosed His righteousness "apart from the law" (3:21), if Christ is the "end of the law" (10:4), if the special privilege of Israel is superseded (3:29 and 3:9)—what is then the position of the Old Testament? The question is as important for ourselves as it is for Paul. Does it mean that God may have changed His plan? Is it the case that to-day He is different from what He was of old? Or are we to regard the Old Testament as representing a misunderstanding of God? For Paul and the New Testament as a whole the answer to this is "no". God has remained true to Himself. He pursues His eternal plan, although His ways are inscrutable (11:33). He is not a God whose action can be confidently predicted. But neither is He an arbitrary tyrant. The new factor in the situation, embodied for us in Jesus Christ, has been foreshadowed and prepared in the Old Testament dispensation. This Paul shows by allusion to the figure of Abraham (ch. 4).

How did the father of Israel, Abraham, arrive at his right relation to God? Paul finds the answer in the Old Testament itself. Abraham believed God (4:3).

Hence he is certainly not the ancestor of those who, as it were, wish to make reckoning with God (4:4); no, he did not proceed by the method of good works, but believed the One who justifies the ungodly (4:5). Hence in truth he is the father of believers (4:11). And circumcision became for him the sign and the seal of the righteousness which is by faith (4:11). Hence he is not the father of such as boast of their circumcision, but of believers purely and simply, whether they are circumcised (i.e. Israelites) or uncircumcised (i.e. born Gentiles). Abraham belongs not to the sphere of the law but to that of the promise (4:13–16) and so to the gospel.

Thus just by the example of Abraham Paul is able to show what faith is. Abraham "in hope believed against hope" (4:18): he did not allow himself to be put off by the incredibility (humanly speaking) of the promise (of an heir) but gave glory to God (4:20), i.e. he really allowed God to be God. To allow God to be God—that spells the attitude of faith! But this God to whom faith blindly gives the glory, is He who gives life to the dead and calls into existence the things that do not exist; He is the Creator (4:17). He is the God who raised from the dead Jesus Christ (4:24). He is the One who justifies the ungodly (4:5). He is the God who does what is impossible with man!

4. *Life in righteousness* (chs. 5:1—8:39)

The four chapters which must now be briefly summarized have been classified under the general heading "freedom". The new reality which God has established for us in Jesus Christ means for the believer that the wrath of God (5:1–11), death (5:12–21), sin (ch. 6), the law (ch. 7), in fact the whole of the old world of the flesh (ch. 8) with all its repercussions, have no longer their old significance. In these chapters it becomes absolutely clear that Paul is not expounding a theory but is bearing witness to an unheard-of new reality, to the new world, to peace with God (5:1), to the new man Jesus Christ, with whom a new creation takes its rise (5:12ff.), to righteousness as the new order of life to which man is now permitted to be subject and which fashions his life anew (6:1ff.). We might also put it thus: a new epoch has dawned, old things are done away. Yet this new age is not like a new epoch in history the coming of which can be observed, and which grows out of previous epochs; it is new in a transcendent sense, utterly other than anything that we can conceive, and hence it can be grasped only in hope and obedience (5:2,5; 8:24ff.; 6:11ff.), hence only by way of total self-surrender. Whoever says "yes" here, is lifted into a new beginning of life—"the old has passed away, the new has come" (2 Cor. 5:17). It is not that something new has taken place within our life but that the direction of our life has been changed, because the relation to God has been restored. Such is the secret of the Christian life, i.e. of life in faith, in the righteousness of God, in Christ.

The new life is a life which has ceased to be exposed to the wrath of God

(5:1–11, esp. 6–10). It is a life which is no longer in dispeace but in harmony with God (5:1), i.e. in reconciliation (5:11). The estranging element has been abolished.

At the same time death has lost its power over us (5:12ff.). Life lived in peace with God is not a life which fears death (or is lived in a frivolous forgetfulness of death) but as certainly as Paul explains that death is a terrible reality (8:38) so is this life lived on the one undivided plane of the eternal reality of God. In 1 Cor. 15:45 Paul describes Christ as the "second Adam", i.e. the one who inaugurates and establishes the new creation. This also forms the background to Rom. 5:12ff. One man brought sin into the world, and all men are involved in the fall of man (Gen. 3). One has rendered perfect obedience and all who belong to Him are justified by His life of obedience. Adam and Christ are the symbols of the two worlds which Paul sets in antithesis.

But in what way do we share in the sufferings and achievement of Christ? Is it not enough that He was obedient? Is not grace as it were an automatic factor so that it does not matter even though we continue in sin? (6:1). Might we not say flippantly that the more we sin, the more can grace operate? (6:1,2).

Paul answers this question in ch. 6 where he speaks of baptism. At that time it was performed by immersion. 6:3 means simply that all of us who have been baptized into Christ have been baptized into His death. Thus the death of Christ is not for Paul a completed fact of the past, but is something which is made effective for us in baptism and faith. He who is baptized and who believes does not remain what he was previously (cf. Gal. 2:20; 3:27). We cannot call Christ our Lord unless we share in His death. Baptism is a baptism into death, "a drowning of the old Adam". But if we are baptized into the death of Jesus and are buried with Christ, we also know that we shall live with Him and share in His resurrection. Thus Paul is led on to the exhortation: recollect that you have died unto sin, and hence live for God in Christ Jesus (6:11). In 6:12ff. this line of thought is developed in more detail. The indicative is changed into an imperative: "let not therefore sin reign over you". The fact that you are no longer like the old man under the law, but under grace (6:14) means that you have another Lord. The new life is a life under a new dominion.

Is this mysticism? We would rather say that it is a mystery, a secret. But for Paul it is a secret which is effective in practice. Whoever has come under the power of the Crucified can no longer wish to be the slave of sin!

But sin has not vanished, just as death has not vanished. They have both lost their mastery and their claim over the believer, but both are still there. Hence the Christian life is a struggle (cf. Gal. 5:16ff.). The Christian is free from sin, but he must still struggle against it. The Christian is indeed justified in Christ, i.e. in a right relation with God. But when you consider his life in itself, he is still absolutely a sinner. He is sinner and righteous at one and the same time.

The freedom from the law which Paul proclaims in ch. 7 has in this situation apparently a dual aspect. On the one hand it is true that the Christian is dead unto the law (7:4,6). He belongs to the new order of the reality of God which in fact was foreshadowed (ch. 4) before the law.

But on the other hand he has to undergo the terrible experience of finding that the law is right in its claim against him just because it is the law of God (7:7–25). If Paul uses the expressions freedom from the law and freedom from sin in almost the same sense (6:14) yet there is one deep distinction that he must make: the law is not sin (7:7) but on the contrary is holy (7:12). Freedom from sin can only be confirmed inasmuch as the believer is fighting against it. Freedom from the law on the other hand consists in the fact that the believer admits the rightness of the law. But he must realize too that the law does not effect freedom from sin—only the awareness of sin (3:20). More it is not able to do: for the man to whom it applies is "fleshly" (7:14) and cannot do justice to the law's demands. Thus the tangled situation into which the law brings us can be summed up by Paul only in that impassioned outburst in which he longs for and expects redemption (7:24).

But the matter cannot remain at that stage. The law indeed condemns us, and is powerless to help us (8:3). But *God* does not condemn us. That in spite of everything we may have confidence (7:25) Paul shows in ch. 8. Here it is apparent that the Christian life is a struggle, but it is not a desperate dualism in human nature. "Flesh" and "spirit" stand in opposition but they are not as it were equally strong combatants. The Christian does *not* live after the flesh but after the spirit (8:4). Spirit is here the epitome of the new reality, the new world which God wills to bring to pass. And the believer "has" the spirit (8:9). He is not a slave but by adoption a child (8:14–16). And because he is a child of God, therefore he is an heir (8:17), which means that he has something to look forward to, a future which no one can snatch from him and in the splendour of which Paul includes the whole of creation (8:19-22). No doubt this future is still hidden (8:24ff.). But the believer knows that it is assured to him—not because his faith is so strong, but because God is for us (8:31). The chapter ends triumphantly with the declaration of this certitude—and 8:31ff. has been rightly called the "song of faith"; it would however be still more apposite to say that here we have a shout of triumph praising the unconquerable love of God.

5. *The mystery of the people of Israel* (chs. 9–11)

A deep gulf in temper and mood separates the end of ch. 8 from the beginning of ch. 9. We notice that although Paul is writing a doctrinal letter, it is still not without a note of passion. The question which most deeply torments him as a missionary and a Jew is not wholly unexpected. The righteousness of God and the new relation to God which God Himself bestows is valid for Jews as well as Gentiles. Is the precedence of the Jews a thing of the past? We have seen that the faithfulness of God is always the same (3:3), but the Jews by their own fault forfeit their privileges (3:9). All have sinned, both Jews and Gentiles. To all salvation is offered, and all may believe. Does the new unheard-of event which has come into the world in Jesus Christ supersede the Old Testament? We have been told (3:21 and 3:31, and even more in ch. 4): no, even the

Old Testament already bears witness to the righteousness of faith. But if this is so, then the further question is unavoidable: why then has Israel (in general) pre-eminently declined to believe, why has it rejected the Christ sent to it, why does it even now (so asks Paul the missionary) harden itself in its harsh opposition? And in view of such an opposition has not the end come upon Israel? Such are the questions which are answered in chs. 9–11. Chapter 9:1–29 speaks of the freedom of God with regard to Israel, 9:30—10:21 of Israel's guilt, and ch. 11 of Israel's hope.

Israel has received much. That is Paul's starting-point (9:1–5; we recollect 3:1–3). But has it not lost all through its own fault? Paul says: no, God's word of promise has always been valid for those who belonged to Israel not merely by the fact of racial descent (9:6,7) but who were rather "children of the promise" (9:8). A deep division has always rent Israel regarded externally: Paul shows this by adducing the examples of Isaac (and Ishmael who is latent in the background of the passage), Jacob and Esau. Why did God choose Isaac and Jacob? Certainly not because of their merits (9:11,12) but by free grace. It is the mystery of the gracious election of God (predestination) into which Paul here introduces us.

Paul does not say: God acts just as it pleases Him. He is not speaking of an arbitrary God, but of a God of grace (9:14–16). But no man by will power or self-exertion can earn this grace. It is freely given. As Paul shows by the illustrations of Pharaoh and the traditional image of the potter, divine grace is incalculable and mysterious in its working. Man is permitted to receive it, but he can neither deserve it nor explain it.

Now Israel (as is argued in the section 9:30—10:21) has repudiated the grace of God. It has shown zeal for God but not an enlightened zeal (10:2). With its concern for its own achievements and its own righteousness it has failed to subordinate itself to the righteousness of God (10:3). It might have gone the way of Abraham (ch. 4). But as a result of its self-righteousness, it has missed the very goal of the law, namely Christ (10:4). Israel desired to strive upwards from below. But God goes to work in the reverse direction: He comes near to us (10:8) especially in the word that we hear and He desires from us faith, such as will respond to Him and acknowledge His reality. Israel too could have heeded the word of the preacher (10:18ff.). But it has failed to hear the word that gives life.

Is the story of Israel now ended? Ch. 11 answers "no". Paul himself, the Israelite, is a proof to the contrary (11:1). There is also the fact of the elect Israel (11:7). God has not spurned His true people. Rather He has turned the failure of Israel to account by making it a means for the salvation of the Gentiles: Israel has rejected its Christ, but precisely through this rejected, crucified Christ the Gentiles have been received into the fellowship of God. If this is so, however, then Gentile Christians should not boast (11:18): they are like a wild olive shoot which has been grafted on the olive tree to share its richness (11:17). And at some future time—and this is the ultimate mystery to which Paul here gives expression—Israel too, all Israel will come to salvation (11:25ff.). In truth we have here the expression of far-reaching insights which constrain the apostle of the Gentiles to break out into the lyric of rejoicing with which his periods reach their final cadence (11:33ff.).

6. *The life of the justified as service* (chs. 12–16)

Paul again and again emphasizes the fact that we Christians are men who have received a gift. But righteousness and the new relation to God, spelling freedom over against death, sin and the law, are not given us to enable us to continue with "Christian" comfort in our self-willed, self-seeking way of life in the thought that these matters do not depend on us. Already in 1:5 Paul spoke of the "obedience of faith". Now (12:1,2) he begins with a review of the "mercies of God" and exhorts us in consequence to devote ourselves (our bodies) to God as a living sacrifice. Such is the "spiritual worship" of the justified. Or to put it in other words: if we believe in God as the One who unconditionally bestows on us His grace, then we can do no other but live in love (13:10). Or again, if we own Jesus Christ as our Lord, then we can no longer live unto ourselves (14:7–9). Here Paul gives us in brief his Christian ethics, i.e. his directions to the believer in regard to the business of living.

The sphere in which this is operative, as is plainly shown by 12:3ff., is the Church described as "one body in Christ" (12:5). But among the admonitions which follow are such as clearly extend beyond the confines of the Christian community (12:14,18–20). How could he who realizes that Christ died for the ungodly hate his persecutor? (5:6).

Hence we shall not be surprised to find that among the spheres of life in which Christian living proves itself as the surrender of self-concerned claims, the State appears in ch. 13, i.e. the heathen State of those times. Paul is not approving of the deification of the emperor but he is saying to the Christian: even this State (which as we see in Rev. 13 could easily become an anti-God power) has a task to fulfil which God Himself has imposed upon it: namely to protect the innocent and to punish the wrongdoer. It is wholly earthly in its mission. But the task of maintaining order here below is one which God Himself has given it. Hence the believer must subject himself (13:1—literally). The kingdom of God is imminent (13:11ff.) and is something wholly other than the State. But here and now the Christian must fit himself into the State and its laws. He must not simply, as the passage has been misunderstood to mean, become a passive subject, but must actively co-operate in helping the State to fulfil its God-appointed task. Hence the Christian's self-subordination to the State (clearly indicated in the intercession of 1 Tim. 2:1ff.) may in certain circumstances mean his responsible opposition, not to the State as such, but to what it does or orders that is contrary to right and the will of God.

Considerable space is given in this section to the question of the peaceful co-operation within the one Church of Christians who are differently disposed and think differently. It is the question of the relation of the "strong" to the "weak" (14:1—15:13). Some Christians make no distinction between various foods (14:2) and in other ways too (14:5) are more liberal in their outlook: they disregard the distinction between clean and unclean which the law enforces. Paul calls them the strong and counts himself among them (14:14). Such no doubt were mostly born Gentiles who emphasized that they were not subject to the ordinances of the Jewish law (cf. 15:8,9). Others on the contrary observe so carefully the prescriptions of the law that they eat only vegetables (14:2) and also strictly observe the traditional Jewish feast days (14:5). Paul describes them as the weak. It was no doubt very difficult for these two groups to live together peaceably. Should not Paul have said: it is only the strong who are right? He does say this too (14:14). But as a matter of general principle he considers it bad if in such questions any Christian asserts that he is right as against another Christian. In that case the freedom from the law would harden into a principle of which man might boast. For Paul the decisive thing is that love should reign—or what comes to the same thing, that the lordship of Christ should be recognized (14:7–9). Freedom is manifested in consideration for others, and in mutual respect. Freedom and love are one and the same! Such, we might say, is the practical consequence which can be drawn from the whole letter.

Paul concludes the letter with a reminder of his special service among the Gentiles (15:14ff.) and an account of his plans for the future. Ch. 16 contains merely greetings and from it we see how closely the Churches of the time were bound together.

According to the information of the Acts of the Apostles, Paul in fact went to Rome (ch. 28) a few years after the composition of this his most powerful letter. But he went there as a prisoner. Whether he was eventually released, and whether he was able to realize his plan to push on into Spain, is more than uncertain. We know very little about his activity in Rome itself (Acts 28:17ff., and cf. also the letter to the Philippians).

The letter which the apostle to the Gentiles wrote to Rome has endured. Very soon Rome was to become the starting-point for that development of the Church which led to the papacy. On the other hand this letter, after whole centuries had passed, became the inspiration of the Reformation, and in more recent times it was an exposition of the same letter (Karl Barth's, in 1919) which became the point of departure for a renewal of the life of the reformed Church.

Chapter 19

PAUL AND HIS CHURCHES

A SURVEY OF OTHER PAULINE LETTERS

Paul was the first to think out the meaning of the Christian gospel in intellectual terms: he was a theologian and the very existence of Christian theology cannot be understood apart from him. He brought to his task all the necessary equipment: in his youth he had enjoyed the instruction of the famous Pharisee exponent Gamaliel, and from his native Tarsus he became learned in the Greek philosophy of his time; above all he was fully at home in the scriptures (the Old Testament). He was a man of tremendous depth and clarity of thought.

But nothing would be more wrong than to suppose that Paul was an isolated thinker in his study or a lecturer on the platform. Rather everything that he has done as a supreme teacher to clarify the gospel for all times is deeply embedded in the service which he rendered as an apostle. His thoughts do not as it were take their own course but always are concerned with the particular situation of living men: Paul thinks as he acts, he does not turn over problems in his mind but solves those questions which are agitating the minds of his Churches. Hence it is characteristic that his deep thoughts are to be found in that type of literature which by custom is most immediately concerned with actual situations: namely the form of the letter. And the interesting thing is that they are real letters (and not dissertations) aflame with passion, penetrated with his anxieties, informed by his love, and constantly interrupted by words of encouragement, exhortation, warning, instruction. Such letters can be the more profitably read in proportion as we know the concrete situation in terms of which they are written. We must never attempt to understand Paul in purely theoretical terms. With Paul, as with the Bible as a whole, it is not a question of abstract problems but of questions which emerge from the actual business of living, or rather of the one great question, and to that Paul here gives an answer.

After attaining a preliminary view of Paul's world of ideas by the study of the letter to the Philippians, we shall now glance at the other letters. Let us not forget that we have here documents with whose understanding and bearing the thought of centuries has concerned itself, and whose ever living power is shown by the fact that each century as it were discovers them anew. How could we in such a case propose anything but the attainment of a few insights, from which to think further?

1. *The letters to the Thessalonians* (cf. especially 1 Thessalonians 1—2:5)

The two letters to the Thessalonians were written in A.D. 51. They are addressed to a Church which had arisen only a few months previously at Thessalonica (or Salonica). Thus we can here observe how matters stood with such a young Church and what Paul had to say to it.

(*a*) *How matters stood.* The first three chapters of the first letter give a very vivid picture of the situation. Men who only a short time before were still heathen (1:9) have experienced something utterly overwhelming; the gospel, the good news of Jesus Christ, has proved to them a life-transforming, creative force (1:5) so that already they can serve as an example to others (1:7). Thus the Thessalonians have not so to speak grown up with their Christianity, it has come upon them as a sheer incomprehensible marvel. But their life as Christians is no easy matter; they have had to suffer affliction (1:6), persecution has been their lot (2:13–16), and they need strengthening in order not to give way (3:3,4). But through his pupil Timothy, whom he sent to Thessalonica, Paul has heard of their "faith" and "love" (3:6): thus the Church is standing its ground.

Paul stresses again and again, above all here, that the Christians in Thessalonica (and everywhere in fact) are Christians not by their own decision but as a result of the action of God towards them: God has chosen them (1:4) and the Holy Spirit has manifested His power among them (1:5) and they received the word spoken to them not as the word of men but as the Word of God (2:13). Thus so certainly as in this town human action, decision, faith and love have been at work, so surely does everything depend on the fact that God Himself has acted upon them and is still acting. Were it otherwise, Paul could not be so unreservedly hopeful for the future.

No letter of Paul is without its warnings and injunctions. None of the Churches to which he writes is in an ideal state. The Bible does not know a perfect humanity, not even among Christians. The Thessalonians too are in need of advice. "Sanctification" and sobriety of temper are what Paul requires for the Thessalonians.

The lack of sobriety and composure was seen above all in the fact that some of these Christians were neglecting their daily work. In this regard we should read ch. 4:11,12 of the first letter and ch. 3:6–13 in the second. Their attitude can be readily understood: they had become so absorbed in the other world, and were so gripped by the idea of the great events to come (we have dealt with the eschatology of the New Testament above, p. 169) that the earthly, the everyday, were lost sight of. Paul explains that whosoever lives thus is not living soberly, and like a drunken man cannot correctly appraise realities. But the Christian is a man who for the sake of the other world, and because he is at home there, is able also to make a sober estimate of the realities of this life too: whoever is sober thus shows that he is a child of the light and of day, and lack of sobriety means that one is at home in the night, in darkness (1 Thess. 5:4–8). We observe that Paul will have nothing to do with uncontrolled ecstasy.

(*b*) *What has Paul to say?* By the previous observations we stand on the threshold of an answer to this question. We have seen that Paul does not scold but points out the right way. Correct doctrine helps towards right living. There is a deep reason for this. For the life of the Christian reflects, both in its action and abstinence, what the Christian essentially is by the grace of God. Thus when Paul shows in his teaching what we ideally are in God (so for example 1 Thess. 5:4ff.) then he at the same time implies what our conduct should be. Hence doctrine and living are so closely bound up together here. And thus it is in all the letters of Paul.

Sanctification. This word denotes the idea to which we are thus led. As we have seen above (p. 160) Christians are "holy" in the view of Paul, i.e. they belong to God and not to themselves. Hence sanctification means that God takes possession of a man, separates him and transforms his being in accordance with His own holiness. Thus in 1 Thess. 5:23 we read that it is God Himself who sanctifies believers; sanctification is the work of God. But the believer answers this work of God by taking seriously the idea that he does not belong to himself, does not live for himself in accordance with his own desires (cf. 1 Thess. 4:1ff.). That Christians do not believe by their own efforts, but that God has acted and still acts upon them, is what Paul teaches, and we find the same trend of thought in 1 Thess. 1–3 constantly. He now enjoins them to the effect that they should respond to and co-operate with the work of God. Thus again teaching and life hang together.

It is similar with regard to the expectation of the future. In 1 Thess. 4:13ff. and 2 Thess. 2:1–12 Paul speaks of things to come (cf. p. 169). Yet he does not teach in order to encourage the curiosity of the inquisitive, but in order to give exhortation through instruction; you belong to the day and not to the night, hence be wakeful and sober! (1 Thess. 5:1–11).

2. *The first letter to the Corinthians* (cf. 1 Corinthians 1; 3:1–11; 6:9–20; 7:27–35; 10:16,17; 11:17–34; 12:1–26; 13:15)

Paul had founded the Christian Church in the port of Corinth in the course of the same missionary journey in which he founded the Church at Thessalonica and in fact in the same year (A.D. 50). These two letters however were not, like those to the Thessalonians, written shortly after the rise of the Church in question, but about seven years later.

As we are told in 5:9, this letter was preceded by an earlier one. Hence our first letter is really the second. We must assume that Paul wrote many more letters than the 13 which have come down to us as his. His work probably covered three decades. Hence we possess only a selection.

(*a*) With regard to conditions in Corinth, we must realize two things for the understanding of this letter: (i) In the Corinthian Church there flourishes a luxuriant sectarianism (cf. esp. 1:10ff.); various groups violently clashed with each other and appealed to the great men of early Christianity, to Paul and Peter and Apollos (who followed up the work of Paul); in fact there were some who wished to make of Christ Himself a party chief. (ii) Many Corinthians were of the opinion that the gospel was a new "wisdom", a source of deep insights for the spirit of man; they regarded the life of the body as a thing of relative unimportance, and some supposed that they could act as they pleased about it.

Both these things cohere. Since the Corinthians were Greeks proud of their enlightenment, they gladly admire the spiritual superiority of leaders and delight to form sects in order to cultivate the special type of wisdom which they owe to particular leaders. Because they are concerned about the soul, they attach so much importance to spiritual factors.

Paul refers the Corinthians to Christ alone: He was crucified for them, in His name they were baptized (1:13–17), and as the crucified Saviour He is not a leader about whom one ought to be or can be enthusiastic. The Jews are offended by the cross—what is the good of a crucified Messiah? And the Greeks find the cross ridiculous—"a sage crucified" one of them later mocked and thereby expressed what all thought. Hence Paul knows that *no man* (the Jews and the Greeks constituted humanity for him) can understand Christ unaided. This he implies in 1:18–31 in powerful words. "To us, who are being saved", the word of the cross is the "power of God" (1:18). But that we belong to this company has nothing to do with our wisdom or our human nobility, but is solely the work of God (cf. esp. 1:26ff.). Hence, he urges, do not suppose this is man's doing, and do not glorify man!

In 2:1–5 and 3:5ff. Paul attacks the glorification of man. He is speaking chiefly about himself. When he founded this Church, what great wisdom had he to offer? He "knew" only the Crucified. And later as the Church took shape both he and Apollos worked at it (3:5ff.). But they were both only servants, "fellow-workmen for God" (3:9). The Church however must heed the foundation which was laid (3:11).

The idea that the gospel was concerned only with the spiritual and hence was "wisdom", deep insight or spiritual triumph over the lower material world, is called gnosis. It is a mode of thought which stems from Greek culture. There were many Greeks who considered the body the mere prison house of the soul. Such people easily came to believe that Christ was the Redeemer of the soul; that He freed the soul from its prison and led it into the hidden worlds of the spirit. The entire first letter to the Corinthians is a polemic directed against this fundamental misunderstanding: you belong wholly to Christ who is in everything your Saviour. In His resurrection He did not abolish the body, but overcame all bondage and opened up for you the way to a new life in the body (1 Cor. 15).

If people undervalued the body, they might become ascetic, and so for example despise or dissolve marriage. But also a contrary opinion might occur to them; since the body is meaningless, therefore one can do as one pleases in regard to the body; the main thing is the soul, the spiritual element. This very opinion was widespread among the Corinthians (as is shown especially in ch. 6:9–20). Here it is plain how Paul answers such people. Contempt for the body cannot grow on the soil of his teaching.

Nor does the much discussed ch. 7 imply a contempt for the body. Paul certainly in regard to himself values the single life above the married state, and that because the single man is freer for service (7:32). In 7:1 also he defends the right to the unmarried state. But he is realist enough (and now for the first time in regard to Christians who live in a specially immoral city) to understand the dangers of the single life (7:2). Hence he attacks divorce (7:10ff.). It must especially be remembered that Paul expects a speedy end of the world (7:29ff.). Why in such a situation should there be concern about changing one's earthly condition of life? One's earthly state in comparison with the one thing that is needful is fairly subordinate, although not unimportant (7:20ff.). We should live out our faith in that condition, whatever it is, and not suppose that by making great changes, by adopting a religiously founded and mystical singleness of life, we can underline our faith. In such matters faith gives us inner freedom.

(*b*) *The Lord's Supper*. From ch. 7 onwards the letter deals with a number of questions which this Church had laid before the apostle. Among these is the question how the Lord's Supper is to be celebrated. Paul has heard how things were going in Corinth (11:17f.) and they were going badly. The Corinthians in fact looked like turning the eucharist into a meal of gluttony where the rich had plenty to eat and the poor went hungry (11:21ff.). In contrast to this, Paul reminds them of what the eucharist really means and sharply warns them against unworthy celebration (11:23ff.).

In the primitive Church the regular custom was that the whole congregation was present at the celebration of the eucharist. It contained two separate parts: a normal meal which was eaten in common (for eating together was considered a visible sign of religious fellowship), and the "Lord's Supper" in the narrower sense, which was intended not for the satisfaction of hunger but for a memorial of the crucified Lord and a proclamation of His death (11:25,26). Later, only the latter part was retained. But the Corinthians did not "discern the body of the Lord" (11:29); they confused the two component parts of the meal and made of the whole thing a quite secular feast in which into the bargain the rich caroused and the poor went hungry. Perhaps they thought that even this rite was merely something bodily, hence fundamentally unimportant and so something which they could treat as they pleased.

In this connexion the apostle reminds them in solemn introductory words (11:23) that this meal in its essence did not arise from any human appetite or other need, but from the institution of the

Lord. He quotes the words of institution as he too had received them from the Lord (through the medium of the earliest Church). The form in which he gives them diverges somewhat from that of the gospels and is most closely related to the account in Luke.

At v. 26 Paul takes up again the course of his own thoughts. The supper is the proclamation of the death of the Lord and therefore is not a memorial celebration of one that is dead, but a meal of joy, for the death of Christ is a redeeming death! But you Corinthians, you behave as though you were simply eating bread and drinking wine—which means that you are eating and drinking unworthily (v. 27). But consider, you will thus be guilty not of mere bread and wine but of the body and blood of Christ. Hence this bread and this wine are not mere earthly things for consumption and carnal enjoyment, but here the Lord Himself gives Himself to you, He who in His body was crucified for you and shed His blood for you! Perhaps we can grasp Paul's thought more clearly in 10:16: the cup and the loaf are (or, in reality effect) the "communion" of the body and blood of Christ.

If this is so, then the lack of discipline prevailing in Corinth is a profanation of the Lord Himself. In their gnostic way of thought, it had not occurred to them that these bodily things (bread, wine) and actions (eating and drinking) were immediately concerned with Christ. But Paul assures them that this is really so, for thus He wills to grant them fellowship with Himself.

(*c*) *Disciplining the Christian congregation.* The assemblies of the early Christians were extremely lively in character. In them many persons one after the other addressed the assembly, as moved by their inner inspiration, flowing from the Holy Spirit (Paul calls this the gift of prophecy in ch. 14). There were also healings of the sick, and other extraordinary happenings, in particular a form of ecstatic speech in which inner excitement prevented clear articulation so that it was necessary for another to say what the ecstatic had not been able to say in words (this was called glossolaly, and Paul describes the other gift as the interpretation of tongues). Worship, marked by such ecstatic phenomena, was not so solemn as with us and not so severely controlled by thought. Paul had been asked by this Church to express his opinion about these goings on. In answer he makes essentially three points. Firstly: all special capacities which any one exercises in your assemblies are gifts of the Spirit (12:4–11); hence they are not to be exploited to puff up the self-esteem of any individual but they must be made to contribute to the good of the whole (which Paul calls the "body", 12:12ff.). Secondly: the supreme gift is that of love; whatever marvellous capacities are displayed, all are subordinate to the gift of love (ch. 13). Thirdly: among these gifts of the spirit prophecy stands first, for it is intelligible to all and serves directly to the increase of knowledge and insight among the other members of the community (cf. esp. 14:1–5,19).

To go into detail here would take up too much space. It is enough to note that everything Paul here says corresponds to what we have already learnt. Wherever man strives to assert himself, he is going to work in the wrong way. To be sure, there are people in Corinth with special gifts (the Christian must believe that every gift which he can use for the edification of his brethren is a gift of the Holy Spirit; gifts themselves change and are in part different to-day from what they were in ancient Corinth). But then as now they are gifts which are bestowed, of which man may not boast and which must be offered in the service of all. The emphasis is on service.

Hence ch. 13 stands at the centre of this brief summary of Church order (chs. 12–14). The hymn in praise of love is indeed an artistically moulded passage. But is not Paul claiming too much? Where is such love seen? We shall have to conclude that Paul is describing the love of God. Our own movements of love can hardly be described as "never ending" (13:8). But this love of God "is poured into our hearts", says Paul in another place (Rom. 5:5). It is bestowed on us that we might spread it further.

(*d*) *The resurrection.* In Corinth there were people who declared that "there was no resurrection of the dead" (15:12). No doubt they were such as considered the gospel to be purely spiritual and so supposed that what was meant was an inner awakening of the soul. The body did not interest them at all. So Paul was asked about this point and ch. 15 gives his answer. Paul's method here is the same as in the case of the eucharist; he reminds the Corinthians of what they had long ago been told, of what Paul himself had received from others, and had accepted and handed on as tradition: viz. the fact of the resurrection of Jesus Christ (15:1f.). The resurrection of Jesus Christ has made it clear that God has broken the power of death and that He "is the God of the living" (Matt. 22:32). Christ, the Conqueror of death, is the "first-fruits" (15:20) and has conquered death for all men; as once the first Adam brought death on all, so is Christ the second Adam who confers on all the life which breaks the power of death (especially 15:21,22,45). Thus the ways of God with man end with the destruction of death (15:26).

Paul is here concerned about the new resurrected body, which has been disclosed through the resurrection of Christ. The latter signifies the dawn of a new order of creation and Christ is for a new humanity what Adam was for the old humanity (Christ is the "second man", 15:47, or the "second Adam", 15:45). "The new has come" (2 Cor. 5:17).

What is doubted or not understood in Corinth is this all-embracing renewal of creation which has dawned for man with the resurrection of Christ. The Corinthians do not doubt the resurrection of Christ itself; Paul can remind them that the preaching of the risen Lord, the basis of their salvation (v. 2) was once accepted (v. 1) and believed (v. 11) by them. But perhaps they thought that Christ rose again only as it were in the spirit or that He had attained only a spiritual immortality.

In what Paul says about the resurrection of Jesus (vv. 1–11) he does not want to assert that Christ simply rose again in the same body which He had before. He does not even speak of the empty tomb as the evangelists do. But what is decisive for Paul is that Christ rose again in reality: the witnesses which he quotes have not merely an inner spiritual awareness persuading them that their Master is not really dead; no, they have seen Him alive in full reality. For this vision of the truly risen Lord Paul adduces with great care a large number of witnesses of whom, he says, some are still alive, and ending with himself (vv. 8ff.; cf. Gal. 1:16; 1 Cor. 9:1). Hence what he experienced before Damascus (Acts 9) was a vision of the risen Christ. We might suppose that this experience was after all a "vision" and if so, then all the appearances that preceded it were also visions. But Paul is not interested in the form or psychological structure which the experience of the resurrection assumed in the believer, but is concerned to reaffirm the basic message of Christianity: "The Lord has risen indeed" (Lk. 24:34). Whatever form the human awareness of the resurrection may have taken, the fact was that these despairing men really saw Him alive with the result that their lives were given a completely new direction. It is important to note that Jesus showed Himself alive only to such as had been in His company as disciples: resurrection and faith belong together. Only the believer in Jesus can know that He rose again. Only because He rose again can there be belief in Him. Hence the resurrection "proves" nothing to those who close their hearts to Christ. But those who open themselves to Him come to know Him as the ever-living One.

Hence we understand Paul when he explains that (vv. 12–19) apart from the reality of the resurrection faith is "futile", lacking in content (the A.V. translates as "vain"; v. 17). The fact is that faith is not concerned with beautiful and deep thoughts, but with reality, and indeed with a reality which has overcome death (v. 19).

Christ is the first-fruits of them that sleep (v. 20); with His resurrection something transcendently new has broken into this world, and this new order will be consummated. Those who belong to Him (v. 23) and even the rest of mankind (v. 24; or "the end")—all will be involved in this new order and the victory of Jesus will manifest itself as a victory over all His enemies (vv. 24–25). Until finally as the ultimate Victor He will subject Himself to the Father, and God will be everything to every one (v. 28).

Paul then explains (vv. 35f.) in more detail what the new body of the resurrection life is. We have insisted that the resurrection meant for him that Jesus in truth rose again and not merely in a spiritual-gnostic sense. For Paul this "in truth" means corporeally. But it now becomes clear that corporeality need not always mean the same thing. The corporeality which the Risen One bore and which He will give to men is "spiritual" (v. 44), it is completely different from natural corporeality (vv. 42–44). *We* cannot imagine any other body but that of nature to which we are accustomed. But Paul dares to express the unutterable, the inconceivable: in the Risen Lord a new corporeality and a whole new creation has emerged into view, and this will swallow up the old frail nature of man: "Death is swallowed up in victory!" (vv. 54ff.). These verses have been called the great psalm of Christian hope, and not without reason.

It must now have become clear that ch. 15 is the centre of gravity of the whole of the letter. Again and again Paul has spoken of the bodily and warned against gnostic spiritualism. Here it becomes clear why he does so and what he implies. We might sum up the matter by saying that in 1 Cor. Paul declares the full *reality* of Jesus Christ as the epitome and symbol of a whole new order of life.

3. *The second letter to the Corinthians* (cf. esp. 2 Corinthians 1:1–14; 2:12–17; 3–6; 7:4–10; 12:1–10)

The two letters to the Corinthians known to us are separated by no great interval of time; probably the interval was no longer than six to nine months. If we read chs. 2:3,4,9 and 7:8ff. of our letter it becomes clear that Paul had already sent to Corinth another letter which is lost to us. Thus altogether we know of four letters to the Corinthians, of which we have only the second and the fourth, our Corinthians 1 and 2. Both must have been written about A.D. 57, the first from Ephesus, where Paul stayed long, and the second from Greece (Macedonia).

A mere superficial glance at ch. 1 shows that this letter is conceived in far more personal terms than the first. If further we look at chs. 11 and 12 we realize even more that this letter springs from a situation of struggle. As can be most clearly perceived from 7:12, Paul has been personally offended and wronged by a Christian in Corinth and in other matters too has had to encounter much opposition from this Church; he has to defend himself constantly against personal reproaches (e.g. 1:17).

In such a situation he does not take the obvious course: he does not take up a defensive position. On the contrary it is just in this letter that he gives the world a glimpse of his own weakness, more clearly than anywhere else (cf. 2:12,13; esp. 12:6ff.). He does not shrink from laying himself bare. "Fighting without, fear within"—thus he characterizes his experience (7:5). Hence he does not seek to impose his authority. But of course as against all attacks and all his own weakness he can invoke one thing: the splendour of the apostolic ministry (cf. esp. chs. 3–6).

We may sum the matter up by saying that in this letter, alike to defend himself against criticism and to overcome his own inadequacy, Paul expounds the purpose and meaning of his office.

In our detailed observations we shall confine our attention to certain chapters; hence we propose to omit whole sections which would require very detailed elucidation.

(*a*) *Affliction and comfort* (1:1–14; 2:12–17; 7:4–10). It is not for nothing that Paul at the beginning of this letter praises God as the "Father of mercies and God of all comfort" (1:3), and incidentally all the letters of Paul with the exception of that to the Galatians begin with words of thanksgiving. He had suffered severe affliction (1:8,9) and is still involved in great dangers (1:10). Obviously he means the violent riotous opposition he has encountered in Ephesus (cf. Acts 19). But in all this God has comforted him and rescued him. Paul has been vouchsafed the experience of the power of God to raise the dead (1:9). But he is certain that also the prayers of the Church have helped to deliver him from his distress (1:11).

But to these afflictions of the apostle have been added in the meantime serious anxieties about the Churches. Paul went from Ephesus to Macedonia (i.e. to Europe). In Troas (on the Asia Minor side) he awaited the coming of Titus, his follower, whom he had sent to Corinth to bring him news. But in vain! And so it turned out (2:12ff.) that he had indeed an opportunity of preaching the gospel but did not avail himself of it because he had no inner composure of mind ("rest", 2:13). That was truly a bitter defeat! And yet in looking back on this sorry failure he can now speak of the triumph of God (2:14).

Verse 14 means literally: "But thanks be to God who in Christ always leads us in triumphal procession (i.e. as captives) . . ." The image is that of a field marshal triumphantly returning home and leading captive his prisoners as the tangible witnesses of his victory. Hence Paul means that such a victor is God. But we (i.e. the apostle and also all other Christians) in Christ (because we are His own) are the captives of God testifying to His victory. This is one of the most splendid interpretations of the apostolic ministry which we have. Thus the most successful missionary of Christianity says that he is not a victor but merely a prisoner.

Once again Paul comes back to the thought of his care for the Corinthians (7:4ff.). He had written to them, as we have seen, and had sent Titus to them probably as the bearer of the letter. He had waited for him in vain. The disquiet which drove him out of Troas (2:13) tortured him still in Macedonia (7:5). To such an extent does this man live with his Churches that their fate can almost make him fall ill. Now comes the word: "Fighting without, fear within" (7:5). This is truly a self-unveiling. Paul makes it freely, he has not his own honour to defend. But he can now also report how he was comforted by the eventual arrival of Titus; Titus brought good news from Corinth where the Church had experienced a healing sorrow (7:7–10) and had brought to account the man who had wronged Paul.

(*b*) *Weakness and strength* (4:7–18; 12:1–10). The two sections to which we now turn stand in close connexion with what Paul can plead against all attacks: namely the dignity of the apostolic ministry (cf. below, (*c*)). But it is obviously important for Paul to emphasize that he cannot possibly praise himself. "Not that we are sufficient of ourselves to claim anything as coming from ourselves", he explains in 3:5. The high office which he fulfils sheds no glow on his own person. We have already seen this in considering the attacks which he had to meet from without. He now speaks openly of the assaults to which he is subject from within.

He has a "treasure" (4:7) but it is in "earthen vessels". As far as he himself is concerned he is a harassed, afflicted, weak man (4:8ff.). He is the servant of God (6:4) but that involves him in sheer distress, weakness and tribulation. What a life poised between deep contrasts! He expresses this most vigorously in 6:9,10: how poor is the servant of Christ, and yet how rich; how powerless and yet how strong! Ch. 12 takes us further into the heart of this life in contrasts. Almost mockingly Paul speaks of the boasting which his opponents try to provoke him to indulge in. He could indeed boast if he wished: for example he might speak of the visions which he has had, of inner raptures which he has experienced (12:1–4). But he speaks of the man who experienced all this as though it were some other. "On behalf of this man I will boast, but on my own behalf I will not boast, except of my weaknesses" (12:5). Hence the Paul who enjoyed these experiences of such a powerful interior kind is an *alter ego*, as it were, "a man in Christ". But the Paul who every day is assailed and engaged in bitter conflict can claim for himself none of all this, he is rather a desperately weak and wretched man and if he must boast he can boast only of his weakness! In fact, providence has taken good care that he shall not be too elated, for it has given him a thorn in the flesh (12:7). Paul does not say what he means by this torment. Is it some sickness? We do not know. Paul traces his tortures to an angel of Satan who beat him with his fists. Inner dejection and despair, possibly. In any case Paul is an unusual man and unusual men have in their inner lives unusual abysses of sorrow to conquer. For us it is important to notice that Paul found no alleviation in consequence of his prayer. But another type of assurance was given him: namely that the grace of the Lord would always be sufficient, for the divine power is made perfect in weakness. Thus the man who so deeply discloses to us his inner being can end with the seeming self-contradiction: "when I am weak, then I am strong" (12:10).

The life of the apostle is fraught with the strongest tensions. But not only his. Every Christian in his way knows of something similar. If our subjective emotional life were the important matter to God, then we could none of us be sure that we were in a state of grace. For it is just the Christian who has to encounter the fiercest temptations. The decisive point is that in these temptations he is allowed to know that though in such experiences we are as those who "have nothing", yet—because we may have Christ for us—we "possess everything" (6:10).

(*c*) *The ministry of the gospel* (chs. 3–6). Our letter shows with especial clarity how little Paul is inclined to ascribe any importance to himself. So much the more clearly it also shows what for Paul is the true content of his existence: the glory of the gospel and the service of it. This suggests also what should be the true content of every Christian life.

"*The ministry of the new covenant*" (3:6) —it is this which is the life work of Paul. This ministry is exercised not in a written code but in the Spirit (3:6). The written code is the law by which God pronounces our condemnation (3:9). Because even the ministry of the written code was instituted by God (3:7ff.) this ministry too had its splendour. Thus when God gave the law through Moses, the effect of which could only be to render man aware of his guilt before God, Moses the lawgiver was clad in a halo of brightness; his ministry had dignity and exaltation. How much the more so must be that ministry by which God gives us life and righteousness (or a right relation to Himself)!

The high worth of this ministry springs from its content, the gospel. Where the gospel is preached and believed the Spirit of God is at work (3:6) and that Spirit gives life. Where the gospel is, there righteousness is freely granted (3:9). Hence the gospel is no sum of doctrines, no world-view, but the means by which the living reality of God is conveyed to us. In this weak human word, the Spirit of God wills to act towards us, to transform our being and give us true life. But where the Spirit of God is—and this is a bold word of Paul!—there is the Lord Himself (3:17). And because Christ Himself acts upon us in the Spirit, the Spirit gives us "freedom" (3:17). Whenever men come into communion with Jesus Christ, then they experience deepest liberation.

It should be noted that in ch. 3 the relation of the law and the gospel is thus again discussed (as it was in Phil. 3 and the letter to the Romans, and as we shall meet it again in the letter to the Galatians).

In ch. 4 Paul says that in spite of its glory and high worth the gospel is by no means rightly received by all men. It is not a matter that can be spread abroad through propaganda tricks (4:2) or with cunning persuasive arts. We cannot "prove" the gospel by valid reasons; it is addressed to the conscience of man (4:2). "Conscience" means in the Bible man as he stands in the sight of God. Where the gospel is not received and remains hidden (4:3) there the god of this world, the Satanic adversary, has intervened between God and man. These powerful expressions could never be applied to a human religious doctrine. But Paul stresses: it is not a question of ourselves (we preach not ourselves, 4:5). Hence he goes on to say that the ministers of the gospel do not reflect in their persons that splendour of which he spoke in ch. 3: "We are afflicted in every way . . ." is now his confession (4:8f.).

The whole letter reaches its climax with ch. 5. Previously Paul had spoken of the many sorrows he had had to bear. Now he begins with a word of Christian hope (5:1ff.): out of the depths of his despair he looks upwards to the eternal building of God which is prepared for all believers. For the believer is here only on pilgrimage (5:6: "while we are at home in the body we are away from the Lord"). Faith is not sight (5:7). But the time of pilgrimage passes in good hope, for the pilgrim sees from afar off the gleams of his "home with the Lord" (5:8). But Paul knows too who this Lord is: He is the Judge of the whole world (5:10). Confident as he is that before the judgment seat of Christ he can count on the help of grace, he is sure that it is a divine judgment which is inescapable.

In view of this earnest hope Paul comes

back to the consideration of his work. It is really not a question of success with men. Of course the missionary must use every endeavour to "persuade" men (5:11); but he does so openly in the sight and fear of God. In other words, he does not aim to please men, much as it is his duty to get to grips with them; his aim is to please God alone who knows the heart of man. (Apparently he is here concerned to defend himself against the reproach of dishonesty.) But that he seeks contact with men, tries to win them over and is "right-minded" with them is the consequence of the fact that he is controlled by the love of Christ (5:14); he cannot fail to plead on behalf of this Christ. He loses sight of every human point of view when he remembers what Christ has done and how a whole new world ("a new creation", 5:17) is now dawning for humanity. Whoever is "in Christ", living no longer by his own resources and for himself, but having his life in and flowing from Christ, is already a new creature, is rightly related to God and participates in the life of God!

Hence man is now permitted to enter into a completely new situation. It is possible for all things to become new with him (5:17) for God has made peace with man and has "reconciled the world to Himself" (5:19) and that "in Christ". Hence up to the present the world has been irreconcilable, it has rejected the love of God (Paul speaks not of a reconciliation of God but of a reconciliation of the world), it has been engaged in conflict with God and has been in revolt against Him: that is the essence of sin. But God, by His own initiative, has ended this situation (5:18). "In Christ" He has become the Reconciler of irreconcilable man, and has made peace. In fact God has loaded the burden of man's hostility to God on to the person of His Son, and "has made Him to be sin who knew no sin" (5:21), and "in Him"—in fullness of communion with Him—by becoming one with Him, we are to be what He is—righteous before God, or literally the "righteousness of God". Here is one of the most powerful passages of the whole Bible. Christ takes our unrighteousness and death on Himself in order that we might share His righteousness and His life. This is the meaning of Paul here. And *this* is the theme which Paul must expound to the world: as an ambassador for Christ (5:20) he shows that God causes peace and reconciliation to be offered to men.

Chapter 6, vv. 1–10 have already been discussed above.

The reader will have noticed that this letter is the hardest to understand of all the letters of Paul. But if we take the trouble to study it carefully, we shall find in it some of the peaks of Biblical inspiration, audacious words of unfathomable depth.

4. *The letter to the Galatians*
(cf. esp. Galatians 1:6–20; 2:1–21; 3:1–14; 3:19–29; 4:1–7; 5:1–6; 5:16–24)

It is not exactly known when the letter to the Galatians was written. In any case the time of its composition falls in the same decade as the composition of the Corinthian letters, and may possibly be a few years earlier. Nor do we know exactly to what Churches it is addressed: there was an old district of Galatia in northern Asia Minor, and there was the Roman province of

Galatia which also included more southern areas which Paul visited on his first missionary journey. However, it is certain that this is a letter of Paul which is addressed to several Churches.

Paul himself had once founded these Churches (in 3:1ff. and 4:13ff. he recalls this). But now he sees them in the greatest danger; they are about to "submit again to a yoke of slavery" (5:1), in particular they are inclined to regard circumcision as a pre-requisite of being a Christian. Hence their idea was that if one wants to become a Christian one must first become a Jew, a member of the old people of God and so keep the Old Testament law (5:3). Thus the Galatians are being stirred by Judaizing notions.

This letter is a polemic of great sharpness. Even the customary words of thanks at the opening are lacking. Paul gets down to the point immediately; you are turning aside to a different gospel and such there cannot be (1:6ff.).

The passionate emphasis with which Paul speaks shows that he feels the whole gospel to be threatened. If someone who was formerly a Gentile causes himself to be circumcised and thus incorporated into the Old Testament people of God he must keep the whole law (5:3). But to wish to be "justified by the law" means that one is "severed from Christ" (5:4). In Christ neither circumcision nor uncircumcision is of any avail, but only "faith working through love" (5:6).

In these sentences we see plainly what is at stake for Paul. If in addition to what Christ bestows on us, we wish to offer something else to God, then we are not putting our whole faith in Christ alone. But if we fail to do this, we cannot be sure that we are right with God; for what we perform is always somewhat imperfect and never really fulfils the demands of the law. "All who rely on works of the law are under a curse" (3:10). It is clear that it is the zeal of the pastor which causes Paul to speak so severely. The Galatians are playing fast and loose with their souls' salvation. We recollect that in a similar case in the otherwise so brightly joyous letter to the Philippians Paul suddenly finds words of great harshness springing to his pen (Phil. 3).

The letter to the Galatians is clearly divisible into three parts. In the first of these (chs. 1–2) the centre is the assertion of Paul that he received his gospel from God Himself and that even the Jerusalem apostles approved his missionary work.

In the second part (chs. 3–4) Paul argues that Christ has made us free from the curse of the law. In the third part the apostle admonishes us to make a right use of the freedom which Christ procures us.

In all three parts we are concerned with the way in which Paul deals with the main question: what has the gospel to do with the law? Hence we shall leave out of account many detailed points.

(*a*) *Paul as the authorized apostle to the Gentiles* (chs. 1–2). Paul flings his curse at every one who preaches any other gospel (1:8,9). Does not this indicate a despotic authority? And is he not insisting with quite unreasonable obstinacy on his own interests? Paul replies "No: I am not at all concerned about the interests of men (not even about my own, cf. 2:20); I am a servant of Christ" (1:10). He appeals to the way in which he was made an apostle: quite apart from any exertion of his own, purely by the grace of God, and also apart from the interference of other men (cf. esp. 1:11–17).

For the readers of the letter this implies that if Paul were speaking from a personal point of view, he could claim no authority in fact. He reminds them that he himself had been a persecutor of Christians (1:13), a zealous observer of the law, even to excess (1:14). But then Another entered his life and the Galatians have to do with that other Person. Paul desires nothing for himself, but works entirely for his Lord, whose servant he is (1:10).

Although Paul did not receive his commission from men, yet he can say that those men who possessed authority in the sphere of Christianity approved of his appointed task. Here he comes to speak about the "apostolic council" (2:1–10). The leaders ("pillars") of the early Church (2:9) in Jerusalem came to an understanding with Paul that he should preach the gospel to the Gentile world while Peter took it to the Jews (2:7,8). Why? Because they recognized the grace which was given to Paul. They realized that God had intervened in the situation and the chief apostles were generous and obedient enough to recognize the work of God (2:9a).

Of course it was painful for them to have to admit this! So much was shown soon after the council. At Antioch, where Jews and Gentiles lived together in common Christian fellowship, Peter refused to eat with the Gentiles (because as a Jew he felt it was not permissible; the Gentiles were considered in the law as "unclean" and incapable of taking part in the cult and its fellowship). Then Paul sharply opposed him (2:11 ff.). It is observable from what follows that this quarrel left its mark; even then the question was whether the law still retained some meaning and authority in regard to the justification of man and his right relation to God (2:16). But Paul is constrained to say that as a born Jew, a sometime zealous observer of the law, he "died to the law" (2:19). For it is no longer he who now lives! The Christ who has gained power over his life is the Crucified and has drawn Paul into His death, and thus the law has lost its authority over him. "It is no longer I who live but Christ who lives in me . . ." (2:20). In these words Paul intimates the entry into his life of something incomprehensibly new and transcendent, which also must mark the life of every Christian. This new and transcendent element puts an end to all that man can do in his own power to make himself right with God.

(*b*) *The law and the gospel* (chs. 3–4). According to the argument of Paul the order should be: the gospel and the law. For at the very beginning of the old covenant we find not the law but faith. "Abraham believed

God and it was reckoned to him as righteousness" (3:6; cf. Gen. 15:6). Thus if any one believes as Abraham believed then he too shares in the blessing which our forefather received (3:9). Quite otherwise is it with those who wish to bring before God their observance of the law; they stand not under the blessing, but under the curse; for no one can keep the law in its entirety (3:10) and only the perfect fulfilment of the law would be of any use. But Christ has freed us from this curse because He took it upon Himself (3:13). By His so doing, the blessing which Abraham enjoyed is now accessible to the heathen (3:14). Abraham himself received of old the promise that through his one "seed" (offspring) the blessing would be actualized for humanity. All this is now fulfilled.

According to this argument the original relation of man to God even in the old covenant rests on faith. Or to put it in other words: man originally and essentially must be so related to God that he trusts Him and dedicates himself to Him—that he allows God to be his God. But that God wills to be the God of man, that He condescends to man, was already disclosed to Abraham by this promise.

But in that case what is the purpose of the law? Paul himself asks the question (3:19). And he answers by referring to the puzzling mysterious fact of sin. In reality man does not love God, does not put his trust in God and does not allow God to be God for him. He rather revolts against God. The law has then a twofold purpose: firstly it discloses to man the wrongness of his way of life (3:22), secondly it operates so that man does not sink into complete chaos, but "is kept under the restraint of the law" (3:23) until the promise of God is fulfilled (esp. 4:1ff.). Thus the law is a custodian (literally: a pedagogue or tutor) working until the advent of Christ (3:24): it places unbelieving man in the wrong, and at the same time preserves his life (it is compared with guardians who take charge of a minor until he attains his majority; 4:1ff.). Hence until the coming of Christ, the law had great significance. Now, however, Christ has come, in the fullness of time (4:4), God "has sent His Son" and thus a completely new situation has arisen. Now the minor and the slave is free (4:7). But at the same time the law has been superseded in its significance for our relation with God; whoever now proposes to fulfil the law by his works, is going back to his minority and is casting aside the freedom "for which Christ has set us free" (5:1). But it is just this which the Galatians are doing by proposing to undergo circumcision and to reintroduce the Old Testament feasts (4:10).

For the purposes of illustration—in accordance with the method of theology at that time—Paul uses an Old Testament story. Abraham had his real heir, promised by God, from the free woman Sarah (i.e. Isaac); but he had also a son by the slave Hagar, namely Ishmael.

Now this word Hagar in Arabia is taken to denote Mount Sinai, on which the law was given (4:25). Thus the law belongs to servitude, not to the promise (4:24).

Let us sum up. Paul intends to say: for the man who is in Christ, the guardianship of the law is ended. This guardianship, however, had been instituted by God Himself; the law retains its full and proper value within its own dispensation. But that dispensation of servitude is now ended. Now our relationship with God, our adoption as sons (3:26; 4:5–7) rests solely upon our thankful acceptance of the love of God which we encounter in Christ—and that means on faith.

But this introduces something so utterly new and other that all earthly distinctions—Jew, Greek, slave, free, male, female—no longer signify anything in the sight of God (3:28). Hence in the Church of Jesus Christ these distinctions have no place. We must recall the conduct of Peter in Antioch in order to realize what this means. Peter was prepared to have table fellowship only with the Jews, not with the Gentiles (2:11ff.).

(*c*) *Life in freedom* (chs. 5–6). We have already seen that Paul regards it as a lapse into minority and servitude when the Galatians have themselves circumcised and so assume the burden of the law (5:1–12). But one question inevitably arises for any attentive reader of our letter: can a Christian who through Christ has been liberated from the bondage of the law, feel free to do what he wishes in this new life? Is there now no more order or discipline in life? Does not this gospel which Paul proclaims open the door to every kind of libertinage? Paul answers "no": quite the contrary! We have already seen that the faith which is acceptable in the eyes of God (5:6) "works through love". We are told something similar in 6:2: the fulfilling of the law of Christ consists in the bearing of one another's burdens, hence is the practice of love.

But Paul can put the matter otherwise, as he does in the section 5:16–26. What does it mean to say that we are God's children and so are free? Have we seized this freedom ourselves? If it were so, then we should not be free, we should be the slaves of the "flesh", of our desires. It is rather that we are the children of God because God Himself has made us so and has given us His Spirit (4:6). And the life of the Christian means that he lives his life under the control of the Holy Spirit who really guides him. Now whoever does this is not under the law (5:18) but what he does under the control and in the power of the Spirit—the "fruits" of the Spirit (5:22)—is certainly not against the law (5:23). The life of the Christian is the scene of a struggle: the flesh (i.e. the man who is self-assertive in rebellion against God) is in conflict with the Spirit, and conversely (5:17). This is certainly no idle life. No, those who belong to Christ "have crucified the flesh with its passions and desires" (5:24).

The detailed exhortations which now follow (6:1ff.) are all concerned with the command of love. This is hardly surprising in view of what we have been saying.

5. *The letters to the Colossians and to Philemon*
(cf. esp. Colossians 1:9–20; 2:16–23; 3:1–17)

These two letters belong together; the recipient of the Philemon letter is a member of the Church at Colossae, and this short letter is brought by the slave Onesimus who belongs to the party which carried the letter to the Colossians (Col. 4:9). The letter to Philemon is a private letter which was dispatched at the same time as the letter to the Church.

Paul is writing from prison (cf. the letter to the Philippians). This is clearly indicated by Col. 4:3,10,18. It seems to be his imprisonment in Rome that is in question. In that case our letter—as is generally supposed—belongs to the beginning of the sixties. Thus it is about five years later than the letter to the Romans.

Paul is not yet personally acquainted with the Church in Colossae (2:1). But Epaphras (1:7), probably the founder of this Church, appears to have been a follower of Paul, and in any event is closely connected with him. Thus it is understandable that the apostle concerns himself about this community.

Although Paul is writing from the narrow horizons of imprisonment, his letter embraces a wide circle of vision. In fact one can say that Paul wishes to open the eyes of this Church to the fullness and breadth of Jesus Christ at a time when it is involving itself in all sorts of restrictions and becoming anxious about ritual cleanness, the keeping of feast days and other such questions (cf. Col. 2:16–23).

The particular errors which had arisen in Colossae need not detain us here. What we read in 2:16ff. reminds us in many ways of the letter to the Galatians. But if we take into consideration 2:8, there is a difference; here the lapse into legalistic thinking is the result of philosophical speculations. In this connexion the "elemental spirits of the universe" play a certain part (2:8). The Colossians suppose that the universe contains all sorts of powers, planetary influences (as astrology to-day assumes also), angelic beings endowed with specific power; in any case forces which determine human destiny, and with which the Christian too must reckon. From this point of view we can understand why just in this letter Paul so vigorously insists on the all-embracing sovereignty of his Lord. He is "the first-born of all creation" (1:15), "in Him all things were created" (1:16). Even the angels—which Paul according to the ideas of his time classifies into "thrones, dominions, principalities and authorities" (1:16)—do not wield power in their own right, but everything, even the upper worlds of which man would otherwise so easily become afraid, "was created through Him and for Him".

Because all the worlds and the whole cosmos have one and only this one Lord, therefore the Christian has no cause for fear. Christ has "disarmed the principalities and powers and made a public example of them, triumphing over them in Him" we read in 2:15. He who has reconciled us with God (very pregnant is the phrase about the cancelling of the bond, 2:14) has triumphed over every sort of power in the universe.

The life and attitude of the Christian is now defined by the statement that he has "risen with Christ", and as a sharer in the victory of Christ over sin, death and the devil, his whole life is directed to the things which are above, i.e. to the world of God in which Christ reigns (3:1–4). From that thought springs the rejection of all wickedness, falsehood, self-will and self-assertive power, as also the exercise of love to the brethren (3:12ff.).

In 3:16 we get a glimpse into the life of the earliest Churches which completes what we know from 1 Cor. 11, and 1 Cor. 12–14.

The *letter to Philemon* is a letter of recommendation from Paul to the master of a runaway slave, Onesimus. The latter had in the meantime got into touch with Paul and had become a Christian (v. 10). Now Paul is sending him back to his master. While he must certainly remain a slave of the master, he must also become much more, namely a "brother" of his lord. Paul begs: "receive him as you would receive me" (vv. 16, 17). Thus the new relation to God transforms the relation of men to each other.

6. *The remaining letters of Paul*

In addition to the letters we have discussed there are four further letters of Paul which have come down to us: that to the Ephesians, which in many ways is akin to the letter to the Colossians, and the three so-called "Pastoral Letters" — the two to Timothy and that to Titus.

These four letters have one negative point in common, namely that their composition by Paul is disputed. Nevertheless it is hardly a matter of dispute that all of them and especially the letter to the Ephesians and the second to Timothy are saturated with the key-ideas of Paul. But it is questionable whether Paul himself is the author.

Of course, this is no more than questionable. The letter to the Ephesians (which can hardly have been meant for the Church at Ephesus; the note about its destination in the first verse is not found in the oldest MSS.) may very well have been written about the same time as the letter to the Colossians. The fact that it discloses thoughts and, even more, stylistic peculiarities which we do not find in the other letters of Paul is not a conclusive proof against his authorship. The pastoral letters offer difficulties because they are not only stylistically so different, but also imply circumstances which are historically quite different from anything we are aware of in the life of Paul: according to 1 Tim. and Titus, Paul has been able to make lengthy journeys which do not fit into the period reported in Acts, and 2 Tim. shows that the apostle is at Rome in strict imprisonment whereas Acts 28 suggests that his detention was a mild affair. However, these very surprising indications would suggest that the letters at least have some connexion with Paul. There is much that would lead us to suppose that Paul was released from his first Roman imprisonment and even fulfilled his intention of journeying to Spain. In that case it was quite possible that he made other journeys too. Finally, as many suppose, he may have been imprisoned again in Rome, and—so much is certain—executed there.

In any case there is good reason to think that the four letters have something to do with Paul. The latter dictated his letters and the final draft of them was left in the hands of his secretary. It is also quite possible that, as a modern critic thinks, in these last letters Paul "gave his secretary greater freedom than heretofore". It is in any event very probable that all four letters were written by followers of the apostle who made use of his dictated phrases.

From the point of view of content, all four letters have one feature in common, namely that the Church has assumed a specially significant role. The letter to the Ephesians in particular gives us a view of the relation between Christ and His Church, the pastoral letters contain directions for the inner life of the Church, given by Paul to his fellow-workers who under his command have charge of particular Churches.

(*a*) *The Church as the body of Christ* (cf. Ephesians 1:15–23; 2:19–22; 4:1–6; 4:11–16; 5:22–33). Ephesians has in common with Colossians a cosmic breadth of vision. Christ is not merely the Saviour of the individual Christian, but, as the Risen Lord, is the Conqueror of all powers and dominions (cf. esp. 1:20–22; 4:8–10). Now Christ belongs fully to His Church as its Head. This thought was already indicated in Colossians (cf. Col. 1:18), but here it becomes a central theme running through the whole.

"Congregation", "church", "assembly" are various terms for the same idea. In 1 Cor. we saw how the Church assembled itself and what went on in its assemblies. Ephesians introduces us into the innermost secret of the life of the Church. It is no mere assembling together of Christians. It is rather the very body of Christ. Through its continued life Christ makes plain that He is the Lord and is really alive, and has overcome death. This is suggested, in immediate connexion with the resurrection, in Eph. 1:23.

Because the Church has one Lord, therefore it is a unity. Earlier distinctions between Jews and Gentiles are now superseded, since Christ "has reconciled both in one body through the cross" (2:16). We are reminded of Gal. 3:28 and generally of the letters both to the Galatians and Romans. The confession: "One body and one Spirit . . . one Lord, one faith, one baptism, one God and Father" . . . sounds very much like a hymn (4:4–6). When the Church splits up into parties—as we saw in 1 Cor.—it is the result of an over-emphasis on the human. The Church is a unity in the one Christ. In 5:22ff. Paul in fact boldly describes the union of Christ with His Church as a marriage bond. Deepest and most complete of all unions!

(*b*) *Order in the Church* (cf. 1 Timothy 2:1–7; 3:1–16; Titus 2:1–15). In the pastoral letters too the manner in which the Church should behave in its assemblies is once again discussed. Thus in 1 Tim. 2, Paul urges that supplications should be made for all in high positions. Even if these authorities are heathen, the Church should remember that God is one and that there is only one Mediator, Jesus Christ, who gave Himself as a ransom for all, even for those who are yet heathen (1 Tim. 2:1–6). Further, the numerous warnings of the apostle that the Church should guard itself against fantastic and erroneous opinions (e.g. 2 Tim. 2:14f.) is directed to meetings for Church worship: the recipient of the letter is to oppose such errors and banish obstinate heretics from the Church (2 Tim. 2:21; cf. also 1 Tim. 6:3–5; Tit. 3:9–11). The struggle which from the first Paul had to wage against confusing wrong teaching, is not yet over.

So much the more important is it that those who enjoy authority in the Church should be the right type of men. For this reason the pastoral letters are especially concerned with the bearers of Church offices. As such there are mentioned "bishops" (1 Tim. 3:1ff. and Tit. 1:7ff.) and "deacons" (1 Tim. 3:8ff.); in addition we have the term "elders" (1 Tim. 5:17 and Tit. 1:5), though in Tit. 1:5 "elder" means the same as "bishop", which is mentioned in the same breath (1:7). These letters contain detailed consideration of the qualities which are needed in such leaders.

"Bishops" (of which there are several in one community) we have already met in Philippians (1:1). They were general overseers and probably to be equated with the "elders" which we meet elsewhere. The "deacons" ("servants") whom we also found mentioned in Phil. 1:1 had above all to look after the ministry to the needy. In the pastoral letters the chief functions in the administration of the Church had already hardened. In place of the liveliness and variety of Church ministry which we see reflected in 1 Cor. 12 and 14, quieter and more orderly working of the Church has come into existence; the good order which in 1 Cor. 14 Paul outlines for Church worship itself is here required for the chief office bearers. Apart from the male leaders of the Church, the service of "widows" is mentioned (1 Tim. 5:3) who devote themselves wholly to the needs of the community. They are to be at least 60 years old (5:9).

(*c*) *Peculiarities of* 2 *Timothy* (cf. 2 Timothy 1:3–5; 2:1–13; 3:10–17; 4:5–8). Whereas the letter to the Ephesians and 1 Timothy and Titus contain relatively little that is personal, 2 Timothy together with Philippians is the most personal of all the New Testament letters. And that in two ways. The apostle openly tells his colleague (who must have been relatively young, see 1 Tim. 4:12) of the disappointments which some Christians have caused him (1:15; 4:10; 4:16), and he speaks frankly of the fact that he feels his death to be approaching, that he has fought the good fight (4:6–8). He begs him to come soon (1:4; 4:9,21) and in fact the whole letter sounds like one single earnest supplication: come soon, I need you! On the other hand, what the apostle says about Timothy shows how closely this young follower of his was bound to him by ties of affection, how formerly he became a Christian through the apostle's preaching. He now encourages him to rekindle the gift that has been bestowed on him (1:6ff.) to fight the good fight (2:1–7) and, like the apostle himself, not to shun suffering for the sake of Christ (2:8ff.). Here we have a picture of the friendship existing between teacher and pupil, such as we do not find elsewhere in the apostolic age, and we see how the common task in which they were engaged gave rise to the strongest personal affection between them. At the same time, and to complete the view we have previously attained, we become acquainted here with the apostle as a man.

Chapter 20

THE LATER PERIOD OF EARLY CHRISTIANITY

1. *A survey*

The letters of Paul which we have just been studying have taken us into the sixth decade of the first century, and in the opinion of some critics are much later in date. With these letters we have reached the period when apostolic Christianity was making the transition to the Church of the sub-apostolic age. This time of transition is covered essentially by the last third of the first century. Both Peter and Paul died the death of a martyr in the sixties of that century. Other witnesses to the early development of the Christian Church had died even before. According to an old but somewhat disputed tradition, John alone lived to the end of the century. The responsibility for the guidance of the Churches devolves more and more on those who were pupils of the apostles or were converted to Christianity by their preaching.

For such men whose names we know in part (Timothy, Titus, Silvanus, etc.) the apostles were the standard authority and the oldest witnesses. Some of them had travelled with apostles, and for a considerable time had been fellow-workers of apostles. Also in the capacity of secretaries or writers they had been busy with the drafting of apostolic letters. Furthermore, many of them will have been in the possession of written notes from the hand of their masters. Thus we can readily understand that the New Testament offers us several letters which bear the name of apostles as authors, though we get the impression that they could hardly have been written or directly dictated in that form by the apostles themselves. We have already indicated this supposition in regard to Paul's later letters. It applies still more strongly to those letters which we propose now briefly to discuss, and probably also to the "Revelation to John" (i.e. the Apocalypse). This does not mean to say positively that none of these documents were written by apostles themselves, but (under their authority) by pupils or other leading Christian men. Yet everywhere we must reckon with this possibility. One of the letters now to be considered appears without any indication of authorship: the letter to the Hebrews. In another, the writer (Silvanus) seems at one point to name himself: 5:12 of the first letter of Peter.

The letters to which we now turn are none of them addressed to individual and specifically named Churches. It has been therefore assumed—what the letter of James (Jas. 1:1) directly states—that these letters were written to several Churches, indeed to the whole of the Christian communion. For this reason they have been called "catholic letters", which is to say, letters addressed to the Christian Churches as a whole.

Questions of individual authorship and date we shall not discuss in detail. For in that respect we cannot really get beyond suppositions. Probably the oldest of the catholic letters are the first letter of Peter and the letter of James; both of these may still belong to the sixties. The latest is the second letter of Peter, which probably belongs to the first half of the second century. The Apocalypse must have been written in the last decade of the first century.

2. *The first letter of Peter*
(cf. esp. 1 Peter 1:3–9; 1:13–19; 2:1–10; 2.21–25)

Of all the catholic letters 1 Peter stands nearest to the letters of Paul. Its relations to Colossians and Ephesians are especially close; a section such as 2:1–10 would fit very easily into either of these two letters. The author addresses himself to persecuted Churches and exhorts them to steadfastness. Christians are "aliens and exiles" in this world (2:11) and they must suffer various trials (1:6), be the victims of much calumniation (2:12) and suffer for righteousness' sake (3:14). How easily they can succumb in a fiery ordeal! (4:12). How easily can an external threat become a danger to their inner life as Christians: if Christ is really the Lord, why does He allow us to suffer so? Hence the letter has as its purpose to bear witness that it is the "true grace of God" in which they stand (5:12). Further, Christians can easily come to despise the State which threatens them (2:13ff.). And this situation can easily lead to disorder in the Church and general disruption. How easy it is for the persecuted Christian to counter hatred with hatred! Hence we can understand the exhortation to have patience even in face of the enemy (3:8ff.); and we also understand that in this letter no less than three times are Christians urged to show brotherly love (2:17; 4:8; 5:14); persecution causes perturbation, which in its turn easily provokes quarrelling; again in such a time of distress nothing is more needful than that the Church should form a single-hearted fellowship in which each finds his spiritual home and has his place. Even the domestic rulings (2:18–20; 3:1–7)—which remind us of the letter to the Colossians—tend in the same direction.

But what the persecuted Churches in their hour of affliction most need is the assurance that they are God's very own, because they belong to Christ. Hence at the very start the letter alludes to the imperishable inheritance which is unfading and is stored up in heaven for the Christian (1:3ff.). For the same reason the Church is described as the new house of God; Christ is the cornerstone, but believers themselves are "living stones" forming an essential part of this edifice of God—a glorious image of the Church (2:4ff.) to which corresponds the promise that they are the "chosen race and royal priesthood" (2:9). In other words the author is saying that Christians are that people of God which once was called into being by the old covenant! We can only fully comprehend the audacity of faith involved in these utterances when we realize that they were addressed to persecuted, afflicted, powerless men —and moreover, it would seem, babes among the Churches (2:2), having only shortly before come into existence.

But no assurance among Christians —however important—must contribute merely to arousing a spirit of proud self-consciousness. This first letter of Peter has in fact a real hall-mark—the hall-mark of requiring from Christians that holiness of life which will reflect the holiness of the God who has called them (1:15). The judge of the whole world is the one whom they invoke as Father, and therefore they must conduct themselves with fear (true childlike fear) (1:17). And what a thing of inestimable worth was sacrificed for their ransom! (1:18f.). Could they do anything else but direct their lives accordingly?

3. *The letter of James*
(cf. esp. James 1:2–12; 1:22–27; 2:14–26; 3:1–12)

The first letter of Peter revealed a certain connexion with the message of Paul. In regard to the letter of James we are tempted to say the exact opposite. It is manifestly (2:14ff.) a polemic against Paul. Yet it is probably the misunderstood Paul against whom it is directed.

Of what use is it for some one to assert that he has faith when this is not proved by his deeds? This is the question thrown out by our letter (2:14). And immediately it goes on to ask: can then faith bring salvation? How can a pious word alone help a neighbour in need? (2:15,16). While to be sure faith is necessary, without works it is dead (2:17). Even the devils believe that there is only one God! (2:19). The case of Abraham proves the need for works (cf. Rom. 4 and Gal. 3); for Abraham was obedient to the point of the uttermost sacrifice (2:21).

Is all this a polemic directed at Paul himself? Superficially it would appear to be. For Paul makes a sharp distinction between faith and the "works of the law" (e.g. Rom. 3:28). But two considerations give us pause. Firstly, faith is here understood in the sense of pious statements (2:15,16) or else the affirmation of a dogmatic principle such as that God is one (2:19). Is that what Paul means by faith? We must answer at once: certainly not! We saw that faith was not to be separated from full, living self-dedication to Christ, from unity with Him and the sharing of His cross and resurrection (cf. Rom. 6). The faith which James has in view is a petrified, hardened, merely apparent faith. And secondly what kind of works are those which James has in mind? He speaks of love for one's neighbour (2:15,16), of obedient self-surrender (2:21), of the daring help rendered in the Old Testament by the harlot Rahab to the Israelite messengers (2:25). Are such actions, in the words of Paul, to be qualified unreservedly as the works of the *law*? Does not Paul just as much as James demand the exercise of love? Or "faith which works through love"? (Gal. 5:6).

Hence we must conclude that the letter of James is opposed to a misunderstood Paul. It is certain that the apostle to the Gentiles was misunderstood in this way. Such a misunderstanding gave birth to a hardened arid faith.

Yet on the other hand it is clear that, taken as a whole, the letter of James tends in a different direction from the writings of Paul. Everywhere he requires the deed (as exemplified in the most famous text of the letter: 1:22f.). In this regard, from the point of view of the history of literature, he shows himself to have been influenced by the Jewish wisdom literature (the well-known admonition against the sins of the tongue is a bit of wisdom writing: 3:1ff.).

All in all, the letter of James discloses its origin in Jewish Christian circles.

4. *The letter to the Hebrews*
(cf. esp. Hebrews 1:1–4; 2:11–18; 4:14–16; 5:11–14; 10:11–25; 11:1–7 (40); 12:1–6; 13:7–9)

We know neither the author of this great letter nor those to whom it was addressed. On a general view this document does not sound like a letter at all; all those characteristic marks of a letter (to which the letters of Paul accustom us) are here lacking. It is more like a solemn written message, or a sort of written sermon.

Once more it is a number of Christians in distress to whom this circular is addressed. Their distress, however, springs not from outward circumstances but from within. They have experienced the bitterness of persecution; but the moving words on this subject (10:32ff.) refer rather to a past event. No, the difficulty here is an inner weariness and dejection, which the letter repeatedly strives to combat (e.g. 12:1–3; 12:12–17, etc.). The suffering of persecution may well have contributed to this state of mind, as indeed it has often in the course of Church history led to such defeatism.

In such a situation our letter is an exhortation to steadfastness and endurance, to faith (cf. esp. ch. 11). The following verses might indeed be regarded as a summary of its whole content: "Therefore, since we are surrounded by so great a cloud of witnesses, let us also lay aside every weight, and sin which clings so closely, and let us run with perseverance the race that is set before us, *looking to Jesus* the pioneer and perfecter of our faith . . ." (12:1,2). The author of the letter opposes to all weariness and despair the portrait of Jesus Christ. Jesus Christ, the heir appointed by the Father, the instrument in creation (1:2), higher than the angels (1:4ff.), infinitely transcending the priesthood and the priestly ministry of the Old Testament (so especially chs. 7–10) is the One to whom the Church must look, He is "the same yesterday and to-day and for ever" (13:8), and it is He, the author urges, who will rescue and uphold you also.

But this same Christ who is clad in such splendour has identified Himself wholly with man: He is not ashamed to call men His brothers (2:11), He has become like them in every respect (2:17); in fact, "in every respect He has been tempted as we are, yet without sinning", and thus He is able to "sympathize with our weaknesses" (4:15). All this means for these Churches that their Lord is powerful enough to stand by them and help them, He is the Mediator who opens up for them the way to God (4:16; 10:19ff.), but He is also willing to stand by their side; for He has borne and suffered all things with man and on behalf of man.

The letter to the Hebrews—as is apparent even from the most cursory survey—is exceptionally penetrated with and moulded by Old Testament ideas and allusions; priesthood, high priest, sacrifice, tent of meeting, Melchizedek, etc. We cannot know precisely whether the writer had any special reason to insist so strongly on the Old Testament background. It looks as if the Christians to whom he was writing had had a special predilection for Judaism, and as if indeed there had been inclinations among them to repudiate faith in Jesus and to return to a spiritualized Judaism.

What is the point of these Old Testament allusions? We notice at once: here it is not (as it is in the letters to the Galatians and Romans) the Old Testament law which is at the centre of the circle of ideas, but rather its cultus. Now as Paul shows that in Christ the law has reached its appointed goal, so this writer demonstrates that Christ has fulfilled and so superseded the Old Testament sacrifices, priesthood, temple cult, in short, the whole ceremonial apparatus of the old covenant. In comparison with what Christ has effected, we must recognize in the law only a shadowy outline (10:1). The sacrifice of Christ is ultimate and final; it brings decisively to an end all those sacrifices which had temporarily foreshadowed it. Christ is the high priest who once for all has offered the atoning sacrifice. To insist on this over and over again in a flood of images, a mesh of mysterious allusions and relations, is the most important concern of our letter.

But with the "once-for-all" of the sacrifice of Christ which suffers no repetition, there hangs together another "once-for-all", a very harsh one; whoever has once become a Christian (6:1ff.) cannot become one a second time; thus if a Christian falls away decidedly from Christ, he cannot be restored to repentance (6:6). Hence the sharp warning against deliberate sinning (10:26ff.).

5. *The letters of John* (cf. esp. 1 John 1:1–10; 3:1–12; 4:1–21)

We have been considering some of the New Testament writings which take our thought and meditation to special depth and also give us wide horizons of vision: Ephesians and Colossians and 1 Peter and, last of all, Hebrews. In Christ—and this is the message of all the apostles—a new world has broken in upon us. And it is necessary to grasp in thought the whole range and fullness of this new world.

But on the other hand, if the mind of Christians were solely concentrated on the task of thinking out the unfathomable significance of Christ for the universe, a real danger might emerge: it might be forgotten (or in fact eventually denied) that Jesus Christ, the Son of God and the sovereign Lord, had become a real man. In other words the mind of Christians might be alienated from this earth and from historical realities in an unhealthy fashion. This danger was the more pressing in the ancient world because the Greeks were in any case inclined to indulge in such remote speculations. The movement through which this tendency of Greek thought, strongly influenced by oriental mysticism, asserted itself also in Christianity, is called "Christian gnosis" (gnosis means insight or recognition, in the sense of a higher understanding of reality, which is not accessible to all).

Those writings we have mentioned above (from Colossians onward) never disparagingly left the ground of earthly realities. But if any one had read them exclusively and then had interpreted them in the light of gnosis, he would have become involved in certain dangers. When in this way the meditation of man withdrew from the scene of earth and from the earthly figure of Jesus Christ, then it was easily forgotten that the Christian here on earth should love his brother. If a man plunges deeply into the origins of things he is liable to lose sight of his neighbour. And he will also be inclined to despise more ordinary Christians who do not entertain such deep thoughts. All this was a very real danger towards the end of the first century.

How necessary it was that in the midst of such dangers warning voices should make themselves heard! And it is a fact worth pondering that the Bible always evinces new aspects of truth to balance others. If we read the Bible in such a way as to concentrate too much on any one particular writing, we are liable to understand it wrongly. We must always hear other voices in counterpoint with that one voice, and only so shall we hear the full rich orchestration of the Biblical testimony.

The first letter of John (we shall leave aside the two others, which are very brief) is one great warning against an unbalanced over-valuation of deep insights, one single long-drawn admonition to practise love (of which Paul said that it was greater than faith and hope; 1 Cor. 13:13).

The Son of God has appeared here on this earth, the eternal "Word of life" was manifested to us (1:1–4) and here He assumed our flesh (4:1–3). Woe to any one who forgets or disputes this. Then the ground would sink from under your feet!

The view that Christ did not really come in the flesh, but had only an apparent body, was much cultivated among the exponents of gnosis.

The plea not to undervalue earthly reality is applicable also to the life of the Christian. Our letter warns readers that no one should consider himself sinless (1:8); whoever does that fails to realize that God is light (1:5) and does not live according to the truth (1:6; 1:8).

Here again the letter has in mind the dangers of gnosis, many of whose exponents claimed that the Christian is sinless, so long as he has the right, deep insights.

Only when sin is recognized to be a grave reality can there be any question of a real atonement (1:7; 2:1–2).

But whoever realizes that he has been reconciled to God through the expiation wrought by Jesus Christ and thus now stands in communion with God, cannot but be astonished at the greatness of the love which God has shown towards us (3:1) and such a one can do no other but practise love. This theme is repeatedly expressed in this letter, most comprehensively in ch. 4 which may be regarded as summing up all the leading thoughts of the writer.

Love to the brethren—but not love to the world! i.e. to all which would estrange us and separate us from God (2:12–17). People of every age and of every degree of Christian maturity are exposed to this danger (2:12–14). Whoever is really mastered and controlled by the love of God and lives in love to the brethren cannot possibly be actuated by self-seeking, whether in its coarser or finer forms.

Even for the reader who has not access to the original text, these letters of John disclose striking resemblances to the gospel of John (in spite of certain differences which research has noted). But it is remarkable that the gospel of John of all the gospels takes us most into the depths and the widest horizons of vision, while this letter which is so closely connected with it brings us back to earth and to the conduct of man on this earth! The two are integrally connected.

6. *The Revelation to John*
(cf. Revelation 1:1–8; 2:8–11; 3:7–22; 5:8–14; 6:1–8; 7:13–17; 13:1–10; 19:6–10; 21:1–8)

The New Testament closes with a message of *hope*, not of course the only one which it contains, but the most wide-embracing and deeply thought out.

We have already seen several times that Biblical faith cannot be without hope. The most important testimonies to this in Paul are to be found in 1 Thess. 4–5; 1 Cor. 15 and 2 Cor. 5.

The note of forward-looking expectation was sounded already in the Old Testament, especially in the Book of Daniel. It is no wonder that Christians meditated deeply on the words of hope and the pictures of the future contained in the Old Testament and in the light of the certitude that with the coming of Jesus Christ the last day of all history had dawned. Thus their minds fed on a copious supply of images with which were also mingled other late Jewish conceptions.

From this point of view we can understand the language and the world-view and pictorial imagery of the Book of Revelation. But this is no product of lonely brooding; it discloses visionary experiences and also rings with the choruses in which the early Churches sang of their eager-hearted hopes for the future (esp. 5:11ff. or 19:6ff.). The Apocalypse too is anything but an academic writing.

This work addresses itself to certain Christian communities living in a particular time. It is a time of rigorous oppression when the Roman empire with its deified head is beginning to turn with conscious hatred against the Christians in its midst (the period of the emperor Domitian, who died A.D. 96). Who will conquer, Christ or the emperor? All appearances suggest that the prospects of success lie with the Roman State. "It was allowed to make war on the saints and to conquer them. And authority was given it over every tribe and people and tongue and nation, and all who dwell on earth will worship it . . ." (Rev. 13:7,8). Such was the impression made by the Roman empire in its glory! But the Apocalypse says that it is a beast, a monster which arose out of the sea, and which derived its power from the dragon, symbol of the might of Satan (Rev. 13:1,4).

Against this lashing monster symbolizing man who has made himself into a god, there stands—a "lamb" (cf. especially 5:11–14). To this Lamb (looking as though it had been slain) the angels sing their hymn of praise (5:11–14), and the Lamb opens the seals of the closed book which foretells coming and indeed imminent events (6:1ff.). Hence in reality it is not the world-power which reigns but Christ, now still hidden, yet soon to reveal Himself as the Lord of all!

Thus we are faced with the real theme of the Apocalypse. It does not propose to tell us in advance the story of future millennia. "Surely I am coming soon!" This is the text which expresses the fundamental ground note of the whole work, heard again and again: all the distresses and sorrows of the present time are the immediate preparation of the victory of Jesus Christ. He who long concealed has held in His hands the destinies of the peoples will soon be disclosed openly.

Of course the approach to that day of final revelation is a way of tribulation. To be sure, at the commencement of all ways stands the majesty and universal dominion of God (ch. 4) and the Lamb that was slain, irradiated in heavenly glory (ch 5). But earthly ways are hard, and so are above all the ways of the Christian Church. Tremendous world catastrophes are immediately ahead (best known is the grim picture of the apocalyptic riders, ch. 6), terrible torments are in store for all those who refuse to participate in the worship of the beast (Rome) (ch. 13). And yet Babylon (i.e. Rome) will fall (ch. 18); the beast and its false prophet (its extoller) are thrown into the fiery pit of hell, and Antichrist, who has snatched all power on earth, is plunged into it too and the kingdom of God stands revealed. "Hallelujah! For the Lord our God the Almighty reigns! Let us rejoice and exult and give Him the glory . . .", thus runs the song of triumph of the liberated Christian fellowship. Now its bridal day has dawned, and it is forever and wholly united in marriage to the Lamb, and is clothed as His bride (19:6ff.). Even so, however, the ultimate victory of God and of the Lamb has not yet been won. Satan is bound for only one millennium (the idea of the thousand year kingdom, ch. 20); then comes the last fearful and fateful clash. But finally God is the undisputed Victor, and the devil, like the beast and his prophet before him, is cast into the fiery pit—all power that is turned against God is now at an end (20:10). This leaves the way open for a new heaven and a new earth (ch. 21) where there will be no more evil or pain—the curse-laden history of the world gripped by the power of evil finally dissolves into the glory of eternity!

All this is expressed in a language not easily understood, heavy with symbol and image, a language which was certainly understood at the time and the allusiveness of which has recently become clear to critics who have worked on it in the last decades. The Apocalypse is a book of comfort designed for Christian communities which were suffering trial and affliction.

But it is also a book of warning and indeed of harsh accusation. This is shown in the seven messages to the Churches with which the book opens. By what token can it be seen whether a Church truly believes in the Lamb, the Conqueror, and not in the power of earthly rulers? By its faithfulness and endurance in the hour of persecution (e.g. the message to Smyrna, 2:8–11; and to Philadelphia, 3:7–13). Where however the Church behaves in a somnolent fashion and is lukewarm, "neither cold nor hot" (Laodicea, 3:14ff.), or where instead of looking only to its Lord it succumbs to all sorts of strange doctrines or vices, then the harshest condemnation is meted out to it.

Is the Book of Revelation out of date? Unquestionably the writer had a specific period in view, and that time is no more. Yet the struggle between the kingdom of God and the power of evil still continues and still underlies history, and indeed at times has been manifested as a struggle between the State which deifies itself and the Church of Jesus Christ. If this conflict between God and the power of evil is the theme of world-history, then it is understandable that just at the climaxes of the struggle the Church has again and again gone to this book and found in it consolation and the assurance of final victory. Of course the Apocalypse can easily be abused. It can be exploited for the purpose of making elaborate calculations about future events, and many have used it in this way. Such attempts have never been successful. But the true consoling message of the book has proved its power ever afresh.

For long the work was neglected under the influence of the idea that this world must last for ever and develop to unsuspected magnificence and splendour. But to-day an opposite tendency of thought is showing itself among many; a gloomy expectation of imminent world destruction has taken hold of many minds. But however our human moods may change, the Book of Revelation, like the Bible as a whole, bears witness not only to the passing away of earthly powers, but (1:8) to Him who is and who was and who is to come, the Almighty.

Chronological Table of Biblical Events

Index of Main Biblical Ideas

CHRONOLOGICAL TABLE OF BIBLICAL EVENTS

B.C.

13th cent.	Exodus from Egypt. Moses. Beginning of penetration of Israelites into Palestine
circa 1110	Gideon
" 1050	Emergence of Samuel
" 1030–1010	Saul
" 1010–972	David
" 972–932	Solomon

932—DIVISION OF THE KINGDOM

Kings of Judah (southern kingdom) 932–588		*Kings of Israel* (northern kingdom) 932–722	
874–850	Jehoshaphat	875–854	Ahab (prophet Elijah)
779–739	Uzziah	*circa* 845	Revolution of Jehu
739	Call of Isaiah	784–744	Jeroboam II
735	Syrio-Ephraimitic war	*circa* 760	Amos the prophet
739–690	Activity of Isaiah (also Micah)	" 750	Hosea the prophet
Up to about 691	King Hezekiah	722	Destruction of the northern kingdom (Assyrians)
701	Siege of Jerusalem by Assyrians		

638–609	King Josiah
626	Call of Jeremiah (active until after 586)
622	Cult reform of King Josiah
609	Josiah falls in battle at Megiddo (against Pharaoh Necho II)
608–598	King Jehoiakim
598	First conquest of Jerusalem by Babylonians: exile of part of the inhabitants, among them King Jehoiachin
597–587	King Zedekiah
587	Conquest of Jerusalem: Second Exile
Up to 538	Babylonian Exile: at its commencement, Ezekiel the prophet; at its end, Deutero-Isaiah the prophet
538	First return of exiles
516	Completion of the new temple
After 450	Nehemiah and Ezra
After *circa* 300	Palestine under the Ptolemies (Egypt)
After 198	Palestine under the rule of the Seleucids
168	Desecration of the temple by Antiochus IV Epiphanes
After 167	Struggles and successes of the Maccabeans

After 141	Dynasty of the Hasmoneans (Maccabees)
63	Conquest of Jerusalem by the Romans (Pompey)
37–4	Herod the Great
Before 4	Birth of Jesus (our dating of the Christian era begins about 5 years too late)
4 B.C. to A.D. 39	Herod Antipas, tetrarch of Galilee and Perea (the overlord of Jesus)
A.D.	
26–30	Ministry, death and resurrection of Jesus
33 or 35	Conversion of Paul
50	Apostolic council in Jerusalem; Paul in Greece
51	Letters to the Thessalonians (oldest writing in the New Testament)
54–57	Letter to the Galatians
57	Letters to the Corinthians
58 (?)	Letter to the Romans
58 (56 ?)	Letter to the Philippians
After 60	Letter to the Colossians; later, letter to the Ephesians and the Pastoral letters
64	Nero's persecution of Christians; martyrdom of Peter
After 64	Martyrdom of Paul in Rome
66	Beginning of the Jewish revolt
70	Destruction of Jerusalem (by Titus)
70–90	Writing of the gospels; the letter to the Hebrews; other catholic letters
90–100	Writing of the book of Revelation, the letters of John and the gospel of John

Index of Main Biblical Ideas

DATE DUE
